20

D0276573

N
Ple
Re.

12. 0

16.

ND
Tel.

12

The Great Swim

The Great Swim

Gavin Mortimer

✳ SHORT BOOKS

This book was first published in 2008
by Walker Publishing Co
New York

Published in 2008 by
Short Books
3A Exmouth House
Pine Street
London EC1R OJH

10 9 8 7 6 5 4 3 2 1

Copyright ©
Gavin Mortimer 2008

Gavin Mortimer has asserted his right under the Copyright,
Designs and Patents Act 1988 to be identified as the
author of this work. All rights reserved. No part of this
publication may be reproduced, stored in a retrieval
system or transmitted in any form, or by any means
(electronic, mechanical, or otherwise) without
the prior written permission of both the copyright
owners and the publisher.

A CIP catalogue record for this book
is available from the British Library.

ISBN 978-1-906021-29-0

Printed in England by Clays, Suffolk

Jacket design: Two Associates

For Margot

Far better it is to dare mighty things, to win glorious triumphs even though checkered by failure, than to rank with those poor spirits who neither enjoy nor suffer much because they live in the grey twilight that knows neither victory nor defeat.

— Theodore Roosevelt

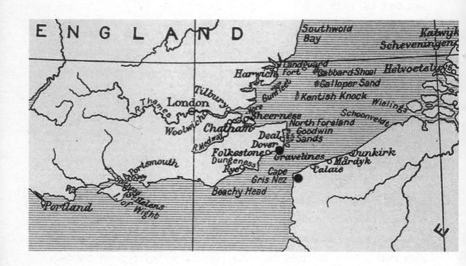

Prologue

AUGUST 18, 1925

THE SEA WAS CALM, the sun was out and Gertrude Ederle felt great. Treading water, the eighteen-year-old New Yorker caught the bottle of beef broth thrown to her by her trainer, Jabez Wolffe, an unsmiling Scot. There was little to see of Ederle's powerful body as she took her first refreshment at 8:15 a.m., one hour into her swim and three miles out from the French coast. Only her head was visible above the motionless English Channel, and that was masked by a pair of dark automobile goggles and a pink bathing cap that concealed her brown bobbed hair. Ederle yanked out the cork with her teeth, and in the same movement the bottle slipped from her hands and sank from sight. Wolffe wasn't amused. "Five shillings' worth of nourishment gone to Neptune," he muttered, reaching for another bottle of broth that lay at the bottom of his small wooden rowboat. Ederle toasted the health of Wolffe and gulped down the contents of the second bottle before tossing it over her shoulder as if she were a cowboy in a Dodge City saloon bar. It was a performance laid on for the reporters on the accompanying tug, *La Morinie*. One or two lounged against the boat's handrail, admiring the view and enjoying the sensation of the early-morning sun on their faces, but most were using the pause to file copy. The click of their typewriters and the sputtering of the vessel's wireless, its series of dots and dashes as tireless as Ederle's swimming, were the

Gertrude Ederle ready to embark on her 1925 attempt to swim the English Channel. Trainer Jabez Wolffe faces Ederle

only sounds that disturbed the early morning tranquillity.

Ederle continued on her way, and soon there was another noise, the bawling of Wolffe as he ordered her to slow down. "Too fast! Too fast! It's not a 1500-metre race, Miss Ederle." His instructions went unheeded as she propelled herself ever closer to England. Wolffe shook his head at the American's wilful disobedience. It had been like this from the moment Ederle had arrived in France two months earlier. Wolffe was consulted for his knowledge of Channel tides and currents, but it was made clear he had nothing to offer in the way of swimming strategy.

Wolffe's humiliation found an outlet in the newspapers that

were following Ederle's attempt to become the first woman to swim the English Channel. "I am sorry she has not followed stricter training but her ideas have frequently been opposed to mine," he complained to one American reporter on the eve of Ederle's swim. "I have told her that this marathon swim is different from anything she has tried but what man can argue successfully with a woman?"

At 1:30 p.m. Ederle was in mid-Channel and looking good to make history. Aboard *La Morinie* Bill Burgess was telling anyone

Wolffe feeding Ederle during her swim

who would listen that Ederle was "the most marvellous swimmer" he ever saw. Burgess knew what he was talking about. In 1911 he had become only the second person to swim the Channel, thirty-six years after Captain Matthew Webb had first succeeded, and no one knew the sea's nuances better than he.

Friends and reporters shouted encouragement as Ederle swigged down a bottle of hot chocolate. Before long the white cliffs of Dover would be visible through the weak sunshine, they told her. In the next hour, however, the weather turned on the

American. The sun disappeared, and a cool wind swept up the Channel from the west, whisking the sea and making the reporters look up from their typewriters as they felt the tug roll. "There's too much up and down to this ocean," Ederle moaned. Wolffe looked at her and shrugged. "No extra charge for that."

As the sea became more agitated, Ederle had to summon more energy to summit the peaks of the white-crested waves. Her stroke rate per minute dropped from twenty-six to twenty-five to twenty-four as the effort sapped her stamina. The temperature of the water was also on the wane. Earlier it had been sixty-four degrees but now it was sixty-one, and Ederle could feel the difference. She cried out for some beef broth, and this time there were no jokes as her trembling hands raised the bottle to her lips. Wolffe turned to the tug and ordered one of Ederle's pacemakers, a big burly Egyptian called Ishak Helmy, to swim alongside her.

Ederle carried on, but every stroke was heavy with pain. Frequently she rolled onto her back and massaged her body and legs. Helmy shouted words of encouragement above the moaning wind, but the end came at 3:58 p.m. Helmy told the *Los Angeles Times* later, "I kept my eye on her all the time. Presently I noticed her gasp, choke and splutter, the water coming through her mouth and nose. I said 'Steady, Gertie, steady. Take it easy.' She appeared to ease up. Suddenly she threw her head back and was on the point of collapse. Then Wolffe ordered me to seize her."

Helmy and Wolffe dragged Ederle into the rowboat, and she was soon back in the warmth of the tug's cabin, broken and bewildered, a strange contrast to the confident swimmer who had left Cape Gris-Nez almost nine hours before. "I just couldn't do it," sobbed Ederle. "That salt water was too much for me."

Chapter One

IT WAS MAY 1926, and life was returning to the small coastal village of Cape Gris-Nez. The fields were crawling with farmworkers, and the hedgerows bursting with wildflowers. The shutters and dust sheets had been removed from the village's two hotels, and the faint whiff of fresh paint was detectable on the sea breeze that sighed up the narrow lanes.

The bigger of the two hotels, the grey stone Hôtel de la Sirène, was on the beachfront and possessed a restaurant terrace from which, when the weather was fine, guests could look out across the Channel and see England twenty-one miles to the north. If the weather was bad, on the other hand, as it frequently was on this stretch of the French coastline, diners could concentrate on the fresh seafood before sampling the chef's speciality: chocolate pancakes fried in liqueur.

There were no guests as yet in the hotel, but the owner, Henri Lenoir, was hoping for a good season nonetheless. Americans were expected to visit Europe in droves to take advantage of the feeble European economy that made one U.S. dollar worth forty French francs. To that end, Monsieur Lenoir had hired as his assistant a young, dark-haired Frenchwoman in her twenties, Louisette, whose fluent English would make life easier for everyone.

Standing on the terrace of the Hôtel de la Sirène facing the

The Hôtel de la Sirène at Cape Gris-Nez

sea, one could look left, or west, for the geographically minded guests, and see the dark grey promontory, shaped like a nose, which jutted out into the sea and gave the village its name. Between the hotel and the promontory was a small sandy beach which petered out into a confusion of rocks, each one rising in height until finally they merged into the Grey Nose.

On top of the grass-covered cliff above the rocks were half a dozen whitewashed cottages, most occupied by the inhabitants of Cape Gris-Nez, but one or two owned by outsiders who came only in the summer when the wind that whipped off the sea wasn't quite as bone-chilling as during those long, dark winter months.

Outside one of the cottages, a large timber building, was a sign in English: THE VILLA OF CROSS-CHANNEL SWIMMING. This was the holiday home of Bill Burgess, conqueror of the Channel on his eleventh attempt in a time of twenty-two hours and thirty-five minutes. He'd staggered ashore a half mile or so up the coast in 1911, disorientated and delirious, and had used the small amount of money he'd earned from his feat to buy a second home. He already owned a flat in Paris, above a garage business that he ran with his French wife.

Beyond Burgess's holiday home, on top of the promontory, and surrounded by an abundance of pink flowers, long grass and grey rabbits, was the Cape's lighthouse, which flashed its warning every thirty seconds. The lighthouse keeper was a friendly soul, a breeder of Belgian hares and a man who, for a small gift, would let holiday makers telegraph cables from his office.

In the shadow of the white lighthouse was the Hôtel du Phare, rival to the Hôtel de la Sirène, and currently undergoing a refurbishment by its proprietor, Amédée Blondiau, a middle-aged man with a face already rich in wrinkles.

The nest of swallows that lived in the hotel porch was still there, and it was clear from a quick glance inside the small, spartan bar on the ground floor that no redecoration had taken place for a good many years. In the corner was the counter, with the single hand pump which filled guests' glasses with frothy yellow beer. Bottles of red wine, their labels hidden by a sheen of dust, were lined up on a wooden shelf, and the chairs and tables were grubby and uninviting. It was a bar made for drinking, not relaxing.

The improvements were all upstairs on the first floor. Over the winter a washstand had been installed in each bedroom, although the pipes had yet to be connected, and there was also a communal hot tub behind a door proudly marked Bathroom. That the smell of damp pervaded most rooms, freckling the wallpaper with mildew, was of little interest to Monsieur Blondiau. To have running water was an indication that the Hôtel du Phare was a progressive establishment. Soon, perhaps, the hotel would also have electric lighting.

The first of the season's overseas guests were scheduled to arrive at the end of May, an American couple, Mr. and Mrs. Edwin Day, and a reporter from the *Baltimore Post* called Nelson

Robins. Bill Burgess had made the reservation, informing Monsieur Blondiau as he did so that there would be two large dogs in attendance. Not a problem, the Frenchman had replied, they could stay in the backyard with his own dogs.

Burgess had also booked in a second party of Americans, which would arrive in the second week of June. Six people with one purpose: to help Gertrude Ederle succeed where she had failed the previous year and swim the English Channel. Blondiau smiled at the name; he remembered her well, a sweet and guileless girl whose only fault in his eyes was her unsophisticated palate.

Burgess would be coaching Gertrude Ederle, as he would Mrs. Lillian Day, better known in America under her maiden name of Lillian Cannon. Neither woman knew it yet, neither woman would like it when they found out, but Burgess was confident they would see the sense of training together. And anyway, his needs came first. The garage business he owned in Paris was as sickly as the French economy, and a double income over the summer would be as restorative to his well-being as Cape Gris-Nez's sea breeze.

Chapter Two

FOR THE LAST YEAR Lillian Cannon had thought about little else other than swimming the English Channel, yet now, on the eve of her departure, she was nervous as hell. She had never left the Eastern Seaboard before, let alone America. Her husband, as ever, was the buoy she clung to. She had married Edwin Day on the last day of June 1925, a wedding distinguished by the attractiveness of the couple. He was a football star from Johns Hopkins University, muscular with brown hair, a lopsided smile and a glint in the eye that hinted at calm self-assurance. Lillian was five foot three and every inch as American as apple pie. She had a blond bob and cornflower-blue eyes she emphasized with eyeliner, in the style of the models in the magazines. She wore her skirts daringly short; sometimes they stopped a couple of inches below the knee. To the tutting older generation who passed her on the street, she was just another feckless flapper, one of the new breed of liberated young women who were giving their sex a bad name.

But on Wednesday, August 19, six weeks after the wedding, Cannon's toothsome figure was splashed across the *Baltimore Post* under the headline: GIRL, MAN WILL TRY TO SWIM BAY. The short story described how Lillian Cannon and George Lake, "lifeguards at Bay Shore Park, will attempt a 12-mile swim across the Bay tomorrow. They will start at Tolchester Beach and hope to finish at Bay Shore. If weather permits they will start at 11:30 a.m. Motor boats and a doctor will accompany them."

When Cannon and Lake finished work at the Bay Shore Park on the evening of the nineteenth, they boarded the thirty-eight-foot *Rosa Anna* for the voyage across Chesapeake Bay to Tolchester in readiness for their start the following morning. Unfortunately the boat's skipper, George Evans, was new to the Bay and lost his bearings. At 11:30 p.m. the *Rosa Anna* ran aground on a sandbar, and for the next five hours Cannon and Lake yelled into the darkness in the forlorn hope someone might hear their cries for help. Only the arrival of dawn, and a fishing boat, allowed the *Rosa Anna* to complete its passage to Tolchester.

They disembarked at 6:30 a.m., impatient to press on with their plans for a morning start. A couple of steaks were demolished for breakfast, washed down with a few glasses of milk, and at 8:35 the pair dived into the Bay. "The morning was bright and the bay smiled," reported the correspondent of the *Baltimore Post*, who was one of a handful of journalists on board the *Rosa Anna*. Even closer to the two swimmers was a skiff containing Lake's brother, Herman, the head lifeguard at Bay Shore Park, and Cannon's younger sister, Loretta.

By 9:30 the first two miles had been knocked off, and Cannon asked her sister for a couple of slices of chocolate cake. "Sure, I'll make it, I feel fine," she laughingly replied to a question from one of the reporters on the *Rosa Anna*. At 11:00, however, the wind picked up and the tide increased in strength. Ten minutes later the accompanying skiff was nearly swamped by a wave, and Herman Lake and Loretta Cannon decided it would be prudent to transfer their encouragement to the sturdier *Rosa Anna*.

Captain George Evans brought his vessel closer in an attempt to protect the swimmers as best he could, but suddenly, in the words of the *Post*'s correspondent, "an extra large wave washed

Miss Cannon within a few inches of the boat. She saved herself from serious injury by a quick side stroke that half flung her out of the water".

The pair were now struggling to keep close to each other in the pugnacious water. Captain Evans told the press corps that he intended to follow George Lake because in his opinion he was the more likely of the two to be able to tough out the storm.

The sun peeped through the clouds at noon but vanished almost at once, as if scared by the Bay's bad temper. At 1:00 p.m. it was raining hard, and George Lake appeared to be tiring. He took a drink of peppermint essence, and for a while it did the trick, fortifying him so that at 2:00 he and Cannon were able to give a little cheer when told they had swum seven miles.

Not long after came Lake's crisis. His head started to loll, and his arms flayed feebly through the water. It was his brother, Herman, who made the decision to get him out, a move applauded by the correspondent for the *Baltimore Sun*, who described the swimmer as "overcome with nausea and weakness . . . [when] he was assisted, pale and shivering from the cold water".

As Cannon battled on alone, the *Sun*'s reporter became possessed by melodrama. "A driving rain and a brisk gale whipped the crests of the wave into hundreds of foaming white caps and high rolling swells which held the 124-pound girl in their grasp," he wrote, "but throughout the tempestuous period of exasperating struggle, when the blue bathing cap and tanned face of the swimmer were tossed up and down by the waves, Miss Cannon forged slowly forward. At times the girl would be raised five or more feet, then dropped suddenly into a foaming trough. Again a wave would break over her head, submerging her face and body for ten seconds."

Cannon, in the bathing cap which she said brought her luck, used the sidestroke to counter the buffeting of the waves. Herman Lake dived in and swam alongside her, offering words of encouragement and monitoring her condition. In the launch

Cannon's sister, twenty-year-old Loretta, told reporters she would never quit. "It's tough going but 'Lil' will make it. She's got the stuff."

Loretta knew Lillian better than anyone else. They were the youngest of six sisters, the eldest of whom was thirty-eight-year-old Maggie. Not long after the birth of Loretta, their parents divorced and Sophia Cannon had to raise her daughters on her own. Lillian and Loretta discovered swimming as a means to forget their unhappiness. At first they raced each other, but when they were old enough they entered competitions, winning several titles in the South Atlantic Championship. It was Lillian, however, who was blessed with the greater talent, and in the summer of 1915 she was invited to compete in the Shawnee Country Club meet in Philadelphia against America's best female swimmers, including the national champion Olga Dorfner. Her mother and five sisters scraped together enough money to pay her fare and waved her off from Union Station. "At that time Miss Cannon weighed less than 100 pounds and was looked upon as more or less of an upstart. . . she was subjected to a good deal of 'razzberrying' comment," said one newspaper. The sniggerers shut up the moment the race started and the Baltimore waif glided through the water, eventually taking the bronze medal, a couple of yards behind Dorfner and Elizabeth Becker, who would later win a diving gold medal for the United States in the 1924 Olympics. Cannon was saluted by the *Baltimore Post* as "the pride of all Maryland swimming enthusiasts", and over the next few years the medals turned from bronze to silver to gold.

There had been talk of competing in the 1920 Olympics, but that would mean remaining amateur and Lillian needed to make money from her talent to support her mother and Loretta. In 1920 Cannon turned professional and began work as a lifeguard at Bay Shore Park. She gave swimming and diving exhibitions, bent on making the most of her abilities while she was in the prime of her life. Only once did she turn down the offer of work, and that was when a carnival manager asked her to perform some high dives for the crowd. Initially Cannon was interested because of the fee. She had never been offered so much money. But in return the manager wanted her to dive three times a day from a seventy-foot tower into a tank of water less than five feet deep. Cannon talked it through with her sister in the North Charles Street apartment they shared with their mother and decided that the risk outweighed the reward. "There is just a chance," Cannon told the carnival owner, "that I'll smash against the bottom or sides of that tank." The owner, seeing his queues outside the box office shrinking, tried to convince her that she wouldn't be hurt. "I'm not afraid of getting hurt," replied Cannon. "I'm afraid of crippling myself so that I won't be able to try and swim the English Channel. And that's what I'm look- ing forward to more than anything else in the world."

Cannon's intention was to use Chesapeake as a stepping-stone to her ultimate ambition of swimming the Channel, but the Bay seemed to resent its inferior status as she entered the last third of her swim. As the wind grew ever stronger and the water ever rougher, Cannon's sister leaned over the rail of the *Rosa Anna* and shouted, "Come on, old girl, you can do it, you're sure to win." Cannon seemed punch-drunk from the pounding she had taken in the water. "It's a terrible strain," she croaked to Herman Lake, who was still swimming in support. She asked for some food and flipped onto her back to shovel some chocolate snaps and a couple of graham crackers into her mouth.

At 3:00 p.m. the weather began to ease, and Cannon was able to revert to the overarm crawl. Charlotte Beehler, her coach, came out in a motor boat and "was keenly enthusiastic". At around the same time the late edition of the *Baltimore Post* was arriving at the city's news-stands with the front-page headline: GIRL BOY SWIMMERS FIGHT CHOPPY WAVES. Underneath was a photograph of Lillian looking ravishing in her bathing suit and a report on their progress from a few hours earlier. Both had been looking strong, said the article, although Loretta Cannon "held herself in readiness to go to her assistance" if her sister didn't make it to the elaborate reception that awaited them.

People read the story and tore helter-skelter to Bay Shore to welcome plucky George Lake and gorgeous Lillian Cannon. One fisherman, sensing a quick buck could be made, charged sightseers a small sum and took them out in his boat for a glimpse of the swimmers. When he returned for a fresh catch, news passed around that only the girl was still in the water. Those waiting at Bay Shore first spotted Cannon's head bobbing up and down at 7:00 p.m. She heard the cheers of the crowd and turned grinning to the reporters on the *Rosa Anna*. "Here's where I really begin to swim!" She reached the shore at 7:20 – nearly eleven hours after leaving Tolchester-to the accompaniment of a local band whose tune was just audible over the tumult caused by the thousand-strong crowd. The photographer from the *Post* tried to push his way through to get a shot of Cannon, but the throng was too dense. "Shucks," he said later, as he took his pictures, "I was hoping to get a flashlight of you coming up to the pier." "No problem," replied Cannon. She dived back into the Bay and swam out fifty yards. "All right now?" she asked the photographer, who gave the thumbs-up and took his last photo as she climbed back up the ladder and onto the pier.

The next morning both the *Baltimore Post* and *Sun* ran lengthy reports on Cannon's achievement. The plight of poor George Lake took only a few lines to dismiss as the papers proclaimed the twenty-two-year-old blonde the new darling of Baltimore. And what legs. The *Sun* published a photograph of

Cannon having her thighs greased before the swim, while the *Post* carried the staged photo of Cannon emerging from the Bay, bathing suit clinging to her body's every contour.

At any other time so much gratuitous flesh on display would have been unacceptable, but newspapers got away with it by pointing out that women's swimming was one of the fastest-growing sports in American society; they were merely giving it the coverage it merited.

But the swimmers could be exploitative, too. Many used their female charms to further their own careers. That might have been Cannon's intention when, in reply to an inquiry from a *Post* reporter as to when she would tackle the Channel, she said it depended how quickly she could raise the funds to cover the attempt. It didn't take the editor of the *Post* long to realise that he and Cannon could be mutually beneficial: the editor would use the paper's money to propel Cannon toward the Channel, and she would use her charms to increase its circulation.

In the week following her swim across the Bay, Cannon pulled in the crowds at the Maryland Theatre, appearing with Odiva, the diving Venus, and some sea lions in what the *Post* declared was a "most attractive act . . . she is on the road to become one of the swimming immortals". Now that the paper had announced its sponsorship of Cannon, the editorial staff intended to use every opportunity to promote her.

Once the run at the theatre was over, Cannon and her husband headed to Florida to spend the winter with Eddie's parents so she could train in warmer climes. The *Post* and other newspapers from the Scripps-Howard syndicate kept America informed of her condition. On December 31, 1925, California's *San Mateo Times* explained in a short paragraph that she was training at Daytona, and to emphasise the point the paper ran a full-length photo of Cannon posing on the beach in her bathing suit.

In April Lillian and her husband returned to Baltimore. While she trained each day in the Magothy River, the *Post*'s editorial team started to think beyond the rather humdrum "Woman battles Channel" plotline. What better way to capture readers' imagination, they agreed, than by turning it into a race between the United States and Europe? Their headline on April 26 was WOMEN FROM AMERICA, ENGLAND AND FRANCE WILL TRY TO ACCOMPLISH DIFFICULT FEAT THIS YEAR. Mercedes Gleitze would be representing England, Jeanne Sion, "that great swimmer and lovable woman", would carry the flag for France, and Gertrude Ederle and Lillian Cannon likewise for America. The article ended by saying that "[Bill] Burgess will train Miss Ederle this year, and is making arrangements to handle Miss Cannon as well".

Burgess's name had been one of several suggested to Cannon by her newspaper advisers. "He was selected after the whole list of trainers had been thoroughly gone over," explained the *Post*, "and Burgess was decided upon as the best possible man to have charge of Miss Cannon's swimming destiny." Burgess said he would be delighted, and cabled a stirring acceptance letter to Cannon in which he informed her that if she was to stand any chance of success she must possess "speed, endurance and luck".

While Burgess was clambering up to the Hôtel du Phare to finalise arrangements with Monsieur Blondiau, Cannon busied herself with last-minute preparations. Her sister and principal cheerleader, Loretta, couldn't afford the trip, but husband, Eddie, was coming, and so was the *Post*'s Nelson Robins.

Robins was a thirty-nine-year-old Virginian who had chosen journalism over the family tradition of soldiering. Apart from his writing and his family, Robins's passion in life was breeding and exhibiting English bulldogs. It might have been Robins who was responsible for the Chesapeake Bay dog gimmick, or perhaps another bright spark at the *Post*, who piped up in an editorial meeting that, seeing as Lillian had swum the Bay last August, why not send her across the Channel with two dogs of the same name? What better way to promote the magnificence of the region?

The editor thought it a scream of an idea, so when Cannon returned to Baltimore from Florida in the spring, she was greeted by William H. Hurst Jr., owner of the Chesacroft Kennels at Lutherville in Maryland. On either side of him were the seventy-five-pound Chesacroft Drake and the equally enormous Chesacroft Mary Montauk, "the two best Chesapeake Bay dogs in the world", in the opinion of the *Post*'s canine expert. "No matter what the weather," he continued, "when a duck is shot the Chesapeake Bay dog goes after him." The breed was descended from the Newfoundland, but now "in most points it has departed from the original type. There is one point in common – their love for the water".

On May 12 the *Post*'s front page was dominated by a photo of Cannon's departure for New York from Baltimore's Union Station. Eddie Day leaned nonchalantly against the open carriage, smiling as he waved his straw boater. Robins had his trilby in the air, while with the other hand he restrained Mary Montauk. Cannon looked resplendent in a white overcoat and matching cloche hat, although her elegance was somewhat offset by her tug-o-war stance. With her right hand she clung to the carriage's handrail, at the same time wedging her right foot against the footplate so she could better keep hold of a disgruntled-looking Chesacroft Drake, who was leashed to her left hand. The article continued on page three, accompanied by more photos. One was of Cannon wearing a bathing suit, oddly, as she was presented with the dogs by Hurst a few weeks earlier.

The *Post* wished Cannon well on her endeavour, proclaiming that "we're all chock-full of confidence that she will do that turbulent bit of foreign water just as she did the old Chesapeake last summer". For her part Cannon told the paper, "You can bet all you've got that I think the *Post* is just about the grandest, greatest newspaper in the whole wide world . . . I've hoped and

Lillian Cannon and Chesacroft Drake

longed and prayed for this opportunity and, now that the *Post* has given it to me, I am going to take a slogan like the Forty-Niners' 'Folkestone or bust'. "

When they arrived in New York City, Cannon and her husband headed to the Astor Hotel on the west side of Broadway, while the dogs checked into a kennel on Long Island. On Thursday morning, wrote Robins, Cannon "started out for a tour of Manhattan's shops, big and little", and took a ride on the subway, which was, she told reporters in the afternoon, "a thrill".

That same afternoon, she and the dogs were scheduled to give a demonstration swim in the Hudson off Ninety-sixth Street, but to the disappointment of the sizable crowd that had gathered – including a number of sailors from the scout cruisers

Rochester and *Cincinnati*, both anchored in the river – it was announced that Mary Montauk would not be taking part-whether because she was unwell or had more sense it wasn't revealed. Cannon dived into the water from a float just astern of the USS *Illinois*, the headquarters of the naval militia. Its decks were lined with sailors, reported the *New York Times*, who gave the petite blonde in the one-piece blue bathing suit a rousing cheer and "even before she started the practice spin, ventured predictions that she would conquer the Channel".

As Cannon struck out with a confident and leisurely stroke, the eyes of the crowd turned to Chesacroft Drake. His paws were rooted defiantly to the pier. When Cannon noticed he wasn't with her, she turned and yelled, "Come on, Drake, come on!" The sympathy of the reporter from the New York *World* rested with the dog. "Drake hung his head and lay down," he wrote. "Finally he consented to be led to the edge of the pier. Coaxing failing, someone gave him a push and the seventy-five-pound champion swimmer went in with a splash. As he came to the surface he looked up reproachfully at the spectators and then chopped his way out to join Miss Cannon." Robins tried to silence the reporters' mirth by explaining that Drake was reluctant to swim only because he was missing Mary Montauk, but his defence only amplified the laughter.

Cannon's promotional tour continued in the evening with an appearance at Earl Carroll's "Vanities", the racy show made famous (or infamous, depending on one's point of view) by Peggy Hopkins Joyce, one of the most outrageous of the incomparable Ziegfeld Girls. During intermission the showgirls, with only their fans of peacock feathers to shield their modesty, formed a guard of honour, and Cannon was introduced to the audience wearing a cream silk sleeveless dress. From the theater Cannon visited the twenty-fourth floor of the McLain Hotel on Broadway and Thirty-fourth Street, where the fledgling radio station WMCA had its headquarters. Once she had been interviewed about her swim, she attended a dinner in her honour in the hotel's restaurant.

Friday followed a similar pattern – interviews, a swimming demonstration and a dinner – before finally, on Saturday, May 15, the day came when Cannon's great adventure really got going. "I just love Broadway," she beamed at reporters on the quayside, in the shadow of the liner *Volendam*, "but I'm afraid of the crowds." Just before Cannon walked up the gangway she relayed a special message for the folks back home: "My Baltimore friends can be sure that I'll do my best to uphold the honour of the city."

There was, however, one last pre-Channel publicity stunt awaiting Cannon before she left America. The *Baltimore Post* had invited three of New York's finest swimmers to wish Cannon "bon voyage" in the spirit of female solidarity. Aileen Riggin, Helen Wainwright and Gertrude Ederle were happy to oblige, even if the latter was a Channel adversary. The quartet posed for pictures on the deck of the *Volendam* with the ship's skipper, the avuncular Captain Wilhelm de Koning, and the two Chesapeake dogs. Then one of the photographers requested a shot of just the four swimmers. And could Cannon and Ederle shake hands? Now that the pair were standing next to each other, the contrast in physiques was glaring: Ederle the slugger and Cannon the sylph. It was the first time they'd met, and Ederle was curious to know Cannon's plans. Did she intend to swim from England to France or vice versa? Where was her training camp? Who was her trainer?

Over the hubbub of the *Volendam*'s imminent departure, the name Burgess ruptured the air like a blast from the liner's horn. Ederle was dumbstruck. Bill Burgess was her trainer, and she'd already paid a retainer to secure his exclusive service. Ederle had no time to pursue the matter. The ship was about to leave, and she had just enough time to respond to one final question from a reporter. Did she have a farewell message for Miss Cannon?

Ederle fixed her rival with an ice-cold gaze. "Good luck, I hope you conquer the Channel." With that, she was gone, storming down the gangplank incandescent with rage.

Chapter Three

ONE MEMBER OF THE ship's company of the USS *Illinois* had watched Lillian Cannon's dip in the Hudson River with particular interest. Mille Gade was the *Illinois*'s swimming instructor, as well as being the mother of two small children and, according to one newspaper, "pretty and blonde".

The previous August Gade had announced her intention to cross the Channel in the summer of 1926. As women's swimming was news that month, what with Cannon having tamed Chesapeake Bay and Ederle's failed attempt to swim the Channel, Gade's disclosure was picked up by several newspapers. They were especially keen to highlight anything that might distinguish her from her rivals and give the story a fresh angle, hence the front-page headline on August 24 in Pennsylvania's *Clearfield Progress*: MOTHER OF 2 WILL MAKE ANOTHER TRY TO SWIM CHANNEL. Underneath, Gade explained that being a mother was no handicap to her ambition, in fact, far from it: "I think no woman is at her best, physically or otherwise, until she is a mother." The paper reminded its readers that Gade had already been defeated once by the stretch of water in 1923, when she was the mother of little Sonny. "Now I have Marjorie," said Gade, "a year and a half old. I almost made it in 1923 with one baby and I believe that with two I can turn the trick."

Lack of confidence had never been one of Gade's shortcomings. She had grown up in Vejle, a town on the east coast of Denmark, in a family that was loving and well-off. Her father bought and sold musical instruments for a living, and melodies could be heard coming from the house most evenings as Mille and her five siblings played for their parents' pleasure. Mille was sent to Copenhagen to study the piano but discovered instead that sport, especially fencing and swimming, offered greater stimulation. While her brother Jacob mastered the violin (he later became a highly regarded composer), Mille spent more and more time swimming. She returned to Vejle, took a job as a swimming instructor and accumulated a plethora of notable endurance records in the water. Soon Gade felt confined by Denmark's small borders and began to contemplate a trip to America, so she could experience another culture, and so she could see her sister who had emigrated a few years earlier.

Gade sailed from Denmark at the end of October 1919 and arrived in New York on November 7. At immigration control on Ellis Island she was asked the standard set of questions for all passengers who came from Europe. Yes, she carried more than fifty dollars; in fact, she had with her two hundred dollars. She would be staying with her sister Helga and Helga's husband, John Carlson, who ran a drugstore in Bridgeport, Connecticut. She intended to remain in the United States for about a year. No, she was neither a polygamist nor an anarchist. Her height was five foot four, her weight 152 pounds, her hair blond, her eyes grey. She was twenty-two years old.

Gade's initial two hundred dollars didn't last long, so she went looking for work in Bridgeport. She appeared at the door of a theatre asking about the job she'd seen advertised in the local paper. The manager sniggered at Gade's strong accent and slight lisp, and dismissed her application, saying he needed an "usher", not a "yusher".

Undeterred, Gade continued to scour the job sections of the newspapers until one day she spotted an advertisement for a swimming assistant at a New York City pool. The pool's director, Anna Wiley, invited Gade for an interview and was impressed with her swimming ability and her tough-as-old-boots character, even if her English was a little hard to decipher. What probably clinched the deal, however, was the gold medal Gade pulled out of her pocket, given to her a few years earlier by the king of Denmark as a reward for rescuing two people from a river.

Gade enjoyed the job as much as life in New York City, and she soon abandoned her plan to return to Denmark. Instead she rented an apartment at 10 West 107th Street and in 1920 applied – and was accepted – for the position of head swimming instructor at the Harlem branch of the YWCA.

Although Gade liked her new role, she still felt she was living within her limits. What she needed was a challenge. One day in June 1921, Gade was sitting by the banks of the Harlem River during a break from work, staring thoughtfully into its turbid waters. Suddenly she came to a decision: she would swim around Manhattan Island.

Unsure of how to organise her adventure, Gade called on the *Illinois* for advice. The superintendent was busy, so he passed her on to his assistant, thirty-seven-year-old Clemington Corson. "Help the lady out, will you?" he instructed. "See if you can't dig up the maps and the information she needs." Corson unearthed the maps, and a boat. Then he offered to row the boat. He couldn't have been more helpful.

A few days later Gade swam around the island in fifteen hours and fifty-seven minutes. The *New York Times* was impressed enough to carry a report in its pages. Gade was back in the papers in September when she swam 153 miles – including detours – from Albany to New York in six days and one hour. The *World* reported that despite being attacked by a sturgeon along the way, Gade was the first person to complete the swim since a man called Cooper did it twenty-five years earlier, although the paper pointed out that he had taken nearly twice as long. It also said Clemington Corson rowed faithfully beside her the whole time.

A fortnight later Gade and Corson were in the *New York Times* celebrating not another swim but a wedding. They were married at the Bridgeport Episcopal Church in a ceremony performed by the fittingly named Reverend Stephen Fish Sherman. Instead of describing the bride's dress, *The Times* disclosed that she "intends to try swimming the English Channel".

Though she became a naturalised American through her marriage to Clem, Gade (she kept her maiden name for swimming) retained great pride in her heritage. Females in Denmark "were big, heavy built and very strong", she said in one interview when asked to compare Danish and American women. Gade herself was unexceptional physically but she was strong and she was hard. On August 6, 1923, nine months after giving birth to her first child, she had come within two miles of swimming the English Channel. Even then, related Britain's *Dover Express* newspaper, "but for the heavy seas at the finish [she] was very near success".

For the next two years Gade forgot about the Channel. She was too busy playing the doting mother to Sonny and, in early 1924, Marjorie. Additionally, she had also taken on her new job as the USS *Illinois*'s swimming instructor. But Ederle's near miss in 1925, and all the publicity it generated, got Gade thinking that it might be time to have another crack at the Channel. She was still mulling it over on the way back from Virginia one summer evening after dropping the children with their aunt for a few days' holiday. Gade lost control of her car, and it swerved off the road and down a twelve-foot bank. A woman who witnessed the accident came running over, sure she would be pulling a corpse from the wreckage. But instead she helped Gade wriggle unhurt from the driver's seat. "Whoever you are," gasped the woman, "you have been saved for something important." Gade smiled. "Yes, to swim the English Channel."

Convinced more than ever that she was predestined to fulfil her ambition, Gade dedicated herself to the task. Throughout the fall of 1925, she rose before her children were awake and ran four times around the Central Park reservoir. She'd be back –

Mille Gade (Mrs. Clemington Corson) with her husband and children Sonny (left) and Marjorie (right)

sweat dripping across the floor of their bungalow in the naval reservation at the foot of West Ninety-seventh Street – in time to dress and feed Sonny and Marjorie.

She also swam each day in the Hudson and on October 27

competed in a special race to celebrate Navy Day. Her particular challenge was to swim the four miles from 181st Street to the USS *Illinois* at Ninety-sixth Street, while Chief Petty Officer Joseph Lamb walked the same distance. Seaman August Friedrichsen, meanwhile, had to run the eight miles from the ship to 181st Street and back. The *New York Times* said that "Miss Gade entered the water off Fort Washington Point lighthouse in the face of a keen, cold wind which whipped the Hudson into whitecaps and kicked up nasty, choppy seas". As ever, Clem was beside her in his rowboat, urging her on and relaying the progress of her onshore rivals. It was soon clear that Lamb was walking his way to victory but that she was neck-and-neck with Friedrichsen. Thirteen minutes after Lamb had crossed the finishing line, Gade completed the four miles in one hour and ten seconds. Friedrichsen sprinted home a minute later. "It took twenty minutes to restore circulation in Miss Gade's hands and feet," said *The Times*, although she was still happy to pose for photographers with her two children, ever mindful of the importance of projecting herself as the Swimming Mother.

Six months later it would be Lillian Cannon and Chesacroft Drake posing for a photograph in the same spot as the press pack fussed around them. What was even more galling for Gade was that her own quest had been largely overlooked. The *Baltimore Post* hadn't mentioned her in its April preview of the Channel swim season, and neither had the Associated Press in May when it listed the "record-breaking entry from Europe and the Americas" all gunning for glory, among them Ederle, Cannon and Helen Wainwright, America's diving silver medallist in the 1920 Olympics.

Gade's problem was that she had no newspaper syndicate prepared to trumpet her bid. She was neither a teenage prodigy like Ederle, nor a winsome ingenue like Cannon. Instead of two dogs, Gade had two children, and even newspaper editors knew they couldn't get away with portraying a mother as a sex object.

And if they couldn't run endless photos of Gade in her swimming suit, what was the point of becoming her sponsor?

Fortunately for Gade, the very characteristics that deterred the newspapers appealed to others. Louis Liebgold, a champion race walker and the *Illinois*'s physical fitness director, had been training Gade since the start of the year and soon had her walking twenty miles a day. He also monitored her diet, telling her to eat all the vegetables she could and restricting her meat intake to three portions a week. Tobacco and liquor were forbidden, but Gade had never been partial to either.

It was Liebgold who introduced Gade to someone else he thought might be able to help her, Walter Lipman Lissberger, the fifty-year-old chairman of the New York Malcom Tire Company. According to many people, Lissberger had the Midas touch. He had certainly pulled off a coup with the Keystone Tire and Rubber Company a few years earlier when, having borrowed five thousand dollars to start the business, it soon had an annual turnover of twenty million dollars. The Malcom Tire Company was Lissberger's next venture, and he was busy constructing a chemical laboratory of Tudor architecture on his sprawling country estate in Norwalk, Connecticut, when his attention was drawn to Mille Gade.

Lissberger identified with Gade. He admired her tenacity and her confidence. She was a battler, like himself. Lissberger had grown up without a father, the second youngest of eight children. He'd fought his way to the top, and now he was in a position to help the underdogs of the world. Lissberger had previously opened his estate to Benny Leonard, the boxer known as the "Ghetto Wizard". Leonard had risen from the Jewish ghetto in New York's Lower East Side to become the undisputed world lightweight boxing champion for seven years until his retirement in 1925. With Leonard enjoying the fruits of his endeavour, Lissberger chose Gade as his new no-hoper to nurture.

She trained on his estate throughout the winter and spring,

swimming in his pool and jogging around the grounds under the supervision of Liebgold. Lissberger defrayed the cost of the trip, giving Gade and her husband three thousand dollars to cover expenses. He readily admitted his motives weren't solely altruistic. It was a "sporting proposition", and as such Lissberger contacted Lloyd's of London to see what odds it would offer. Lloyd's knew all about Ederle but Gade was unknown, so it proposed 20-1 against. Lissberger rubbed his hands in glee and wagered five thousand dollars that the unfancied Mille Gade would swim the English Channel in the summer of 1926.

Chapter Four

IN THE OPINION OF Lissberger and other conservative Americans of his generation, Gade represented the cream of the country's young womanhood. She was a devoted mother and a loving wife. She eschewed tobacco, alcohol and rouge, wore her hair long like her skirts. She wouldn't dream of dancing the Charleston or the Black Bottom, with all of its vulgar backside slapping.* In short, Gade was the antithesis of the flapper generation, and as Lissberger had told her, that was why he was helping her out: "Because you are a mother, don't bob your hair and aren't a flapper."

The flapper had been exercising the mind of Americans since the end of the First World War, but in 1923 she had been brought vividly to life by Colleen Moore in the film *Flaming Youth*. Moore portrayed a bobbed-hair girl who smoke, drank, danced and powdered her knees as well as her nose. For many, a monster had been created every bit as ghastly as Mary Shelley's Frankenstein. Simultaneously, F. Scott Fitzgerald waged a

---

* The dance originated in New Orleans and involved slapping the backside while hopping forward and backward and stamping the feet. Henry Ford was so appalled by the Black Bottom he launched a campaign to "revive the good old-fashioned dances like the waltz in order to counteract the wave of lasciviousness" crashing over the modern dance floor.

literary assault on Middle America's sensibilities, inventing flappers as alarming as their celluloid sisters. "I was the spark that lit up *Flaming Youth* and Colleen Moore was the torch," crowed Fitzgerald. "What little things we are to have caused that trouble!"

By 1925 many of America's authorities were trying to douse the flames of female youth. The chief of police in Dixon, Illinois, ordered his officers to arrest any woman found smoking on the streets and charge her with disorderly conduct. In Jamestown, North Dakota, two women were fined five dollars for smoking cigarettes in public, and Mayonne Bayer spent a night in Manhattan's Mercer Street police station after she was caught smoking in Washington Square. The dean at Rhode Island State College warned, "Any girl I catch smoking anywhere and at any time will not be permitted to remain in this college."

The flapper's sartorial choices also came under attack, particularly the shortness of the skirt, which offended the men and women of the 1890s "Gibson Girl" generation. Then there had been nothing more sensual than a large bust squeezed into an impossibly tight corset under a lavish evening gown. An exposed female ankle was considered brazen, so it was no wonder they couldn't accept that the young women of the 1920s saw nothing wrong with wearing short skirts that showed off their stocking-clad legs to great effect. Where they could, the self-appointed guardians of American morals fought a dogged rear guard. In May 1926, in the same week that Lillian Cannon appeared on stage at Earl Carroll's "Vanities" in front of a hundred peacock-feathered showgirls, two teachers at Overland Park School in St. Louis, Ethel Larkin and Gail Cochran, were fired because their skirts stopped only two inches below the knee. "They didn't show our knees," protested Larkin, "and besides, we sat behind a desk all the time."

College was seen by some conservative Americans as the root

Colleen Moore, the epitome of the "flapper"

cause of the flapper's decadence. From these dens of iniquities came dark tales of "petting parties", where amid the fug of cigarette smoke young women's lipstick was smudged by excited paramours. At the start of 1926 Yale promised to rid its campus of flappers, with the *New York Times* reporting on January 23 that "the round-up of girls followed the recent sensations" involving the elopement of two of their number with a pair of male students. Four months later the *World* published a letter from Alonzo B. See, a wealthy lift manufacturer, in which he demanded that "a child born to a woman who has been to college should be taken from the mother as soon as weaned and placed in some institution where it would be properly cared for."

Many colleges rallied to the defence of their students. What was happening, one dean told the *World*, was that young women in 1926 were "demanding the same freedom to experiment in sex matters that men have always claimed for their own". In the same article Mary Fretts, assistant dean of women at Lawrence College, Appleton, Wisconsin, agreed that "barriers between the sexes are undeniably becoming less rigid. This change undoubtedly has a side which is less pleasant to look upon but I consider it wholly possible that from this period of experimentation women may be able to make saner, wiser marriages".

That a wife could ever be accorded equal status to her husband was heresy for many Americans, who pointed to the increasing number of divorces as evidence of what happened when women were encouraged to pursue happiness over duty.* A woman belonged at home, they said, ensuring everything was in order for the husband when he returned from work and then, in time, looking after the children. Motherhood, not financial independence or job satisfaction, was the greatest attainment for any young American woman. When, on May 9, 1926, James Davis, the secretary of labour, delivered the address at Arlington National Cemetery for the American War Mothers Association, he pronounced: "The best in any man is what he has derived from his mother . . . let us continue to have that faith in woman and motherhood that has always been one of our most cherished possessions."

For Davis, as for many like-minded Americans, what separated the mothers from the flappers was the length of their hair. The former liked to wear it long, spending the quieter moments of the day – when the children were napping and the housework was done – grooming it in readiness for their husbands' return. Flappers, on the other hand, went in for a "bob" because it was less troublesome to manage in the early-morning rush to work. As one woman told the *New York Times* on August 21, 1921, just as the fashion was taking hold, "Cutting my hair has set the clock back ten years. It is the most rejuvenating influence that has come into my life, as well as the most practical and sanitary one.

---

* In 1926, 186,868 divorces were granted in the United States, ten for every 56 marriages, the highest number ever recorded in a single year.

It is the only sensible fashion for a busy woman who has little time and less patience for the intricacies of an elaborate toilet." The bob came almost to replace horns as the mark of the devil in the eyes of the religious Right. "All of you who 'bob' your hair will become bald," thundered the Reverend M. E. Dodd from the pulpit of the First Baptist Church of Shreveport, Louisiana, while in Letcher County, Kentucky, the Reverend Arlie Brown told his congregation that no virtuous woman would ever bob her hair. In 1921 the Chicago department store Marshall Field forbade any female employee to bob her hair in the future because it signalled sexual promiscuity, at which point twenty women walked out in protest, and in 1924 a Pennsylvania school board voted a one-hundred dollar salary increase to all school-teachers who kept their hair long, because they offered a more wholesome image.

Arranged against the forces of conservatism were flappers and their rather more thoughtful allies, the National Women's Party (NWP), established in 1913 and by the early 1920s at the forefront of the battle for gender equality, with the launch of what was described in many American papers as "the Feminist Magna Carta". Joan Grayson, the party's publicity director, released a copy of this document to the *New York Times*, which published it in its entirety in December 1922. The last of its twenty-nine declarations stated that "woman shall no longer be in any form of subjection to men in law or in custom, but shall in every way be on equal plane to rights, as she has always been and will continue to be, in responsibilities and obligation".

In the opinion of the *New York Times* it was an "imposing declaration", although, it continued, "it would have gained in vigour if it had been put in half the space, but that a woman should be contented with a thousand words is in itself a triumph."

Watching from the edge of the battlefield were the likes of Walter Lissberger. Unable to intervene in any significant way in the war of the sexes, he was nonetheless in a position to raise a flag in support of women such as Mille Gade, a mother, not a flapper, with lovely long hair.

The twenty women who resigned from Marshall Field weren't the first martyrs in the feminist cause. There had been others before, fined or imprisoned or vilified, either for defending their rights or for drawing attention to oppressive legislation. Some were small personal stances like those who refused to be told how to wear their hair, while others had far more dramatic repercussions.

The bathing suit that Cannon wore so well had been unimaginable a generation earlier, until the Australian swimmer Annette Kellerman toured Europe in 1906, giving swimming exhibitions. At the turn of the twentieth century women were still expected to take to the water wearing a neck-to-knee bathing dress over woollen tights and shoes. Bloomers had been shed only a few years before, but it was considered risqué for a woman to go wading without her shoes. Finding the bathing suit impractical for her vaudeville act, Kellerman experimented by sewing a pair of black stockings onto a boy's swimming suit. The figure-hugging outfit covered her flesh and enabled her to perform her aquatic acrobatics in a glass tank. Having played to sold-out theatres in Europe – including one performance in front of the British royal family in London – Kellerman took her act to America in 1907 and wowed audiences across the country. But when she went for a dip at Revere Beach in Boston wearing her latest innovation, a bathing suit that stopped just above her knees, she was arrested and charged with indecency. The case was dismissed when the judge accepted Kellerman's defence that the Victorian bathing dress was cumbersome and inhibitive.

Yet despite Kellerman's victory, the revolution in women's

bathing suits took time to gather momentum. The seminal year
was 1919. Young women who had spent the previous two years
replacing men in the country's factories and offices, as they
fought in France, were dismayed to discover they were expected
to resume their old existence of drudgery and subservience now
that the First World War was over. In addition, the thousands of
women who had dutifully passed their American Red Cross life-
saver's certificate, in order to occupy the lifeguards' chairs vacat-
ed by the conscripted soldiers, were now asked to step aside and
go back to ornamenting the beach in the paraphernalia of their
absurd costumes.

When America's most popular female swimmer, Ethelda
Bleibtrey, was arrested on California's Manhattan Beach in 1919
for removing her stockings, there was an angry response from

A 1923 gathering of champion swimmers in Buffalo, NY. Gertrude
Ederle stands in the back centre, Aileen Riggin leans on the stairs
and in the front centre is Johnny Weissmuller – a great swimmer
better known as Tarzan

women. Fortunately Bleibtrey was cleared of "nude swimming", and, although the ban on women's bare flesh wasn't unequivocally lifted, many felt empowered by the court's decision and followed the examples of Kellerman and Bleibtrey. Within two years Atlantic City hosted America's first beauty pageant. More than five hundred nubile young women, nearly all attired in one-piece bathing suits that, as one paper noted with eyebrows raised, "suspended publication half a foot above the knee", paraded in front of ten thousand spectators.

The relaxation in women's swimming apparel led also to an explosion in competitive female swimming, with New York's Women's Swimming Association (WSA) taking a leading role. Women at last were able to enjoy swimming unencumbered by what Kellerman had once described as "more stuff than you hang on a clothes line".

Swimming had been introduced for women in the 1912 Olympics (the United States wasn't represented) but only in the 100-metre freestyle and the 4-x-100 freestyle relay; the Games' organisers doubted whether the fairer sex was capable of swimming farther than 100 metres. But in the 1920 Antwerp Olympics a third event was added to the programme, the 400-metre freestyle (which finished with an American one-two-three and Ethelda Bleibtrey taking gold). When the Paris Games came around four years later, the 100-metre backstroke and 200-metre breaststroke had been incorporated into the women's schedule.

Simultaneously, women were pushing for recognition in other sports, most notably athletics, in which a Frenchwoman named Alice Milliat was in the vanguard. She petitioned the International Olympic Committee (IOC) to include track-and-field events in the 1920 Olympics but was told that it was unfeminine for women to sprint and jump and throw. Undeterred, Milliat established the Fédération Sportive Féminine Internationale (FSFI) to promote women's track and field, and its first meet was held in 1921 in Monte Carlo. The following year Milliat was informed by the IOC that there was no chance of female athletic inclusion in the 1924 Olympics, so she organised the inaugural Women's Olympic Games in Paris. It was a triumphant spectacle with America as one of five countries that sent athletes to compete in eleven events in front of twenty thousand spectators. Even more satisfying for Milliat was the public anger of the IOC at the use of the word *Olympic*. Well then, Milliat told the IOC, let's negotiate.

The newspapers joined in the female sporting revolution with gusto, and swimming came in for particular attention. It was, after all, a legitimate form of pornography. Editors dispatched photographers to beauty pageants and printed reports from women's swimming meets, all invariably enlivened by pictures of the competitors. The *New York Times* said of a 1922 race off Coney Island that "nothing like it had been known before in natatorial [*sic*] annals; so many youngsters of the gentler sex treating Father Neptune to a surprise that well might have caused him to drop his trident to the bottom of the sea".

The winner of that 1922 race, the three-and-a-half-mile Joseph Day Cup, was an unknown fifteen-year-old named Gertrude Ederle, who had finished ahead of the Olympians Helen Wainwright and Aileen Riggin. The trio all swam for the WSA, and in the next three years they became good friends. The papers dubbed them "Mermaids", and at the end of 1925 they turned professional and gave a series of exhibitions at New York's Hippodrome, in the glass tank that had once belonged to Annette Kellerman.

At the start of 1926 the three young women had a short stint working as instructors at the exclusive Deauville resort in Miami Beach, Florida. They had a gay old time of it, bobbing, rouging and dancing, and wearing the WSA one-piece bathing suit that stopped at the tops of their thighs.

Ederle found the woollen suit ideal for the innocuous waters of Deauville, but when she had worn it during her first attempt to swim the English Channel in 1925, it had, she said, "crawled up on the back of my neck and chafed me, and it bulged out and caught water, too, and that delayed me". When her engagement

1924 Olympic swimmers, Ederle in the centre

in Miami Beach ended in spring 1926, Ederle returned to New York and began experimenting with Margaret, one of her sisters, to find a bathing suit better able to meet the demands of long-distance sea swimming.

If Ederle was unconcerned with the brevity of her suit, she balked at the thought of following the many male swimmers who discarded their costume once they were a respectful distance from the shoreline. She was familiar with the story of Enrico Tiraboschi, the Argentine swimmer, who swam the Channel in

1923 in a new record time of sixteen hours and thirty-three minutes. Fifty yards from Shakespeare Beach in Dover, one of his friends in the support boat reminded him that he'd kicked off his rubber costume several hours earlier. "What do you think I'm going to do," mumbled an exhausted Tiraboschi, "swim back to France?"

Ederle lacked that Latin insouciance, but she was coming round to her sister's suggestion of wearing only trunks and a brassiere. Silk had performed well as a material in her trial swims, but a more rigorous examination was required in the Channel. The bathing suit had been one of Ederle's main preoccupations during the spring of 1926; but ever since she had stood on the deck of the *Volendam* with Lillian Cannon, and learned of Bill Burgess's treachery, she could do little more than count down the days until the moment when she would confront him at Cape Gris-Nez.

Chapter Five

"I REALISE THAT it is going to be a fight all the way and that it will get harder as the hours go by. I am going to start my fight as soon as I get to Cape Gris-Nez because above everything else in the world I want to be the first woman to swim from France to England." Captain Joe Medill Patterson's thin lips broke into a smile; this was just the sort of fighting talk he wanted, the reason he had signed Gertrude Ederle to write exclusive columns for his *Chicago Tribune-Daily News* syndicate.

Patterson, the founder and owner of the *Daily News*,* ran his eye down the rest of Ederle's column from the June 3 edition: "I'm no Jack Dempsey," she lectured readers, "and I don't get half-a-million dollars for my efforts. So if I dance in the evening or pick up a ukulele for pleasure I don't think it should be reported as a scandal . . . I don't want to be nagged at my training. I want to talk about clothes and shows and the Charleston." Perfect! The words of a flapper, yet a flapper who might well be on the brink of achieving something monumental. Women would idolise her, and young men would be smitten by her; more important, all would want to follow her progress in the *Daily News*.

* This is the predecessor of today's *New York Daily News*.

Patterson had a reputation as a populist with socialist leanings, the result of a novel he had written, *A Little Brother of the Rich*, which had scandalised Chicago society for its portrayal of the city's rich as idle and dissolute. From the moment he had turned over the running of the *Chicago Tribune* to his cousin, Robert McCormick, in 1919, and founded the *Daily News*, Patterson had created a tabloid every bit as lurid as the British ones that had inspired him during his war service in Europe. The lives of the New York working class were drab enough without being fed endless stories about Bolsheviks and business; they wanted sex and scandal and sensationalism. Patterson knew this because he often dressed in a slouch hat and tatty overcoat and wandered the streets of Manhattan, listening to what the working men and women were talking about, eavesdropping on conversations in bars and on street corners.

In the first few months of its existence, the circulation of the

Cape Gris-Nez, 1925. Gertrude Ederle plays the ukulele while Ishak Helmy dances with Jeanne Sion, the French swimmer

Daily News had been stuck at a risible 26,000. Other papers laughed at Patterson and called his newspaper "the servant girl's bible". The ridicule only strengthened Patterson's resolve to succeed with the *Daily News*, and slowly, as the 1920s blossomed into the decade of unprecedented prurience, the circulation rose – 400,000 in 1922, 750,000 two years later – until in 1926 just under one million New Yorkers were buying the paper each day.

Patterson – Captain Patterson, as the staff were ordered to call him – liked to think he never missed a trick, but even he had been surprised by the interest shown in Lillian Cannon when she'd swept through the city the previous month. People were buying newspapers because of her. If Cannon succeeded in swimming the Channel, the *Baltimore Post* and all the Scripps-Howard newspapers would see their circulation soar as people clamoured to read the exclusive story. Patterson turned pale at the thought. He turned even paler when he considered the consequences should either of the *Daily News*'s two main New York rivals snap up Ederle to write for them.

In 1924 two other newspapers had been launched with the sole aim of muscling in on the territory won by the *Daily News*. Patterson didn't think much of one of them, the *Daily Graphic*, better known to its enemies as the "Porno-Graphic", so lowbrow was its content and so weird was its proprietor, the health nut Bernarr Macfadden, who liked to start each day with a glass of beet juice. Nonetheless, Walter Winchell's salacious gossip column, "Your Broadway and Mine", was reason enough for many people to buy the *Daily Graphic*, and by 1926 its circulation was 200,000.

But it was the second paper that Patterson considered the real danger. This was William Randolph Hearst's *Daily Mirror*, another addition to his newspaper empire that now consisted of twenty dailies and eleven Sunday editions in thirteen cities. By 1926 the *Daily Mirror*'s circulation was 370,000 as its innovative and uninhibited use of photographs proved a hit with the public, living up to Hearst's promise to provide readers with "90 percent entertainment and 10 per cent information."

Patterson had to fight back, but he knew from frightening experience that Hearst was a man who would go to any lengths to win a circulation battle. The launch of the *Examiner* in Chicago a few years earlier had precipitated a long-running feud with the *Chicago Tribune*, which resulted first in street battles between rival distributors and then, in 1921, in a cash giveaway competition that was stopped only by the intervention of the postmaster general,* who told the protagonists, both of whom were offering money prizes totalling $700,000 to drawers of lucky numbers, that they were undermining the morality of America.

If Hearst couldn't be beaten on the streets, thought Patterson, he had to be defeated in the content of the papers, and one way to achieve that was to contract Gertrude Ederle to write exclusively for his *Chicago Tribune-Daily News* syndicate and pray she beat Cannon across the Channel. On May 29 Ederle, accompanied by her father, signed a deal with Patterson's organisation. She would write regular dispatches from France, and Patterson would pay her $5,000 with an additional $2,500 if she was successful.

Ederle had already booked her outward passage on the *Berengaria*, sailing June 2, so Patterson didn't have long to find a journalist willing to spend the summer in a bleak, isolated, windswept French village with a shy nineteen-year-old swimmer. Protocol dictated that it would have to be a female writer who accompanied the unmarried Ederle, so she could be portrayed as the swimmer's chaperone. One candidate stood out above all others: thirty-one-year-old Julia Harpman. She was an

* Until 1971 the postmaster general was head of the Post Office Department and also a member of the president's cabinet with the power to intervene on such matters

able staff writer on the *Daily News*, but more significantly her husband was Westbrook Pegler, a hard-hitting *Chicago Tribune* sports columnist with a good turn of phrase and a weekly salary of $250.

Patterson knew that the tall, slim Pegler wouldn't mind a trip to Europe. His father was an Englishman, albeit one who had emigrated to America in his youth and become a journalist, for a time with the Hearst media empire, before he had been sacked for remarking that a Hearst newspaper resembled a "screaming woman running down the street with her throat cut". Pegler had followed his father into journalism, joining the United Press in Chicago in 1910 on a ten-dollar-a-week salary and being sent six years later to Europe to cover the war. In London Pegler came under the wing of the legendary *Chicago Tribune* war correspondent Floyd Gibbons. He told Pegler that if he wanted his dispatches to stand out he'd better change his byline from the cluttered "J.W. Pegler". "With a 'Pullman-car' name such as Westbrook you will be better remembered," explained Gibbons. By late 1917 Westbrook Pegler's trenchant reports on the doughboys were being pored over at American breakfast tables, but some of them were indigestible for the military. Pegler's accreditation was revoked when he refused to have his columns censored.

Pegler returned to America fearing banality but instead found himself covering the extraordinary murder of Joseph Bowne Elwell, the "Wizard of the Whist" who had tutored the king of England in the nuances of the game. Elwell was also a drinker, a gambler, a philanderer and a secret agent, and in June 1920 someone entered his Manhattan flat and shot him dead. The real headline grabber, however, was that the assassin left the body in a room locked from the inside. Pegler and Julia Harpman met as they crawled over the crime scene in pursuit of the key facts of the case, and love blossomed as they compared notes. Although there was no happy end for Elwell's family — his killer eluded detection – Harpman and Pegler married in New York in 1922. Thereafter Pegler concentrated on sportswriting, mainly baseball, football and boxing, and he was appointed eastern sports editor of the *Chicago Tribune* in 1925. Pegler had known about Gertrude Ederle since 1922 when he'd reported on her victory in the Joseph Day Cup, but it wasn't until June 2, 1926, that he got to meet her for the first time.

Ederle had dressed for the voyage in a light brown serge suit with a cloche hat. She and her married sister Margaret Deuschle posed for a photograph at the request of Arthur Sorenson, an employee of Pacific and Atlantic Photos, who would be working for the *Daily News* for the duration of Ederle's Channel attempt.

The thirty-two-year-old was perhaps the most important member of the team. Like all good photographers, Sorenson got the shots he wanted by sweet-talking his subjects. On the deck of the *Berengaria*, he snapped Aileen Riggin kissing Ederle goodbye, and then he persuaded Henry Ederle to come and join his two daughters for a photo that would please lonely Mrs. Ederle in the weeks and months to come.

The photos appeared in the *Daily News* the following day, along with Ederle's debut column and Harpman's opening dispatch. She described why the Channel was such a formidable foe, and how that accounted for the fact that only five men had ever swum across the twenty-one miles that separated England from mainland Europe. Then Harpman painted a picture of the woman who hoped to make history as the first female to defeat the Channel. "She is sturdily built with wide shoulders and powerful hands. She has a wide-eyed, happy face and a queer way of wrinkling her nose and forehead when she is puzzled or perturbed. Her very dark brown hair is short and straight and caught on the right side with an inexpensive barrette. She seems even younger than her few years and amazingly unsophisticated, in spite of a manner which at first acquaintance, seems a bit brusque. Her laugh is booming and full-throated and always at attention."

At dinner on the first night the Ederle party sat down to a meal of roast beef. There was a symphony of popping champagne corks as passengers toasted Prohibition on the British liner. Pegler and Sorenson clinked glasses and talked about Babe Ruth and Jack Dempsey for a while. Then Pegler turned his attention to Henry Ederle, or "Pop" as he preferred to be called. He owned a butcher shop on Amsterdam Avenue as well as a figure that suggested he enjoyed his own produce. The black hair on top of his chubby face was slicked back, greying above the ears, and he sported a thick moustache, glossed with champagne.

Ederle on the *Berengaria* sailing for Europe in June 1926

Pegler soon discovered that Pop was a talker, particularly when the subject was himself. He had arrived in New York in 1892 as a sixteen-year-old travelling on a twenty-dollar ticket, desperate to build a new life in America and escape the family home in Germany, where he had had to live among his twenty brothers and sisters.

Pegler refilled their glasses and sat back as Pop poured out his life story. Ederle, Pegler wrote later, "started life in the new country as a delivery boy and apprentice cutter at six dollars a week, in the same Amsterdam Avenue meat market that now carries his name above the door". By the time the owner had tired of the work, Ederle had enough saved up to buy him out for two thousand dollars. "Pop now owns not only the shop and the building, and the block of railroad flats, including the one that Trudie was born in, but half of a city block on Amsterdam Avenue."

It was his money taking his daughter across the Atlantic, he told Pegler, and the moment his Trudy* socked it to the Channel, his butcher shop would be the most famous in the whole of New York, if not America.

The only one at the table not drinking was Gertrude. She sipped on a lemon soda not because she was a prohibitionist; "I merely am not acquainted with alcoholics [sic] and I do not desire to make the acquaintance," she explained. After clearing her plate of beef, Gertrude excused herself and retired to her cabin to finish reading Rex Beach's *Winds of Chance*. Pegler had scarcely had a chance to say a word to her, but even in the short space of time she had been at the table, it was obvious why she could be considered brusque – a dose of measles when she was a small child had left her partially deaf.

She had a habit, when trying to catch what someone was

---

* Some reporters used the spelling "Trudie", but Ederle herself spelled it "Trudy".

saying to her, of pushing her hair back behind her ears in the hope that would make their indistinct words clearer. Ederle's poor hearing frustrated her and sometimes made her impatient. The background noise in a ship's dining room she found especially trying, and Pegler noted that she "spoke in a slightly modified bawl", but when the waiter appeared to take her order "she boomed her desires in such a thundering bellow that the passengers at tables forty yards away thought Wild Will Lyons * had somehow stowed away and crawled out of concealment demanding rations". Ederle felt the stares of her fellow diners, which made her even more self-conscious. Soon her cabin became her haven, and her books became her companions.

Her family told Pegler her hearing was a temporary problem, an occupational hazard for modern swimmers who "plough along with their heads almost submerged" using the overarm crawl. They were confident her hearing would improve when she stopped swimming.

Fortunately for Ederle, Cunard's *Berengaria* was a vast ship measuring 277 metres in length so it was easy to hide from the other two thousand passengers as the four turbines drove her across the Atlantic at twenty-three knots per hour. She rose early each morning, while most of the other passengers lay in bed with their champagne sore heads, and took a brisk walk around a 300-metre circuit laid out on the ship's decks, completing sixteen laps on the first morning so fast that, as she put it, "I almost gained a mile on the ship itself." She also liked playing golf on the upper deck with Margaret, and there was a swimming pool that she used more out of habit than for any other reason. As she explained in her column of Saturday, June 5, the hour spent in the pool the day before had been fun, "but for a distance

---

* Wild Will Lyons, also known as Wild Bill Lyons, was a bodyguard to the stars in the 1920s. He had a colourful reputation and packed two pearl-handled pistols and had a host of tales about his days Out West.

swimmer preparing to swim the English Channel this was a good deal like a whale training in a rain barrel . . . one good crawl stroke carries me halfway across".

Ederle enjoyed the time she spent with Harpman composing her newspaper columns. There was no literary pretension to them; they were just the chatty comments of a young woman, which made them all the more readable. She weighed 149 pounds when she left New York, she said in one, but needed to add ten pounds of insulation before tackling the Channel. In this respect, Ederle told readers, she would be helped by their New York steward, Jack Chorley, thirty years in the business, six of which were on the *Lusitania*, and a man happy to pile her plate high with food.

Arthur Sorenson meanwhile did his best to keep Ederle's weight down by asking her to pose for a series of photographs for use in future editions of Patterson's newspapers. He snapped her striding around the ship's track, in her bathing suit, and in another he had Gertrude leapfrogging her sister.

On Sunday, June 6, there was a vaudeville concert on board the *Berengaria*, and Ederle sat in the audience hissing along with the other passengers as Ernest Torrence skulked across the stage. Torrence was Hollywood's "bad man", a Scot who was continually cast in villainous roles, either as Clopin in *The Hunchback of Notre Dame* or Captain Hook in *Peter Pan*. There were also songs and magic tricks, nothing too sophisticated but the type of lighthearted entertainment that temporarily helped Ederle forget Bill Burgess and Lillian Cannon.

But the next day, as she composed her final ocean-crossing column, Ederle had only one thing on her mind. She explained that once the ship docked she would take the train from the port of Cherbourg into Paris, and then back out to the coastal village of Cape Gris-Nez, a convoluted journey but quicker than going from Cherbourg to Gris-Nez because it cut out the hours of waiting for connecting trains. Ederle told America she had no wish to tarry in Paris but wanted to get to Gris-Nez as quickly as possible because she was "anxious to see Trainer William Burgess".

It was cold and grey when they docked at Cherbourg on Tuesday, June 8, and the weather in Paris was the same when they stepped from the train in the early evening. A flock of reporters was waiting, and they found Ederle in a fractious mood. Recognising a journalist from the previous year who had reckoned she could never achieve her Channel dream, Ederle told him: "You wrote a story that I wouldn't make it this year. But, oh boy, how I'm going to make you eat that!" What makes you so confident this time around? another reporter asked her. "I have a regular gang with me now," she replied, "and the training won't bother me." Someone asked her father if he had faith in his daughter. Pop's moustache bristled indignantly: "The hell she can't swim that Channel," he snarled. "The ones who say that she can't don't know my Trudie."

They had supper that evening in a restaurant of high repute on the Champs-Elysées. Pegler watched in cheerful astonishment as "Trudie pushed the bill of fare [sic] away and asked if they could provide her with a bowl of chop suey and a large dish of ice cream". Pegler calmed the chef, who had taken the request as a "personal affront", and from somewhere a bowl of chop suey was produced.

Despite Ederle's desire to get to Cape Gris-Nez as swiftly as possible, she and her team spent Wednesday in Paris, and it wasn't until early on Thursday morning that they boarded the train to Boulogne with the press pack in tow. Pegler was familiar with this part of France, but he noted that "most of the other Americans on board were popping their heads out of the window to be a few inches nearer the wonders of another land". All

A full-page news article presenting the case for Gertrude Ederle's
Channel-swimming abilities

except Gertrude. She "sat gathered up in a corner of the compartment, her brown bare knees showing beneath her short skirt,
reading a fifty-cent novel".

From Boulogne they jumped in two taxis to Cape Gris-Nez,
travelling along a small road which cut through a patchwork of
green and brown fields. Now and again they saw a large square
stone sunk into the ground on which a few years earlier had
stood a coastal gun battery. Pegler well remembered the boom of
such guns, but for his wife everything was new and exciting. As
they turned down a narrow lane into the village of Cape Gris-
Nez, Harpman was charmed by "its little cluster of stone

houses, all neatly whitewashed as to walls and many red tiled as to roofs, while others are thatched . . . moss and vines grow out from the high stone walls surrounding the gardens which are dark with undergrowth dotted with beds of beautiful flowers of varieties not seen in America".

Once they arrived at the Hôtel du Phare, Ederle went hunting for Burgess, with her gang running to keep up. When she found him she demanded an explanation. Why was he training Lillian Cannon when he had agreed to coach only her? Wasn't that why she had paid him ten thousand francs? Burgess shifted from foot to foot and mumbled something about a misunderstanding. If that was the case, he wouldn't have any objection to severing all ties with Cannon and fulfilling his original promise, would he? Burgess apologised and explained that that wouldn't be possible. Cannon's newspaper had paid him twenty thousand francs, and what with the collapse of the French economy because of its war debt to America, he needed the money to prop up his garage business. Of course, if Gertrude's newspaper were to match what Cannon was paying him, he would be delighted to coach only her.

Pegler shook his head with disgust at Burgess's knavery, but he knew it was a well-conceived piece of deception. The Englishman wasn't as stupid as he looked. Ederle didn't need him for his coaching methods, just for his intimate and unsurpassed knowledge of the Channel's tides and currents, and Burgess knew it. Through eyes narrowed with hostility, Ederle told him he would get his extra ten thousand francs. But there was a warning, too: in the future it "would be wise to live up to his contract".

Chapter Six

BY THE TIME Gertrude Ederle had her showdown with Bill Burgess, Lillian Cannon had already benefited from two weeks of his advice. On the day Ederle arrived at Cape Gris-Nez, Thursday, June 10, many of the Scripps-Howard newspapers published Cannon's column, the latest in a series she was writing as part of her sponsorship deal, along with a photo of her emerging from the Channel side by side with a bedraggled-looking Burgess. The previous day Cannon had told the *Baltimore Post*, "Being a good trainer . . . [Burgess] is watching me closely and bringing me along slowly. I am never ready to stop when Burgess calls a halt on a swim, or a walk, but he has warned me against overexertion in these early days of my training."

Cannon also described how the idea to bring over the two Chesapeake Bay dogs had proved a great success in France. "'*Merveilleuse*' was the word of the Paris papers and of the crowds everywhere when they saw the dogs," she trilled. Cannon declined to mention, however, that on the other side of the Channel reaction to the dogs was far from favourable. One Dover newspaper warned on May 28 that a formal protest would be made if there was any indication that the dogs were being forced to swim against their will.

On the same day, Cannon had taken her first dip in the Channel, with the water an icy forty-four degrees. Burgess kept her in for ten minutes before ushering her out of the water and into the restaurant of the Hôtel de la Sirène for a mug of hot chocolate. "It feels exactly as if there is an ice pack all over the body," Cannon wrote when she'd regained feeling in her fingers. "There is a numbness that comes over one that is absolutely paralysing."

In the next fortnight Burgess had gradually increased the length of time Cannon spent in the water, first to twenty minutes, then half an hour, until by the morning of June 10, an hour in the Channel was no great hardship. Cannon had also adjusted to the greater buoyancy of salt water compared to the fresh water of Chesapeake Bay and Maryland's Magothy River.

On the advice of Burgess, Cannon and her husband took long walks down the lanes and across the coastal paths surrounding Cape Gris-Nez to add variety to her training. Some days they walked eight miles, with Chesacroft Drake and Mary Montauk loping alongside, relieved to be out of the freezing water.

One or two tourists had arrived for a holiday, before the summer rush began, but most people Cannon encountered were locals. They warmed to the pretty blonde American, regaling her with stories about how this stretch of coast was "where Caesar came and crossed, Napoleon came, gazed long and turned back . . . of how they narrowly escaped invasion by Germany a dozen years ago". Some of the villagers told her about the time in 1917 when a German submarine caught fire just off the coast and the crew swam ashore, to be captured near the village a day later.

Burgess also took a shine to Cannon and her husband. Eddie was a likable, steady young man, unobtrusive and a great support to his wife, while she was every trainer's dream: hardworking, obedient, disciplined and attentive. Each day started in the same fashion with Burgess appearing on the beach wearing an ancient bathing suit that now struggled to contain its wearer's girth. "Come along, girl," he bellowed, shuffling toward the surf, "it's us for the ice bath." Cannon's response was always the same: "Yes, sir!"

"She's fast," Burgess was quoted as saying in the *Baltimore Post* on June 23. "She's too fast. One of my jobs is going to be to slow her down. But she isn't afraid to take orders. She is eager to profit by the experiences of others. A very nice personality, very nice indeed."

The more Cannon became inured to the Channel's temperature, the more her spirits rose. To inspire her each day, she had painted a motto on the front of her sweater, England or bust, and she became infected with the same Channel obsession as her trainer. They spent hours poring over Burgess's dog-eared sea charts, and he advised her to go up to the top of Cape Gris-Nez, among the buttercups and the rabbits, and study the Channel as it rounded the promontory. Cannon did as she was told. "I spend hours gazing in fascination at the water," she confessed in one column, ". . . [and] see the different currents sweep past, their colours are different and they rush like mill races, each on its separate course. I didn't understand what Burgess meant last winter when he wrote me that I would have to be a fast swimmer, would have to have good weather, and would have to have a world of luck, but I do now."

On the eve of Ederle's arrival, Burgess had planned to intensify Cannon's training programme. The following week she would start to do one long swim a week of six hours. Depending how she fared, Cannon might swim from Cape Gris-Nez to Boulogne at the start of July, to test her "mind, heart and bodily endurance".

An hour or two after the contretemps with Burgess, Gertrude Ederle and Julia Harpman sat down to write the column for the June 11 edition of the *Daily News*. They agreed it wouldn't look good if they disclosed the sordid argument, so instead they laced the copy with insinuation. "An attempt at swimming the Channel is each year becoming more expensive," said Ederle, who added that she'd had a surprise encounter with a fellow American: "Lillian Cannon of Baltimore. She also is in training here for an attempt to conquer the Channel."

Supper that evening at the Hôtel du Phare wasn't particularly convivial. Burgess had at least been able to scuttle back to his villa, but Cannon and Ederle had to eat in the same small dining room. It was an uncomfortable meal, wrote Pegler, who described the two swimmers as "not quite kissing friends".

There was only one long table for guests, Harpman noted, and "the white paper covers are not changed with regularity". She dangled a stained napkin between thumb and forefinger and estimated that it "must last a person 10 days." Lined along the centre of the table was a column of onions, pickles, ketchups and sauces, all of which Ederle used to try and bring her food to life.

Relations deteriorated further over the weekend when Burgess insisted he would continue to train Cannon until he received the money from New York. Ederle had no choice but to comply; already two weeks behind Cannon in her training, she couldn't sit idle for another two days. The trio took to the water watched by a reporter for the United Press agency. It didn't take him long to figure out who was the better swimmer: Ederle uses a "brilliant crawl stroke that has always distinguished her swimming", while Cannon "is trying to adapt her breast and overarm strokes to Channel conditions. She will change from one to the other frequently . . . she says to use all her muscles without tiring herself with any one system".

A Paris-based photographer working for the Scripps-Howard agency accosted the trio as they left the water, and asked for a photo. Again, Ederle was in an invidious position. It wouldn't look good if news reached America that she was playing the prima donna, but the last thing she wanted was to take part in an absurd charade. Ederle solved the dilemma by posing for the photo – each woman sat on either side of Burgess with his arms around their shoulders – but while Cannon and Burgess turned their heads and smiled at the camera, she looked straight ahead. The result of her small act of defiance worked in her favour when the photograph was published in the American papers. Ederle looked like she was gazing out to sea, so focused on the job at hand that she forgot to pose for the camera. Over the weekend of June 12 and 13 news of the dispute leaked out in America, and Ederle felt obliged to use her column on Monday, the fourteenth, to issue a public statement.

I find no joy in misunderstandings and I would much prefer to say nothing about one which has slightly exaggerated the natural climatic chill along this side of the English Channel these last few days. After I failed to complete the crossing last year I immediately determined to repeat the endeavour this year and at once began preparations which are far more complex than the uninitiated would expect. Months ago, after an interchange of letters, I made an agreement with William Burgess, the English swimmer, who was the second man to succeed in swimming the Channel, and whom I considered the best qualified to train anyone for the attempt.

Our agreement provided that he was to train me and no other woman of the dozen who have announced their intention to attempt the crossing this summer. I was particular about specifying that I should have his services exclusively because in a certain sense all of we would-be negotiators of the difficult swim are competitors, and also because it is impossible for one trainer to handle two women and give each equal attention and opportunity for success.

For instance, suppose one man handles two women,

William Burgess struggling ashore after his successful Channel swim

both desirous of making the attempt on the first good day. One is a slow swimmer and the other a sprinter. Obviously it would be impossible for the trainer to accompany both in the water.

Now when Miss Lillian Cannon, of Baltimore, the famous Chesapeake Bay swimmer, left New York recently I paid her a courtesy call on shipboard to wish her "bon voyage" and good luck in her attempt. I was greatly surprised when she told me she, too, expected to have Burgess as her trainer.

When I arrived at Gris-Nez last Thursday I discovered Miss Cannon unhappily situated because Burgess had only agreed to train her, too, if I gave my consent.

I felt it necessary for the protection of my own interests to refuse my consent to such an arrangement and thus Miss Cannon is temporarily without a trainer, although doubtless another good one will be found procurable.

I am sincerely sorry this situation has arisen, but I'm sure it is from no fault of mine and apparently neither is

Miss Cannon to be blamed entirely for, being inexperienced in Channel swimming, she was largely unaware of conditions.

Ederle's statement was seized upon by the *Baltimore Post*'s main rival, the *Baltimore Sun*. On page three of its June 15 edition it ran a piece headlined CHANNEL SWIMMERS QUARREL, under which they printed two photos of Ederle and Cannon in their bathing suits. The *Post* responded by asking Cannon to refute the claims in her column, which she did on Friday, June 18. "I reiterate that there is no dispute of any kind between Miss Gertrude Ederle and myself," she wrote. "On the contrary, there is complete friendliness as we continue our training for the gruelling competition of the Channel swim." Not according to Ederle, who, on the same day, reported in words which dripped with satisfaction, that "Lillian Cannon, the Baltimore Channel swimmer, moved from our hotel to the other nearer the beach".

Cannon was forced to flee the Hôtel du Phare and seek refuge in the Hôtel de la Sirène as the altercation took a turn for the worse. While Cannon sobbed on her husband's shoulder, Ederle turned to her sister for support.

Margaret was two years older and a competent swimmer in her own right. When Gertrude had won the Joseph Day Cup in 1922, Margaret finished a respectable twenty-sixth out of fifty-two entrants, seventeen minutes behind her sister in the three-and-a-half-mile race. But she had always swum for fun; it was Gertrude who had the talent, if not the ambition to match. With the connivance of the Women's Swimming Association, Margaret entered Gertrude for events if she hadn't bothered to fill out the forms herself. In 1925 Margaret had been in the support boat when Gertrude swam twenty-one miles from the Battery to Sandy Hook in seven hours and eleven and a half minutes, six minutes faster than the existing record. A mile from the finish the tide had turned against Ederle, and she began to wilt.

Her coach and one or two concerned members of the Women's Swimming Association had been trying to prod her forward with gentle encouragement, when suddenly Margaret stood up, cupped her hands to her mouth and yelled, "Get going, lazy bones, you're loafing!" It was a brilliant piece of psychology. Stung by the accusation that she was dawdling, Ederle redoubled her efforts and battled through the tide to Sandy Hook.

But Margaret was astute enough to know when to hector, when to cajole and when to comfort. The dispute with Burgess and Cannon, and the headlines in the newspapers, had upset her already self-conscious and sensitive sister, so Margaret took her on a long walk along the cliffs on Friday, June 18. Then they borrowed a car and drove into Boulogne, to an Anglo-American grocery store Margaret had heard about. There they loaded up the car with what Gertrude described as "food I've been craving since our departure" and returned to the hotel to indulge in a marathon session of comfort eating.

Chapter Seven

THE NEW YORK TIMES was one of the few newspapers to ignore the squabble on Cape Gris-Nez. Its publisher, the venerable Adolph Ochs, probably thought it would be undignified to write about the incident. Having taken control of the paper in 1896 when daily circulation had dwindled to just nine thousand, Ochs had a strategy against the rise of the tabloids: to make *The Times* the exact opposite. All the news fit to print was emblazoned on the masthead, and he gave much prominence to literature and arts, establishing an influential weekly books section. *The Times'* circulation quadrupled within three years, and by 1926 it was selling 362,000 copies each day, second only to the *Daily News* and 15,000 more than the *World*, its greatest broadsheet competitor, whose noble tone was as impressive as the gold dome and red stone of the Pulitzer Building in which the paper was housed.

But if Ochs was loath to dwell on the fracas between Ederle and Cannon, *The Times* nonetheless continued to take an interest in the Channel swimming race. In the week that Ederle left New York, the paper assessed her chances as well as those of her adversaries. "Unquestionably Miss Ederle has the best prospects," said *The Times*. "She is by long odds the speediest of the five candidates." As for the others, Cannon had proved her mettle the previous summer when she swam Chesapeake Bay;

Eva Morrison had several notable exploits to her credit.* Gade "makes up in stamina what she lacks in speed", and as for the fifth, Clarabelle Barrett, well, *The Times* didn't know what to say about her. It couldn't even decide whether her surname was spelled with one t or two, in the end opting for one of each in the article. It also misspelled her first name – Clarebelle instead of Clarabelle. "Of Miss Barrett, little is known," confessed the author of the piece. "Nevertheless she has done a great deal of long-distance swimming and is well equipped physically for a severe test."

A week later the *Baltimore American* published a two-page article about the race to swim the Channel. It didn't even mention Barrett's name, though it gave much prominence to the French swimmer Jeanne Sion, who had spent fourteen hours and thirty-five minutes trying to swim the Channel in 1922, an endurance record for a female swimmer. The *American* article concluded by predicting that "unique laurels await the woman who first swims the Channel . . . she will earn an undying fame".

Clarabelle Barrett wasn't much interested in fame; it was the money that had attracted her to the Channel. She wasn't after a fortune but just enough to help her realise her dream of singing professionally. For the last four years she had been taking lessons – when she could afford them – to improve her contralto voice, but the money she might make from the Channel would enable her to hire a singing coach, the best available, and perhaps one day she would perform in New York's Carnegie Hall. Barrett was a few years older than her other Channel rivals. She had been born in New York in August 1891 to Nathan Barrett and his

* Eva Morrison soon withdrew her name from the Channel list, as did Helen Wainwright.

Five Women to Try to Swim the English Channel

Champions Answering Challenge to Sex to Meet the Supreme Test of Physical Endurance---Only Five Men and No Women So Far Have Accomplished This Feat

The bathing beauties of Channel swimming

wife, Clara. Nathan was a Civil War veteran, one of General Philip Sheridan's boys, who had been wounded at the battle of Cedar Creek in 1864.

With the war over, Barrett trained as a landscape architect and soon proved himself a natural. When Clarabelle was born — the last of his four children but the first daughter — Nathan was considered one of America's foremost landscape designers, the man responsible for designing, among others, the town of Pullman in Illinois. In 1893 his star soared higher when he helped create the grounds of the World's Fair in Chicago. He built a majestic house for his family in Rochelle Park, New Rochelle, which was known locally as the "most beautiful half acre in the world". In June 1906 Barrett hosted a fund-raising event on the grounds of his home, which was attended by an enraptured correspondent from the *New York Times*. "The grounds abound with Alpine peaks spanned by rustic bridges, Italian lakes, deep canyons – miniature reproductions of those in Colorado – while brooks fall in cascades into lakes, in which water fowl swim about. This scene was illuminated last night with myriads of coloured incandescent lights which produced an indescribably beautiful effect."

Barrett was back in *The Times* two months later, but on this occasion it was tragedy that brought him to the public's attention. Clarabelle's sixteen-year-old brother, Detmar, an enthusiastic student of telegraphy, had been fixing a broken telegraph pole with some friends when his hand brushed the high-power wire. He crashed to the ground, and the official cause of death was a crushed skull and broken back.

In a bid to escape their grief, the family moved from New Rochelle to nearby Pelham, and soon Detmar's two older brothers, John and Nathan junior, left home to work. One of Nathan senior's few remaining pleasures in his dotage was swimming with his daughter. He had taught Clarabelle to swim when she was six, using the same technique for her as he had for his sons. Having sailed some distance from the shore in his small dinghy, Barrett tossed his offspring overboard and advised them how best to stay afloat.

Clarabelle joined the National Women's Life-Saving League in New York City, and a photograph of her, along with other members of the league, appeared in the *Washington Post* on July 18, 1914, under the headline YOUNG WOMEN WHO IN SWIMMING RACE COVERED A FIVE MILE COURSE IN ATLANTIC. Two years later on March 31, 1916, Barrett, then twenty-four, competed in the biggest race of her life, the Amateur Athletic Union (AAU) Handicap in the West Sixtieth Street municipal pool. The event was billed as America's first national female championships, graced by the likes of Claire Galligan and Lucy Freeman. The crowds jostled for space around the outside of the pool, among them the correspondent of the *New York Times*. At the halfway mark of the 100-yard handicap, there was nothing to separate Galligan, Myrtle Pavitt and Barrett. Only in the last quarter of the race did Galligan edge ahead, recounted *The Times*, and at the finish "not the length of a contestant separated the first three", with Barrett taking the bronze.

Galligan, like Barrett, was a member of the National Women's Life-Saving League, the organisation formed by Charlotte Epstein in 1914 so women could participate in a sport that until then had restricted them to a splash in the surf. The success of the AAU championships in 1916 encouraged Epstein to push for further recognition for women's swimming, and the following year the New York Women's Swimming Association (WSA) came into being. Epstein's wish was to see American women compete in the Olympic Games, just as men did, although the motto of the WSA underscored her overriding belief: GOOD SPORTSMANSHIP IS BETTER THAN VICTORY.

With no money to hire coaches, the WSA had to rely on the generosity of volunteers, one of whom was Louis de Breda Handley, a Roman who had emigrated to America in 1896. Handley had won gold for the United States in water polo and relay swimming in the 1904 St. Louis Olympics, before he had turned to coaching. By 1917 he was a man ahead of his time; not only was he a far-sighted and innovative swimming instructor, but he also supported female emancipation in every walk of life.

When Handley had been growing up in Rome in the 1880s, the most popular swimming stroke was the "Trudgeon", named after the English swimmer who brought the technique to Europe from Argentina a few years earlier. It was an ugly stroke, one that required the swimmer to keep his upper torso out of the water while bringing his arms up and over and executing a scissor kick with his legs.

At the beginning of the twentieth century the Trudgeon began to be replaced in Europe and America by the Australian crawl. This stroke had more rhythm and fluency to it, characterised by a very fast overarm action and a simultaneous leg kick. Handley and other New York coaches, most notably Gus Sundstrom and Otto Wahle, experimented with the Australian crawl, putting greater emphasis on a quicker leg action and an extended reach with the arms. They christened their invention the American crawl. When Handley volunteered to coach at the WSA pool in the basement of 145 West Fifty-fifth Street, he had refined the stroke still further, introducing a breathing technique that involved just a slight turn of the head as opposed to the traditional rolling motion and devising something called the "six-beat crawl".

The six-beat crawl required the swimmer to use three leg kicks to each arm stroke. It wasn't easy for the enthusiastic but inexperienced swimmers of the WSA, so Handley answered their questions in one of their regular newsletters. "What is the best way to acquire the six-beat crawl after one has become accustomed to the four-beat?" asked one student. "Make the leg movements faster and narrower," replied Handley, "occasionally counting one-two-three during the drive of the top arm and four-five-six during the recovery of the same arm. Time the action by counting as each leg starts its downward movement." Another wished to know if "it is advisable to finish the arm drive vigorously in swimming the crawl". Handley recommended that "one should keep pressure on the water to the end of the drive, but any jerk at the finish causes unnecessary waste of energy".

Barrett was one of the first women to learn the six-beat crawl when, having transferred her membership from the National Women's Life-Saving League to the WSA in 1917, she came under Handley's tuition. Even though she was twenty-six, she still harboured ambitions of competing for America in the 1920 Olympics.

Then in October 1919, Nathan Barrett died, and the course of Clarabelle's life changed irrevocably. She and her mother were now alone in their large Pelham house, relying on handouts from her two brothers and the money left by her father, which turned out to be much less than expected.

Nathan Barrett had never been one of life's hoarders, preferring instead to lavish money on his patronage of the arts, for which he had a reputation as something of a philanthropist, and on ensuring that his family wanted for nothing as long as he was alive. One of his indulgences had been to pay for Clarabelle to have singing lessons with Mrs. Roland Howell, a contralto singer of some repute. In the report of Barrett's funeral carried by New Rochelle's *Standard-Star*, Clarabelle was described as a "professional singer", but she had never given a performance to anyone other than small gatherings of family or friends, and always accompanied by her mother, who had sung professionally in her youth.

Clarabelle's dream of becoming a concert singer died with her father, as did her ambition to compete in the Olympics. In need of money, she relinquished her amateur status in 1920 – and her membership in the WSA – and accepted a job as a swimming teacher at Public School No. 40 in New York City. Barrett's involvement in the Olympics was reduced to reading the newspaper reports about the WSA's Ethelda Bleibtrey winning three gold medals.

Barrett was still teaching four years later, when WSA swimmers again dominated the Olympics, and the following year, 1925, she was appointed head of the swimming department at the new James Monroe High School in the Bronx. She was now thirty-four and hadn't swum competitively since her father's death. But with middle age bearing down on her, Barrett's mind turned to her unfulfilled ambition of becoming a concert singer. In October 1925, on her way to work from the home in Pelham that she still shared with her mother, she read in the paper about Mille Gade's intention to swim the English Channel the following summer. This was Barrett's epiphany, the moment she realized she had one last chance to avoid an old age burdened with regret. She started to catch an earlier train to work so she could swim four miles each morning before the school bell rang at 9:00 a.m. She took on classes after hours, to earn a bit of extra money, and most nights she arrived home bleary-eyed at 10:30.

In March 1926 Barrett spent some time training in the waters off Pine Island, in Maine, where in previous summers she had taught swimming at summer camps. She swam her first mile when the temperature was thirty-seven degrees, a feat of endurance so impressive it made the sports pages of her local paper, the *Standard-Star*. The report added that not only would Barrett attempt the "treacherous waters of the English Channel in the latter part of July", but she was also "a big woman".

The next time Barrett's name appeared in the *Standard-Star* was at the end of May. The reporter on this occasion was more appreciative of his subject: "Miss Barrett is of superb physique, being six feet tall. She has auburn hair and has not followed the fad of her sex in having it bobbed." The accompanying photo depicted a woman not short on flesh and ill at ease with her body. Barrett sat cross-legged in a baggy bathing suit, her arms folded defensively over her knees and her hair long and unruly as if she had been out in a gale. Her uncomfortable smile, more like a grimace, hinted that two hours training in the freezing waters off Pine Island was far preferable to five minutes in front of the camera.

Before she had started training for the Channel, Barrett weighed 220 pounds, but in the interview with the *Standard-Star* she proudly revealed she had "lost 22 pounds", adding, "Physical examinations have shown my heart to be perfect after these long swims as I have been an endurance swimmer for many years. I am able to make a mile in 38 minutes, using what is known as the six-beat American crawl stroke, which I will use in making the struggle to conquer the Channel."

On Sunday, May 30, Barrett swam across Long Island Sound from Hudson Park to Sands Point in three hours. The *Standard-Star* was impressed. It ran a couple of paragraphs on the swim and noted – with a Brr! – that the temperature of the water had been fifty degrees. But the paper didn't feel the urge to sponsor its local heroine on her Channel odyssey, even though it was aware she was having difficulty scraping together the funds. Twenty of Barrett's friends had each loaned her a hundred dollars to cover her return fare to England and the cost of a cheap boarding house for three weeks. So at least she would be able to get to the English Channel. Now she had to try to find a way to hire a trainer and a tug and a pilot to guide her across the twenty-one miles of sea. She was probably around $1,500 short, loose change for a newspaper but a towering sum for a Bronx swimming teacher. Barrett's handicap was her body. She didn't look very comely, in or out of a bathing suit, and the only thing eye-catching about her physique was its sheer size. Newspaper editors weren't interested in a "big woman" in her mid-thirties. When Barrett's photo did make the pages of the *Daily News* on June 21, the day she swam twenty-one miles across Long Island Sound, it was an action shot of her in the water, head to one side gasping for air. The caption ran: CLARABELLE BARRETT, PELHAM-WOOD, NY, 200-POUND SWIMMER, YESTERDAY SWAM FROM NEW ROCHELLE TO WHITESTONE, 21 MILES, IN 10 HOURS.

Ridiculed and rejected by the newspapers, Barrett nonetheless booked a passage on the SS *Leviathan* on July 3 with the money loaned to her by her twenty friends. There would be no photographer to snap her leapfrogging on deck, no journalist to write down what she read or what she ate, no sister or father to offer words of comfort. All Barrett had to spur her on was her best friend, Grace Leister, a registered nurse and also her training partner, and a bloody-minded determination to prove people wrong.

Chapter Eight

NOTHING WAS GOING right for Lillian Cannon at Cape Gris-Nez. Burgess was no longer her trainer, and wasn't it strange how the sea seemed much colder now that she was swimming alone? Burgess had kept up her spirits when she swam, imbuing her with the belief that she had what it took to beat the Channel. But now the water seemed to penetrate her skin and chill the marrow of her bones. "The water is still icy cold," she told the *Baltimore Post* on June 18. "Indeed, thus far, it is colder than Chesapeake Bay in winter."

It had become too cold for her two dogs, Chesacroft Drake and Mary Montauk, to the disappointment of the *Post* and the relief of England. The *Post*, as if in an effort to boost the morale of its readers in the wake of the Ederle fight, had taken to publishing photos of Cannon walking Chesacroft Drake on the beach wearing only her bathing suit. A collective groan ran through the editorial office on June 18 when Cannon announced that "the English Channel has added two more to the long list of defeated challengers". She explained that the dogs "have had a taste of its difficulties and given up the job as too tough for them. Though they have never refused to follow me into any water before, they came out of the icy Channel water after several attempts to swim shivering and almost exhausted. I fear I must send them back home. I cannot coax them back into the water. I have got to succeed now, if only to show my dogs that my courage is superior to theirs." Cannon had also come under pressure from organisations as well as from individuals in Britain to release the dogs from their obligation. They were being coerced was the gist of the correspondence, and that stuck in the craw of a certain type of Briton who, while tolerating children living in squalid tenement slums, couldn't bear the thought of cruelty to dogs. From Bournemouth on the English south coast came a letter signed simply "A well-wisher": "We all in England wish you the greatest good luck in your attempt to cross the Channel, providing you do not take the dogs with you. It's not quite sporting because your dogs are so faithful that they will follow you, even if they are suffering. I know I am voicing the thoughts of thousands in sincerely asking you not to attempt to let the dogs accompany you."

Meanwhile another letter arrived from Charles R. Johns, secretary of the National Canine Defence League of England. He informed Cannon that he was writing on behalf of his members who could not "conceive of the possibility that a dog could swim 30 miles without serious injury to its health". Would she not reconsider her plan? Cannon used her column to reassure the dog lovers the world over that "these appeals, just a sample of many, impressed me so much that I've decided to send the dogs home".

On Saturday, June 19, the day after Chesacroft Drake and Mary Montauk received the good news that they were being posted home, Cannon was stung by a jellyfish. That evening her skin prickled with pain and the rash "had spread over several square inches, causing a disagreeable itch and threatening real trouble". Her husband, Eddie, rubbed balm into the wound in their room in the Hôtel de la Sirène, and offered sweet words of comfort, but Cannon was running short of pep.

The Scripps-Howard syndicate dispatched reinforcements to the beach, with orders to launch a charm offensive. Milton

Bronner arrived from Paris with his pen at the ready. "If 24-karat [*sic*] grit, plus swimming ability, will do it, then smiling, blue-eyed, golden-haired Lillian Cannon of Baltimore will be the first woman to cross the English Channel," he gushed in the *Baltimore Post* on Wednesday, June 24. "You ought to see her on one of these cold, windy, rainy June mornings. In her black bathing suit she's a compact, solidly built youngster of 23. Her arms are not large, but they are firm and hinged to a powerful chest. Her legs are strongly built. There should be plenty of swimmer's kick in them." The *Post*, in a contemptuous swipe at the *Daily News*, printed an old photo of Cannon and Burgess standing on the beach drinking hot chocolate, and described him as her "confidential adviser and guide".

Cannon joined in the insolent fun – now that the jellyfish rash had subsided – and crowed: "[I have been] extremely fortunate in that I arrived at Gris-Nez two weeks before the other aspirants to Channel honours arrived. That means that I had the whole attention of Bill Burgess during that time and he has taught me all that I could absorb."

It was Cannon's revenge for a cheap shot by Ederle a week earlier when she had told the *Chicago Tribune-Daily News* of a visit to Gris-Nez by Gaston Smith, the American consul in Paris, to wish the pair well. "He said the [American] flag would fly from the consulate during the period of our attempts to make the crossing," Ederle wrote, adding that unfortunately "Miss Cannon was not present to receive him, being asleep after her early-morning workout, but her husband, Eddie Day, received the consul's good wishes on her behalf." It had been an embarrassing disclosure for Cannon, who a few hours later had written in her column, "[Smith] wished me success and we chatted about my feats in the Chesapeake."

Following the humiliating put-down by Ederle, Cannon was determined to jab at her rival whenever possible. "I have taken up golf on the beach," she said in the *Baltimore Post* on June 19, describing how she and her husband had built a four-hole course in front of their hotel. "I am going to challenge Gertrude Ederle at golf after a day or two more of practice and hope to put a little variety into our friendly rivalry."

As June lengthened, Cannon's sarcasm began to give way to a more contented frame of mind. She enjoyed her new hotel, la Sirène, preferring it to the Hôtel du Phare where Monsieur Blondiau was not only looking after his guests, but his sick wife. It was still far from luxurious – she went to bed by candlelight– and the modest facilities trained her "for simple living", but she had made friends with Monsieur and Madame Lenoir, and their assistant, Louisette, who was teaching Cannon basic French. Henri Lenoir had even procured a Stars and Stripes, which he flew above the hotel in Cannon's honour.

The temperature of the Channel had risen – on good days it topped fifty-six degrees – which further invigorated Cannon, but she still had the problem of finding a trainer to replace Burgess. She and her team returned to the original list of coaches they'd drawn up earlier in the year. The names they discussed were all middle-aged men with a lot of experience and their own specific methods: Billy Kellingley of Brighton, Walter Brickett of London, Jack Wiedman of Dover and a Scotsman called Jabez Wolffe. The only one of the quartet known in America was Wolffe, unfortunately for all the wrong reasons. But before Cannon had time to put a line through his name, Wolffe strolled into Cape Gris-Nez.

The leonine Jabez Wolffe was well acquainted with Cape Gris-Nez, though not as well as he would have liked. The forty-nine-year-old Glaswegian was one of those unsmiling Scots who believed nothing in life should ever be easy. He had tried and failed to swim the Channel twenty-two times, and "Wolffe watching" had become something of a summer tradition on the Channel coast. Families sat on the beach, dipping into their picnic hampers, and watching as Wolffe set off for France, and waiting for his disconsolate return aboard his support boat. Since 1906, the year of his first attempt, he had been back nearly every summer – barring the war years when submarines and mines were too much even for Wolffe – and each time the newspapers reported every fresh defeat and listed the causes: leg cramps, a collision with a plank of wood, an encounter with a bottle-nosed shark and, most agonisingly, a change of tide when he was three hundred yards from Cape Gris-Nez, which swept him back out to sea.

Although Wolffe had never made it across the Channel, his name had made the voyage across the Atlantic, and into the American newspapers, where his defeats were routinely described. In July 1914 the *Indianapolis Star* carried news of attempt number fifteen, and the *Syracuse Herald* ran a piece on Wolffe in 1919, although the post-war tone had changed from frivolity to pity. He was too old now, said the *Herald*, and "it is a sad case for Wolffe would have made a fortune making a tour of the music halls and he was under contract to a patent food concern, whose broth he was using during the swims".

Wolffe made one last attempt in 1921, but it was more for old times' sake than a serious belief he could swim the Channel in his forty-fifth year. From then on Wolffe, dragging his thwarted ambition with him, had turned to coaching and styled himself as the man who knew more about the Channel than anybody else.

Wolffe had a steady turnover of Channel hopefuls in the early 1920s, all men, but none was able to achieve the success that had eluded their coach for fifteen years. Then in the summer of 1925, he was hired by the Women's Swimming Association to coach its eighteen-year-old prodigy, Gertrude Ederle. Like the rest of the world's swimming community, Wolffe had become familiar with the teenage sensation during her record-breaking exploits of the previous two years. In October 1923 Ederle had established a new world record of 1:12.2 minutes for the 100-metre freestyle and 5:54.4 minutes for the 400-metre freestyle. She began 1924 as the overwhelming favourite to win gold at the two distances in that year's Paris Olympics, but a knee injury in training never fully cleared and instead of gold Ederle had to settle for a pair of bronze medals. It was a grave disappointment, particularly as the winning time in each event was nowhere near her world record. (The American Martha Norelius won gold in the 400-metre freestyle in 6:02.2, nearly eight seconds slower than Ederle's 1923 record.)

Jabez Wolffe and Sunny Lowry, whom he coached in the 1930s

Ederle did get one gold, however, as a member of the 4-x-100-metre freestyle team, which finished a phenomenal 18.2 seconds ahead of the British team in second place. In June 1925 Ederle sent a message to her rivals: I'm back. Racing the 150-

metre freestyle at Long Beach, Ederle covered the first 100 metres in 1:05 minutes and finished in 1:41.6 minutes, a second quicker than the time she herself had set in 1922. Less than twenty-four hours later Ederle had broken another record, this time an endurance one, "thus displaying her amazing versatility", in the words of the *World*. On the front page of the paper was an article describing how she had swum from the Battery to Sandy Hook in seven hours and eleven and a half minutes, demolishing George Meehan's eleven-year mark by six minutes. "The success of the trial and the striking time she made augurs well for her coming Channel swim," the *World* predicted.

When Ederle arrived in France a fortnight later, Jabez Wolffe told her from the start that her previous feats were irrelevant. The Channel was like no other stretch of water in the world, and if she wanted to be its champion, she would have to do things his way. The same message was communicated to Louis de Breda Handley and Elsie Viets, her WSA chaperone, both of whom were staying with Ederle at the Hôtel du Phare.

Training went well at first, and Wolffe was soon telling Alec Rutherford, a British correspondent covering the attempt for the *New York Times*, that "Miss Ederle will succeed". In Wolffe's opinion she might even lower Enrico Tiraboschi's Channel record of sixteen hours and twenty-five minutes. "Theoretically, under the best possible weather conditions, it should be possible for a swimmer to make the distance in 14 hours," he added, although he thought Ederle needed to decrease her stroke rate. "She swims approximately 28 strokes to the minute, and we want to reduce this pace to 24. There is no doubt that she can maintain 28 for eight or nine hours, but I would prefer a slightly slower stroke for a swim which may require 16 to 20 hours."

Ederle, however, didn't see why she should alter her training regime when it had hitherto served her so well. Like most eighteen-year-olds, swimmers or otherwise, Ederle thought she knew best. A week after he had praised Ederle to the *New York Times*, Wolffe told the *Chicago Tribune* on August 8 that he didn't "expect her to succeed . . . [because] she refuses to train and plays the ukulele all day. She made her records without training and does not see why she should train now".

When Ederle and her team got wind of Wolffe's comments, they launched a scathing attack on the Scot. Elsie Viets was interviewed by a news agency reporter, and her comments were eagerly published on August 13 by a host of newspapers that weren't going to hold their noses at the first whiff of scandal. "[Wolffe] contends that Miss Ederle ought to do more work in the water, Miss Viets holds for road work with about two hours in the water daily. Wolffe advises heavy massage by a strong man to harden the muscles to immunise them against the fatigue and cold but Miss Viets insists on massage by female experts, whose methods Wolffe claims are insufficiently severe . . . Miss Viets on her part says the trainer may know all about the swimming conditions in the Channel but that he knows very little about the temperament and feelings of an 18-year-old girl."

Now it was Wolffe's turn to be outraged. Viets's assessment of his coaching ability so angered him, reported the *Baltimore Sun* on August 16, "he was on the verge of quitting", and only the intervention of his friends stopped him returning to Dover. With coach and swimmer barely on speaking terms, it was thought best to send Ederle on her way before Wolffe did pack up and go home, taking his Channel knowledge with him. As Viets and Handley oversaw Ederle's final preparations for her swim, Wolffe had an idle chat with a correspondent from the Associated Press (AP), perhaps over a beer in the bar of the Hôtel du Phare. During the course of the conversation, Wolffe told the reporter how he hoped Ederle would succeed, but, of course, his main concern was that she didn't get bitten in half by a shark. As the American's eyes widened in astonishment, Wolffe roguishly explained that so far this summer the "temperature of the water to a higher point than usual is responsible for the presence of the man-eaters".

The very word *man-eater* conjured up for Americans memories of the killer shark that had terrorised the Jersey shore nine years earlier, and the *Washington Post* knew it. SHARK'S NEW MENACE was the headline above the story filed by the AP reporter from Cape Gris-Nez on August 17.

Unfortunately, the journalist hadn't sought to corroborate Wolffe's outlandish claims of man-eating sharks in the English Channel. If he had, he would have soon learned that the only sharks that occasionally strayed into the cold and dirty waters were the harmless bottle-nosed sharks and the large but gentle basking sharks. Then again, perhaps the correspondent had checked Wolffe's statement and decided that the word *man-eater* gave a certain lurid tint to his copy.

Ederle dived off the rocks of Cape Gris-Nez at 7:15 a.m. on August 18, 1925. She swam past Wolffe in his small boat, which also contained the Egyptian swimmer Ishak Helmy, and a few yards farther on passed the tug *La Morinie*, packed to the gunnels with, among others, Viets and Handley, the French swimmer Jeanne Sion, Bill Burgess, over twenty newspaper correspondents and photographers and a four-piece jazz band who, on Ederle's orders, were to play "real American jazz – hard-boiled music – nothing in the minor chord" for her.

Wolffe took no satisfaction from Ederle's collapse after nearly nine hours in the water, the equivalent of a marathon runner "hitting the wall". On the eve of the attempt his heart still had hope that she might surprise him, but his head told him otherwise. As Wolffe said to the United Press correspondent, "Her remarkable speed may carry her over . . . she will either blow up or establish a record."

It was the former, and even a humble Ederle appeared to recognise she had underestimated the Channel's strength as she arrived back at her training camp in France. "It was funny the way I sank," she told reporters. "The last thing I remember was I began to cry. I don't know why. I wasn't sad, and I wanted to go on."

By the next morning, however, August 19, having had a night's sleep to mull things over, Ederle had mysteriously changed her attitude. The blame for her defeat shouldn't be placed on her powerful shoulders, she insisted, sulking in a way that would have done any teenager proud. "You guys are crazy saying I collapsed," she snapped at reporters. "You must have been affected by seasickness. I thought I was going good."

The United News correspondent was as incredulous as the rest of his colleagues and said that her outburst "proves that she did not comprehend during the last hour in the water what the observers aboard the tug saw – her drawn mouth, uneven strokes, glazed eyes and confused shakes of her head. If Helmy had not been alert to grab her, when Jabez Wolffe, the trainer, commanded him to, Miss Ederle, would have been in a most dangerous position".

But Ederle demanded a scapegoat, and the obvious choice was Wolffe. By the end of the day Elsie Viets had fired him and announced that Bill Burgess would prepare Ederle for her second attempt sometime in the next fortnight. The weather, however, didn't allow her to redeem her honour, and for two weeks Ederle was hemmed in on the bleak promontory by a fierce southwesterly wind.

With no sign that September would usher in a period of warm weather, Ederle reluctantly sailed for America in the second week of the month, arriving in New York in no mood to play the gracious loser for the dozens of reporters crowding around her. "I was swimming with Helmy, the Egyptian, and was going strong when my trainer shouted to him to grab me and I quit the swim," she explained to them. A protective arm was thrown around Ederle by Charlotte Epstein, founder of the WSA, who said her swimmer would say nothing further until she had been debriefed by her organization. But Epstein did ask reporters to question Wolffe's motives throughout the training period. "Just imagine his coming into her training quarters one day and exclaiming: 'What do you know, Gertie, I saw a shark today.' Imagine the effect that it would have on a young girl attempting the most difficult of swims." The *World* reported that someone else in Ederle's party intimated what a growing number of people suspected: that Wolffe had been unable to accept that an eighteen-year-old American girl was likely to succeed where he had failed twenty-two times, and so he sabotaged her attempt.

The controversy dominated the American newspapers for the next week, with Wolffe giving as good as he got. "Unadulterated nonsense" was his response to claims that he had been against Ederle from the start, adding, "I absolutely refuse to believe that Gertrude Ederle is responsible for these suggestions . . . and propose to treat the report with the contempt it deserves." But when the American reporters assured Wolffe that she was the originator of the comments, he launched a furious counter-attack. "Her statements are quite untrue," he was quoted in the *New York Herald Tribune* on Sunday, September 20. "I take it her story was meant to cover her non-compliance with my repeated efforts to get her to train. It was evident, both to the French and English observers, that her training consisted mainly of sitting about and playing the ukulele."

Ederle replied with her own fusillade of indignation. "Wolffe is a liar when he says I did most of my training on a ukulele," she told the *World* on September 20. "I played the ukulele only during idle moments, and then mostly to drown out Wolffe's chatter about how hard it was to swim the Channel and what a tough time he had the tenth or fifteenth or twenty-first time he tried it and failed." Ederle suggested that rather than rubbish her attitude, Wolffe should ask himself a few questions because in her opinion he was "one of the poorest coaches in the world".

The Atlantic duel continued with the protagonists calling on their seconds. Elsie Viets disputed Wolffe's version of Ederle's collapse – and also presumably the reports filed by correspondents who had stood next to her on *La Morinie* – by telling the *New York Times* that Ederle had climbed into the tug unaided, said "I'm all right, Elsie", before disappearing below decks to keep warm. The same newspaper recorded Bill Burgess as saying that he felt Ederle was in difficulty, and "in fact, if he had been closer to her, he would have himself gone to her assistance." With both sides standing their ground, *The Times* reflected that perhaps the WSA would be best advised to call the contest a draw and let matters rest, particularly as its motto was GOOD SPORTSMANSHIP IS BETTER THAN VICTORY.

The WSA followed the advice of *The Times* and the row seemed to have blown itself out, but on September 23 Ederle reignited it during an address on the WOR radio station. She had "many suspicions and even facts" against Wolffe, she told listeners, and if the WSA didn't make them public within thirty days, she would do so herself. The WSA rushed out a press release the following day, which was reproduced in many newspapers. The release was more like a charge sheet against Wolffe. It reiterated earlier claims that he had wilfully obstructed Ederle from the start; but the most damning comment came from Alec Rutherford, a compatriot of Wolffe's who had covered the swim for the *New York Times*. "It seemed to me that Wolffe on every possible occasion jammed down her throat the difficulties she would meet, the struggles she would have, the possible illnesses she would experience," he was quoted in the release. "I feel very strongly on the matter of the disgraceful attitude Wolffe adopted toward Miss Viets and Miss Ederle." The last word went to Viets, who wished to straighten out one particular matter: there are no man-eating sharks in the English Channel, she said. "Wolffe must have known the fish seen were porpoises."

Wolffe arrived in Cape Gris-Nez at the end of June 1926 vowing revenge on Gertrude Ederle. His reputation had taken a battering in the nine months since the undignified and very public spat with the American, and there was no longer a queue of Channel hopefuls outside the door of his Kent bungalow. So when word reached Wolffe of Ederle's ruckus with Cannon, he realized he could hurl one stone and kill two birds: guide Cannon across the Channel and skupper Ederle's dream in the process.

But the first American swimmer Wolffe encountered when he turned up on the French coast with his wife wasn't a blue-eyed blonde from Baltimore, but a steely-eyed New Yorker who just happened to bump into him on the beach. They gave each other a welcoming stare, before Wolffe extended his hand and said: "Come, Trudie, let bygones be bygones. You are the greatest swimmer in the world and if you have luck you will swim the old Channel this year." Ederle accepted the peace offering. "Put it there. I guess we were both to blame."

The veneer of civility didn't last long, however, just the time it took Wolffe to realise the extent to which his reputation in America had been traduced by Ederle. Cannon wanted nothing to do with him, no thanks, not after last year's antics. Wolffe reacted churlishly to the rejection, telling the Associated Press that a woman was incapable of swimming the Channel. There were the torments of seasickness, the indigestion, the inflammation of the eyes, the debilitating cold and other disagreeable features which might prove too much for a woman, although he didn't warn of the perils of man-eating sharks. But he was also adamant that "as a woman loses ten seconds in 100 metres to a man she may not be able to reach the English coast". In conclusion, he stated, "The victory of a woman over the Channel is possible, but is it probable? I will not say it is."

Wolffe could have guessed what the consequence of his rant would be. A few days later Ederle described to the *Daily News* how Wolffe had rolled into town, "bedecked in a blue coat with brass buttons, and white trousers, any leg of which could be used for a sail for sailing a boat". Then she explained, "[Wolffe] is a trainer of Channel swimmers, but just now, has no subject upon whom to apply his wits . . . [he] came here from England a few days ago expecting to find someone to train for a Channel attempt."

Ederle went on to say that Wolffe intended to stick around in the hope of coaching Clarabelle Barrett, a woman she herself had never met, but who was "reported to measure six feet and weigh over 200 pounds . . . Mrs. Wolffe sits nearby scanning the horizon for large females [and] not the least of Wolffe's worries is the fact that in trying to locate Miss Barrett he has spent five pounds, which, translated into francs, is too much money to speak of except in whispers".

Having been shunned by Cannon, Wolffe hung around in the hope of encountering Clarabelle Barrett, who he understood was due to arrive from America any day. But when she didn't show, Wolffe decided to return to England. Before he departed he had one last swipe at Ederle, telling Burgess that he was wasting his time; she was incapable of lasting more than nine hours in the water.

Chapter Nine

MILLE GADE SAILED from New York aboard the SS *President Roosevelt* on Wednesday, June 16, the day after the brouha-ha at Cape Gris-Nez became public knowledge. If she had bought some newspapers to learn more about it during the crossing, they remained unread until she was out of sight of New York. The only thing she wanted to do as the liner slipped its moorings was wave goodbye to her husband and two children. Gade blew them a final farewell kiss and shouted, "This time I will do it!"

She would be reunited with Clemington Corson in a month when he sailed to England to lend his support, but three-and-a-half-year-old Sonny and two-year-old Marjorie wouldn't be coming; they would stay with their aunt in Virginia.

The idea of not seeing her children again for three months made it a melancholic voyage across the Atlantic for Gade. Alone on the ship, she thought only of her family and vowed that such a sacrifice must have its reward. She must swim the Channel, not so they could move out of their shoebox of a bungalow on the naval reservation into something better, but so Sonny and Marjorie could have a decent education.

When Gade disembarked at Southampton, she had the Channel in her sights. She held it responsible for separating her from her kids, so she would teach it a lesson. The smattering of

British journalists waiting for Gade never knew what hit them. "You bet I will swim the Channel!" she snorted, irritated at the audacity of the question. "What do you think I have come over here for? What do you think I've left my husband and two children at home for?" She paused for a moment, just long enough to catch her breath. "This isn't a pleasure trip. Gee! You make me feel homesick, asking if I can do it."

Waiting for her at Southampton was a dapper man in a well-cut suit. He had an alert and handsome face, and his mane of dark blond hair – flecked white on closer inspection – made him appear younger than his forty-eight years. It would have been easy to mistake him for a company director or a partner in a legal firm, but this was one of England's most respected swimming coaches. Billy Kellingley introduced himself and accompanied Gade by train to the lodging house he had arranged for her in Dover.

Gade liked Kellingley and his wife, Ethel. The pair had been exceptional swimmers on the south coast of England a generation earlier, and on their sideboard was a panoply of swimming shields and cups. But neither had ever felt the urge to challenge the Channel, even though Billy had coached thirty-one swimmers who had.

Kellingley may have been half the size of Wolffe, but more than just a few pounds of muscles separated the pair. Kellingley had no ego, nor the insecurity of a man with something to prove. His father had spent his life as a railway car examiner, and Kellingley's first job had been in a bakery. He was just happy to be earning his living from something that was satisfying as well as stimulating.

Among the subjects discussed by Kellingley and Gade in the early days was the poisonous atmosphere at Cape Gris-Nez and her good fortune in being far away from it all. Although Gade's intention was to swim from France to England, she would train in Dover and journey across to the French coast on the day of her attempt. For a woman who needed distractions to keep her thoughts from her absent children, there were worse places to be than Dover. Unlike Gris-Nez, Dover had more things to occupy a person than cliff walks and beach golf.

Gade's boarding house on Liverpool Street was close to Marine Parade, the avenue that ran in a big sweep along the seafront and under the cliff tops on which stood Dover Castle. Marine Parade was a long terrace of nineteenth-century houses, many of them covered in creepers and hanging baskets, and at its eastern end, on the immaculate Clarence Lawn, was a bust on a marble plinth of Captain Matthew Webb, the first man to swim the Channel in 1875. Just behind Marine Parade was Granville Gardens, where each evening that summer the band of the Second Battalion, the Queen's Own Royal West Kent Regiment, gave a performance in the spectacularly illuminated pavilion. During the day, the band played on the seafront, entertaining bathers, picnickers and promenaders.

A few hundred yards inland from the beach was Connaught Park with its fabled velvet lawns and the shady nooks where courting couples held hands. The park also had public tennis courts and a children's playground, and there was an eighteen-hole golfcourse just a short ride from the town.

There were shops on Biggin Street, a cinema on Queen's Street and a vaudeville theatre on Snargate Street. There was Admiralty Pier, a tongue of grey concrete sticking out nearly a mile toward France; there were walks along the cliff tops – east toward St. Margaret's Bay or west to Shakespeare Cliff, to the spot where England's greatest playwright had once stood with other members of his theatre company and marvelled at what he called the "silver sea".

For Gade, accustomed to the twenty-four-hour hustle of New York, Dover possessed a sweet gentility which wafted through the town on the sea breeze. Gentlemen doffed their hats at ladies on the pavement, and shopkeepers always had time for

Mille Gade and Billy Kellingley

a smile and a chat. For most of the year the local weekly paper, the *Dover Express*, reflected the harmony, reporting on incidents such as the damage caused to the mudguard of a motor car belonging to Mr. P. J. Waller by a delivery barrow, or describing how old Mr. Shepherd, whose eyesight wasn't what it once was, had fallen into a trench dug for an electric cable. The soldiers stationed in Dover Castle did their best to ginger up the paper's editorial office from time to time by getting into drunken fights with locals or stealing policemen's bicycles, but for most of the year the big news passed by Dover.

The one exception was Channel swimming. For a few weeks each summer the *Dover Express* was the oracle whom *The Times*, the *Daily Telegraph*, the *Daily Mirror* and the rest of the London-based national press consulted. The popinjay reporters who arrived from the capital in their trilbys and pinstripe suits, all swagger and poise, had no idea about tides and currents, and they spent much of their time checking facts with the *Express*.

The week after Gade arrived in the town, the *Dover Express* upbraided one of the London papers, the *Daily Sketch*, for neglecting to include Frank Perks in its list of Channel aspirants. The Express then ran through the other eight contenders: Madame Sion, Miss Mille Gade, Ishak Helmy, Miss Gertrude Ederle, Omer Perrault, Miss Lillian Cannon, Georges Michel and Colonel Freyberg, VC (Victoria Cross), DSO (Distinguished Service Order).

The *Express* commented on the fact that Cannon was the only one of the eight without previous experience of the Channel, and added that Gade had shown up well in her first attempt in 1923. Ederle, on the other hand, sniffed the paper, which was proud of its long association with Jabez Wolffe, "has many speed records to her credit but failed to last eight [*sic*] hours in her Channel attempt last year."

Frank Perks and Colonel Freyberg were both Englishmen, though their nationality was all they had in common. They came from different ends of Britain's rigid class structure, and the newspapers kept it that way. It was plain "Perks" most of the time for the forty-seven-year-old jeweller from Birmingham who had been trying to beat the Channel for the past three years despite having to fund it all from his modest income.

Colonel Freyberg, VC, DSO – the letters stuck to him like barnacles to a rock – was an officer and a gentleman, and a friend of Sir James Barrie, the creator of *Peter Pan*. The British press bent its collective knee to the handsome six-footer, bandying about adjectives such as gallant and heroic whenever his name was mentioned. His first sally across the Channel in 1925 had ended in miserable disappointment just six hundred yards from the English shore, the *Dover Express* reminded its readers, before going on to reprise his war record: "He won the VC at Beaucourt in 1916, and was awarded the D.S.O. earlier for one of the most spectacular feats of the war. He swam ashore at Gallipoli and, by lighting flares, convinced the Turks that a landing was in progress. He was wounded seven times." Freyberg's wife was a glamorous society beauty, and together they were Britain's answer to Hollywood's Douglas Fairbanks and Mary Pickford – only they had more class, or at least that was the tacit opinion of the English newspapers.

The omens, however, were not good for Freyberg in early July. One of his seven war wounds, a leg that had been peppered with shrapnel, had become infected, and he'd been unable to train properly throughout June. Perks had no such concerns. He slipped into Dover almost unnoticed in the first week of July and booked himself into the cheapest lodgings he could find, more confident than ever that this season would bring success. He had trained hard during the winter and increased his weight from 154 to 196 pounds so he was better insulated against the Channel's chilly temperature. Kellingley had told Gade that he would be overseeing Perks's training, and she wasn't in the slightest bit concerned. In her eyes the Englishman was a training partner, not a rival, and having someone to share the monotony of practice swims would be a blessing.

Nor did Gade appear to mind when Kellingley made a couple of day trips across the Channel to coach Lillian Cannon. Having rejected Wolffe's advances, Cannon was still searching for a trainer at the start of July, and she was put in contact with Kellingley. He explained that he was coaching Mille Gade but would be able to get across to Cape Gris-Nez at least on a couple of occasions during her rest days. Cannon first mentioned Kellingley's assistance in her newspaper column on Thursday, July 8, when she described him as her "superb trainer." Two days later Cannon wrote that she and Kellingley had spent two hours in the water on July 4 when the weather was "cold and blustery

[with] a strong north wind and a heavy sea". But when Perks arrived in Dover, Kellingley apologised to Cannon and told her that with two swimmers to train he now had his hands full. Once more she was without a trainer.

Chapter Ten

THE DOVER EXPRESS hadn't been quite as well informed as it imagined when it had scolded the *Daily Sketch* for excluding Frank Perks from its list of Channel contenders. The *Express*'s own list of July 2 had omitted not only Clarabelle Barrett but also an eleventh hopeful: Mercedes Gleitze.

It was a careless error because Gleitze was Britain's only female swimmer, an English Rose who might – with the connivance of a canny editor – have done for the circulation of the *Dover Express* what Lillian Cannon was doing for the *Baltimore Post*. Gleitze's beauty was almost flawless. Dark brown hair, intense blue eyes and a china white complexion that gave her looks a fragile quality. There was something else about her, too, an undercurrent of melancholy, which intrigued her many male admirers. They knew her only as a talented swimmer and a strong-willed young woman who worked as a London typist and lived alone; they knew nothing of her unhappy childhood.

Gleitze had been born in Brighton in 1900 to Heinrich and Anna Gleitze, two economic migrants who had arrived from Germany a decade earlier. When she was still a baby Mercedes – the youngest of three daughters, all with Spanish names – was sent to Bavaria to be raised by her grandparents because her mother couldn't cope. Mercedes returned to Brighton when she was ten, but four years later war broke out and Heinrich Gleitze was arrested. The British authorities didn't care that he had lived in England for nearly twenty years, or that his three daughters were British subjects; he had been born in Germany, so he was a threat to national security. In protest at her husband's internment, Anna Gleitze took her three daughters to Germany and vowed that neither she nor her daughters would ever come back. But in the final year of the war, as the arrival of American troops hastened the collapse of Germany, Mercedes began to pester her mother to return to England. When it became clear that Mrs. Gleitze refused to countenance the idea, Mercedes ran away from their Bavarian home and set out for England. As she tramped west in early 1919, Mercedes' rash pledge began to take shape in her head: "My plan was to walk to the coast of Holland, cross that country until I reached the sea's edge, then follow the Dutch coastline south until I encountered that part of the French coast where the English Channel is at its narrowest, and from that convenient landmark walk into the sea and swim across to England."

Finding the German-Dutch border too heavily guarded to cross, Gleitze swung north, up through Lower Saxony, until eventually she stood on the shore facing the Frisian Islands. Gleitze was a strong swimmer, but her belief that she could swim in stages from Germany to England was suicidally stupid. Nevertheless, she waded out into the North Sea and struck out west. Within minutes the currents had grabbed her and were pulling her northeast toward a miserable death in the North Sea. After a frantic struggle, Gleitze managed to make land at Wangerooge, the most easterly of the cluster of islands. She was found by Hermann Rosing and his daughter, Elfriede, who owned a group of holiday cottages on the island. Elfriede pleaded with Gleitze to abandon her crazy idea, but the Englishwoman shook her head. "How can one suddenly still a drive to somehow or other look for an opportunity to reach one's native land?" she replied. Left with no choice, Hermann Rosing extracted her

Mercedes Gleitze

home address and sent a letter to Mercedes' mother. Perhaps, however, Mercedes gave the address to Herr Rosing as part of her Plan B. For when Mrs. Gleitze arrived a few days later, her daughter was ready with her conditions for returning to Germany: she must be allowed more independence and given the right to earn her own keep. Her mother accepted the terms, and the pair returned to Bavaria. Mercedes took a job, and the moment she had saved enough money she was gone, travelling to England by train and then boat.

Gleitze got a job as a bilingual shorthand typist and rented a small flat in Belgrave Road, a mile south of Buckingham Palace. With no family and few friends, she joined the Amateur Swimming Club (ASC) and swam regularly in one of its two pools at Holborn Baths. In the summer Gleitze swam in the

River Thames or, on weekends, took the train to Folkestone on the south coast, six miles west of Dover, where she swam for hours in the Channel. With the ASC's encouragement she made her first official attempt to swim to France in August 1922, but after three hours she abandoned her bid because of a painful shoulder.

She tried twice again in 1925 – using her favoured breast-stroke – but failed on each occasion and gave no indication that she was a serious contender. Perhaps she hadn't been right mentally, having learned the previous year that one of her sisters had died of illness in Germany. But despite her triumvirate of failures at the hands of the Channel, Gleitze travelled down to Hythe, a village on the outskirts of Folkestone, in July 1926 and began training for attempt number four. She didn't have enough money to hire a full-time trainer, but Mr. Hirst of the Amateur Swimming Club and Horace Carey, a decent local swimmer, promised to assist her when time permitted.

Not that any of this aroused the interest of the British newspapers. They were as indifferent to Gleitze as they had been during her previous three attempts. Perhaps they wondered if she was really one of them, what with her strange name and odd accent, a hodgepodge of English and German. Or perhaps editors didn't approve of turning Channel swimming into a race. For many Britons, swimming the Channel was the aquatic equivalent of climbing a mountain. It was man against nature, a noble struggle and one of unsullied human endeavour. When George Mallory, the English mountaineer, had vanished on Mount Everest in 1924, the question of whether he had reached the summit was largely immaterial to the British. What mattered more in their eyes was that Mallory's death had matched the quixotic nature of his life. He had pitted his wits against the world's biggest mountain to bring honour to his country, not to make money. "Why climb Everest?" Mallory had been asked shortly before his death. "Because it's there," he replied. This remained the British attitude toward the Channel – at least on the surface. It should be swum only as a test of human endurance and not because you might make money from it. How vulgar, how crass, how American.

The London *Star* devoted nine lines to Gleitze on July 14, saying that she hoped to "start from Folkestone about the same time as the American swimmer, Miss Gertrude Ederle, enters the water at Cape Gris-Nez". Word then reached the *Star*'s editor that a photo of Gleitze might be a pleasant adornment to his newspaper, and on July 17 a large photograph of the smiling swimmer appeared incongruously in the news section, sandwiched between a story of a lovers' suicide pact and the accidental shooting of a little girl by her brother. The only words to accompany the photo were: "Miss Mercedes Gleitze, a pretty young London typist, who is training at Hythe for a Channel swim". There were compensations, of course, for not training under the scrutiny of the newspapers. Gleitze had no obligations to fulfil, no column to write, no agenda to follow and no rivalry to stoke. She could just get on with her training. She already knew Frank Perks through their shared Channel suffering, and on her occasional forays into Dover she talked amiably with Mille Gade.

Gade and Perks were also able to train under coach Kellingley knowing that their every move wasn't being dissected over a breakfast table in New York or London. Perks had children of his own, teenagers now, which was another topic to discuss as they ploughed through the waves. Anxious to get back to his Birmingham jewellery shop as well as his family as soon as possible, Perks had pencilled in July 15 or 16 as his likely start date from Cape Gris-Nez.

Gade herself was still weeks away from being ready to challenge the Channel. She had become acclimatised to the water – although having grown up in Denmark it hadn't taken long – and now she was experimenting with the details vital to any

Channel swim: what food to eat, what stroke rate to maintain and whether or not to wear goggles.

On July 11 she embarked on her first real test, setting off without goggles from Dover at 10:33 a.m. to swim the twenty miles north to Ramsgate, a town that jutted out into the North Sea. Escorting her in a small motor boat were Kellingley and Perks, who the previous year had set a new record for the distance of six hours and fourteen minutes.

Gade started well at a steady stroke rate of seventeen per minute. Not long after midday Harry Pearson, the boat's pilot and a member of Bill Burgess's support team in 1911, diverted the craft to break up a shoal of porpoises that were harrying Gade. At 1:22 p.m. she swam past Deal Pier, almost the halfway point, and received a hearty cheer from the small crowd that had assembled. Gade heard their shouts, but she couldn't see them. Her decision to try swimming without goggles had soon been proved foolish. With her eyes red and puffy, she could only just make out Kellingley and Perks on the support boat. Nonetheless, she refused to quit, and one mile from Ramsgate she paused to suck on her final lump of sugar. Kellingley told her how far she had to go. "Very well," replied Gade, "I'll stick it." Perks swam alongside her for the final stretch, helping her up the stroke rate from seventeen to eighteen a minute. She finished the twenty miles in six hours and twenty minutes, narrowly missing Perks's record. Kellingley was impressed. "You're as hard as nails," he told her, "the most tireless woman I've met."

Chapter Eleven

NOT FOR THE FIRST TIME in its history the English Channel was all that stood between England and conflict on mainland Europe. On the other side of La Manche (the sleeve), as the French call the Channel, the warring factions faced each other across the beach. New Rochelle's *Standard-Star* carried a battle field dispatch in its edition of July 16: "The cross-Channel swimming camps are a white heat of rivalry," it began. "Jabez Wolffe, the English trainer, added tensity [*sic*] to the situation today when he announced that he plans revenge upon Gertrude Ederle."

After his earlier retreat from the beach, Wolffe had returned to Cape Gris-Nez to search once more for the large yet elusive Clarabelle Barrett. "I have never seen Miss Barrett," he told the *Standard-Star*, "but the Canadian swimmer Perrault, who is training at Dunkirk for the Channel swim, tells me she is good, so I am going to do my best to get her across with only two weeks' training."

As he roamed the cliff tops and searched among the white-washed stone cottages of the village, its verges now awash with blood-red poppies and yellow and purple wildflowers, Wolffe muttered that he would make Ederle sorry for what she'd done. He bore Cannon no grudge, but every time he saw her with her new trainer, old Jack Wiedman, his bellyaching increased, as did his hunt for Barrett. The *Standard-Star* noted that Wolffe, if nothing else, was a fighter: "Perhaps with the purpose of continually confronting his critic, [he] has taken quarters at the Hôtel du Phare, and will direct the training of Miss Barrett from there."

If Wolffe wasn't sitting in the dining room of Ederle's hotel wondering aloud if that wasn't a dorsal fin he could see in the water, he was repeating to Burgess that his charge didn't have it in her to swim the Channel. But Burgess had other things on his mind. For one, his relationship with Pop Ederle was becoming more fractious. Pop had yet to forgive Burgess for his double cross, while the Englishman resented the heavy German accent that too often queried his coaching methods, comparing them to the strategy that Louis de Breda Handley had written for his daughter before she left New York. It was left to Margaret to keep the peace, calming her father when she saw the colour rise in his cheeks, or massaging Burgess's pride.

Burgess's second source of vexation was the appearance of Jack Wiedman, yet another ego jostling for space on Cape Gris-Nez's already overcrowded beach. The sixty-three-year-old Wiedman had been taught to swim as a young boy by the great man himself, Captain Webb, and ever since he had worn the fact like a lapel badge, forever reminding people that he was an apprentice of the Old Master. It was the story that came before all others: the yarns he hoarded from his years spent sailing the world's oceans, the tales of his days as a Channel coach, even the boast that he had swum alongside Bill Burgess for several hours during his successful Channel crossing in 1911. "Wiedman adds a little interest to the rivalry here by announcing that he is the man who trained William Burgess for his successful swim across the Channel," reported the *Standard-Star*, unable to believe its luck in stumbling upon another treasure trove of strife. "Burgess, who is training Miss Ederle, comes right back with a denial of Wiedman's statement and alleges that his success in swimming the Channel was due to his own efforts. All Cape Gris-Nez therefore is divided into hostile camps . . . and it is said that after the rumpus over the services of Burgess there is very little friendly communication between the Cannon camp and the Ederle camp. The fact that both the Ederle and Cannon ventures are tied up with newspaper syndicate promotion has not lessened the sharpshooting in the least."

The *Standard-Star* dashed from camp to camp, over the beach that was an unofficial no man's land, trying to eke out information on possible start dates. Wiedman dropped his guard for a moment and blurted out that July 23 or 24 was a possibility because the tides looked favourable. He was quickly silenced by Cannon and her husband. The *Standard-Star* speculated that this might have been a ruse by Wiedman to lure Ederle into the Channel before she was ready. "There may be some secrecy about her [Cannon's] departure," explained the paper, "as there is considerable rivalry between newspaper correspondents in engaging tugs and the promoters of Miss Cannon are anxious to keep the news of her swim entirely to themselves . . . there are many rumours of secret trials, much discussion of probable failures, and gossip galore between the rival camps. A spell of rain and Cape Gris-Nez may break out in open warfare."

If an American wanted to avoid a bitter enemy, there were few worse places to be stranded than the bleak and isolated promontory of Cape Gris-Nez, where sheep outnumbered villagers and what people there were spoke little English. Ederle disliked small talk in any language, so she did her utmost to avoid the locals whenever possible, most of whom, anyway, were doomsayers. "I do get fed up on the Channel-swim talk," she wrote. "It seems like everybody I meet insists on talking on nothing else, and especially I am weary of the many who delight in telling me how terrible the Channel is to swim." Ederle nicknamed the self-appointed experts her "Channel croakers". To escape them, she hid behind the pages of fifty-cent novels. "I can forget all about the croakers when I sit down to read," she said. "For they can be talking all about me and I don't hear a word." There was also her sister and Julia Harpman to shield her, the latter having become a trusted confidante during and after the Burgess ballyhoo. Julia's husband, Westbrook Pegler, had been a support, too, in the first few weeks, but he had returned to New York on June 27. In her darker moments, Ederle told Harpman that without her emollient presence she might also have "packed up and gone home".

Since the end of June Ederle had another good friend to help chase away her mulligrubs, the giant Egyptian Ishak Helmy, who had pulled her out of the Channel twelve months earlier and was now staying in the same hotel. Despite his involvement in Ederle's 1925 debacle, Helmy had been absolved of blame and was deemed to have been simply following Wolffe's instructions when he took hold of her in mid-Channel.

He was one of the twenty-one children of a wealthy Cairo pasha, Ahmed Helmy, who had sired his considerable brood with the help of four wives. Everyone who encountered Helmy was bedazzled by his build and his bonhomie. To Lillian Cannon, the twenty-eight-year-old was "huge, dark-skinned and handsome, his glorious teeth constantly are on exhibit because he is always smiling". Julia Harpman described him as six foot three and 253 pounds and added that "he has never worked a day in his life, is hardly ever serious and is a person of explosive temper and quick contrition. He is fond of dancing and of alcoholic drinks." Helmy was fluent in English and French, but whatever language he spoke, he did so in a big booming voice, housed within his fifty-inch chest, that even Ederle could hear without trouble. He liked to sit in the hotel's dining room – the wooden bench straining under his enormous weight – refilling his wine glass as he declared with a mischievous grin that it was intolerable that

Egypt had now outlawed polygamy. What was wrong, he demanded of Ederle, with a man having six wives? In retaliation Ederle teased Helmy about his weight, warning him that if he added any more pounds he would "be able to float across" the Channel to that "tight little isle", as he called Britain. If Helmy thought Ederle required a boost to her spirits, he disappeared in his car to Boulogne and returned with a trunk stuffed full of biscuits, chocolate, oranges, strawberries, figs, sardines and cheese. At other times he treated Ederle's camp to lunch in one of Boulogne's best restaurants.

Even when Helmy and Ederle trained together, a joke was never far from the surface. Of course there are no man-eating sharks in the Channel, he would say earnestly; they have all been eaten by the giant octopus that has recently arrived at Cape Gris-Nez. Nor was Pop immune from the incorrigible Egyptian. One day the pair organised a hundred-yard dash across the beach with Helmy allowing the portly Ederle a twenty-five-yard start. Despite the thundering noise of Helmy bearing down on him, Pop held on to win by a nose, but awoke the next morning, so Ederle wrote in one of her columns, stiff and sore and "feeling as if he had been riding horseback for a week".

Helmy's arrival in France brought with it a lighter touch to Ederle's *Daily News* articles, especially as Cannon was no longer in the same hotel. After her "putting-the-record-straight" column of June 14, Ederle no longer mentioned her rival's name. She had ceased to exist.

Cannon, however, still burned with a sense of injustice at the furore that in her opinion had not been of her own making. Burgess had got his money, Ederle had got her trainer, but she had been left high and dry. From time to time she was unable to resist having a sly dig at the *New Yorker* in her newspaper column. On June 25 she described Ishak Helmy, reminding readers that "he has pulled many a floundering girl from the water just in time to save her from the wicked tides". Those wicked tides,

Cannon continued, were why Burgess took nearly twenty-four hours to swim the Channel. "That, he says, was because he didn't know the currents and tides. Now he does know them, and he is telling me their secrets." A fortnight later Cannon wondered what had happened to Clarabelle Barrett but was sure she would find her way over to Cape Gris-Nez eventually. "I shall be glad to welcome her, and shall at once invite her to have workouts with me," she wrote. "I think we girls should stick together, though we may be rivals."

Cannon returned to the theme a few days later, just in case Ederle had missed it the first time around. Under the headline CHANNEL SWIMMING GAME KNOWS NO NATIONALITIES, the Baltimorean told everyone of her friendship with the Frenchwoman Jeanne Sion. "Madame Sion and Perrault [the Montreal swimmer] are training together at Dunkirk, but they visited me at my hotel here and we at once decided on a jaunt together. Dear old Helmy joined us, and I could not stop thinking that there is no nationality in sport." After their "jaunt", in fact Cannon's euphemism for a hard training swim, Sion and the American played golf on the beach and then had dinner at the Hôtel de la Sirène. "We had heaps of fun," Cannon was delighted to report. "She laughs very easily, this Frenchwoman who is old enough to be my mother. Over dinner Sion passed on to Cannon some "friendly tips" about Channel swimming that she had gleaned from her own unsuccessful attempts. "Isn't it fine," Cannon reflected in the *Baltimore Post*, "that she is such a great sport?"

Jeanne Sion wasn't the only French person with whom Cannon had struck up a rapport. Without Ederle's shy sensitivity, Cannon sauntered through Cape Gris-Nez making friends at will. On July 10 she wrote that she liked nothing better "than rambling about the quaint little farming places. The people are so friendly and kind that all the days are short . . . I am passionately fond of Gris-Nez". While Ederle shielded herself from locals with her book, Cannon took French lessons; while Ederle made regular trips to Boulogne to stock up on biscuits, cakes and strawberries, Cannon devoured the local cuisine. "Of all the things I like about France – and there are a lot of them – perhaps I like best the food which I consume four times a day," she wrote. "First there are 'hors d'oeuvres'. Next comes a bit of fish, caught off the Gris-Nez beach. Then meat and at last four different vegetables – cooked, oh, so deliciously!"

The spirit of Franco-American friendship in Cannon's training camp was symbolised by the Stars and Strips that Henri Lenoir, the owner of the Hôtel de la Sirène, flew from the rooftop in her honour. Cannon's greater popularity with the locals had a lot to do with her staying in the more accessible beach hotel, but they also enjoyed her wide-eyed willingness to sample their culture. Her husband, too, was a hit with the locals. Eddie's fresh good looks and joie de vivre reminded them of the American doughboys who had fought alongside their own sons and fathers a decade earlier. Consciously or otherwise, the inhabitants drew comparisons with Ederle's German-born father.

Ederle didn't give a hoot if Cannon was the darling of the locals. She had come to swim the Channel, and that was all that concerned her. When she wasn't swimming or reading, she was studying tidal charts with Burgess or discussing bathing suit designs with Margaret. Her sister disappeared to Paris at the end of June, to "buy silk to make me a brassiere, which I will wear with short trunks while swimming the Channel". She returned a day later having been unable to find the new type of lightweight silk she had wanted, but she had bought some dark blue jersey silk to make a brassiere and shorts.

As Margaret sat in her room cutting and sewing, her sister

took to the water wearing another of her creations. Back in New York during the spring, Margaret had helped Gertrude design a pair of goggles that they hoped would be waterproof. Instead of two separate eyeglasses, which had proved inadequate in 1925, the sisters took one straight piece of yellow glass and bound the edges with metal and leather. Initial trials in the WSA's pool in New York had gone well, but the ultimate test could only be provided by a lengthy swim in the Channel.

On June 29 Ederle and Helmy set out to swim the seven and a half miles to Wimereux – roughly halfway between Gris-Nez and Boulogne – in hostile conditions. After only a few minutes she threw the goggles to her sister in the attendant rowboat, complaining that they leaked water over the bridge of the nose. Two hours later her shoulders were being chafed by the straps of her WSA bathing suit. Her father urged her to quit, as Helmy had done, but Ederle insisted on staying in the water for at least another hour. The *Chicago Tribune* related that as Ederle battled the sullen Channel, "those who accompanied her sat huddled under their sweaters and heavy robes shivering in their rowboat". When she got back to the hotel, Ederle was given a massage by Mrs. Burgess, and Margaret rubbed a balm on her flayed shoulders. Then she tucked into a plate of roast pork and baked beans, followed by custard pie. "I suppose you are all as disgusted with me as I am with myself," she said to her team as she pushed her empty plate to one side. "I had intended staying in the water four hours and I stayed only three."

Ederle didn't sleep much that night because of the pain caused by her red raw shoulders. The next day, while Margaret rushed to finish the silk swimsuit, Ederle went to Boulogne to inspect the tug, the *Alsace*, that would accompany her on the swim. Considered to be the best craft for accompanying swimmers across the Channel, the *Alsace* had been hired by Captain Patterson's newspaper syndicate for as long as it took Ederle to achieve her goal. It was costing Patterson three hundred francs an hour, but that was a small price to pay to ensure that no other Channel swimmer had access to the vessel. The tug's French skipper, Joe Costa,* the self-styled "Commodore of the Channel Swimmers", could neither write nor read, except when it came to sea charts. He was fond of holding sway in Boulogne's Café Lieboise and telling anyone who would stand him another cognac that he had piloted thirty-three Channel swim attempts. Westbrook Pegler had met him earlier in the month and found him "amusing [but] cheap and phony", a man on the make especially where young naive American swimmers were concerned. While Ederle looked on, Costa ran the American flag up the mast and promised it would remain there until she had beaten the Channel.

Ederle was revitalised by the inspection of the tug, and by her meeting with Costa, who had a knack for making people believe that the impossible was always possible, even if he didn't believe so himself. She had started to ask herself if it was all worth it, the endless hours in the cold, grey Channel, but the sight of the tug was tangible evidence that there would be an end to the tedium. The next day, July 1, Ederle was up early, her shoulders still painful. Enough is enough, she decided.

Margaret's balm hadn't lessened the irritation, so it was time to try a more robust remedy. Creeping down to the beach before even the fishermen of Gris-Nez had stirred, Ederle ran topless into the surf. "I was trying a heroic method to cure my shoulders," she explained in her column the next day. "After the first shock the salt water in the sore places felt good and I believe it has been more beneficial than all the creams and powders my sister has been applying since I was hurt. I did not swim, but I jumped about, letting the waves beat against me. And I proved I

---

* The contemporary reports of the time couldn't agree on the spelling of the name Costa, with some opting for "Corthes" and others "Corthez". Although I was unable to trace any of Joe's ancestors, the few families of that name in northern France all spell it "Costa".

was correct in my belief that salt water will cure any cut."

For the next fortnight Ederle did little else other than train. There was a brief interlude of fun on July 4 when she and her team bought some fireworks from a store in a neighbouring village to celebrate Independence Day, but her columns were becoming as tired as their author. With little to talk about other than how far she had swum or walked, Ederle filled her copy with details of sheep shearing, crop gathering or the latest cattle disease to affect the local farmers. It wasn't the "absorbing story" the *Daily News* had in mind when it signed up Ederle at the end of May. Harpman was instructed to spice things up, which she did on July 9 with an article headlined SEA MONSTERS CAPTURED NEAR EDERLE'S CAMP. Harpman explained breathlessly that "twenty-four hideous sea beasts were caught last night just off the rocks here". But before readers started to imagine giant squids or Wolffe's infamous man-eating sharks, Harpman confessed that the monstrous creatures were in fact tope, which only ate fish smaller than themselves. Nevertheless, continued Harpman, they "closely resemble the tiger shark except that the tope has two sets of teeth, whereas the man-eaters have three".

While Harpman strove to make the news from the Channel less vapid, Arthur Sorenson was told to take some more exciting photographs. The *Daily News* had had enough of Ederle swimming. Sorenson went to work, snapping Ederle in a variety of poses, some dignified, others less so. There were the cute animal photos, one with Ederle cuddling Stroke, the brown and white mongrel dog that was her mascot, and another showing her astride a sheep in a field with the caption describing her as Little Bo Peep; there were "At Play" photos, riding piggyback on Helmy's shoulders or pedalling a bicycle through Gris-Nez; there were "At Work" photos, churning butter on a local farm or carrying pails of milk to the breakfast table which, as the caption said, "keeps those stocky champion shoulders in trim".

Ederle enlivened her columns by omitting references to

farmyard animals and instead talking about evenings in casinos watching Helmy win on the roulette wheel, or dancing late into the night in hotels with Margaret. It was better, more peppy, but the overriding question remained for Captain Patterson and his readers: when would Ederle swim the Channel?

When she had sailed from New York on June 2, Ederle had breezily forecast that she would "take the plunge about the 13th or 14th of July". Six weeks was a long time to hold the interest of its readership, but the *Daily News* had played along, running her daily columns and even featuring her in its "The Question" feature. Each day the paper canvassed six New Yorkers, chosen at random on one particular street, to give their views on a topical issue. On June 27 the *Daily News* asked four men and two women walking down St. Nicholas Avenue, between West 181st and West 191st streets, if Ederle would succeed in her Channel endeavour. George F. Lacker said she would not: "She hasn't the strength . . . I don't believe any woman has." Edward Hickey, a chauffeur, agreed that the feat could only be achieved by a man. The other four predicted she would succeed. "What is mostly in her favour," said the student Blanche Berkowitz, "is that she herself feels certain that she can do it."

But what was unpredictable, and unmanageable, even for a man like Captain Patterson who was used to getting his way, was the Channel weather. It had been one of the coldest Junes on record, with the temperature of the water never rising above fifty-six degrees. Even when the weather improved in mid-July, the Channel remained a degree below its seasonal average of sixty-three degrees. On July 19 a frustrated Ederle informed America that it was unlikely she would start her attempt before the first week of August: "We have had so little warm weather thus far this summer that the Channel water is still icy, and during the last two days the wind has been so frightfully high and the water so rough that long practice swims were impossible." That was the bad news. Then came the good news: yes, of course, the delay was hard to bear, but it hadn't weakened her resolve. On the contrary, she was more determined than ever to swim the Channel. "I don't want anyone to suggest taking me out of the water no matter what the conditions may be until I'm on English soil or have fainted from my attempt to get there," she wrote. "I've never fainted in my life and I don't think there is any reason to believe that I will begin fainting now."

On the same day that Ederle confirmed the Channel weather had delayed her intended start date, Lillian Cannon was thanking an old friend, Viola, who sold popcorn at Bay Shore Park, for her letter that had just arrived at Cape Gris-Nez. "She urged me to 'hurry up' and swim that canal," Cannon wrote in her column. "I wish Viola could be here when a north wind was blowing, and get a good look at the way the sea breaks, and have a feel of the currents and the strata of icy water. If she did she wouldn't want me to make any undue haste and try this 'canal' before I was sure I was fit."

After weeks of antipathy and distrust, Cannon and Ederle had at last found some common ground: their frustration at the weather. Cannon was in her ninth week at Gris-Nez, and the coastal walks among the wildflowers had begun to lose their allure. Blithe letters like those from Viola might have caused her a pang of irritability, but at least they helped "break the monotony of Gris-Nez". The training under coach Jack Wiedman was going well, but his earlier suggestion to reporters that Cannon might be ready to try the swim on July 23 or 24 had proved to be grossly inaccurate. Like Ederle, Cannon hadn't been able to rack up the distances she needed in training because of the inclement weather. "I feel wonderfully fit and should like to get away," wrote Cannon on July 15, "but summer has been tardy. There were some fine days in June, but not enough to take the biting edge off the water . . . we shall probably have to wait until about Aug. 10 when, according to the chart, we shall have a succession of good days."

This was discouraging news for the *Baltimore Post* and the Scripps-Howard syndicate, which had been concerned that in the past fortnight Cannon had started to prattle in her daily dispatches. True, there had been the odd interesting revelation, such as her plan to start her Channel attempt at night so that near the end of the swim, when she was tired and vulnerable, she would be swimming in daylight, but these were the exception. Too often her copy, save for the odd jibe at Ederle's expense, was insipid: another game of golf on the beach, another friendly chat with Jeanne Sion, another bleat about the weather. Hell, even the bathing suit photos had petered out. Something needed to be done, and quick, if readers weren't to become bored with reading about Cannon's French holiday.

But what to do? Her platitudinous columns couldn't really be helped if she was stuck in the middle of nowhere with not a lot to do but swim. The editorial staff at the *Baltimore Post* put their heads together and came up with the perfect solution. On Saturday, July 17, the front page of the *Post* carried a full-length photograph of Cannon in her bathing suit displaying more curves than the Potomac River. HOW TO SWIM BY LILLIAN CANNON ran the headline, and underneath was an announcement that starting Monday, the city's most glamorous swimmer would present the first in a series of thirty-six articles teaching readers how to swim. Each lesson would be illustrated with a photograph to aid in mastering the different strokes.

As if the front-page advertisement wasn't enough to encourage the *Post*'s red-blooded readers to rush out and buy the paper on Monday, the eroticism of Cannon's column that Saturday was intended to have them camping outside the news-stands. With an accompanying photo, Cannon explained the greasing procedure involved in a Channel swim: "I shall be made to lie down and my sun-browned body will be smeared first by an oily concoction that is designed to keep the pores of my skin open. Then I shall be covered from toes to chin, by a thick, dirty grease . . . [then] I must manage to squirm into the flimsiest kind of costume and then I shall be greased all over again . . . the awful stuff will probably get into my hair, and cake about my neck, and make me feel slimy as a fish."

The first "How to Swim" lesson duly appeared on Monday with Cannon explaining how to breathe in the water. There were three photographs, each one showing Cannon on her hands and knees (a waterline pencilled in) demonstrating the correct breathing techniques. Thereafter the *Post* ran daily swimming lessons and explanatory photos. The photographer who took the pictures was also told to shoot Cannon looking sexy, sultry, sassy, whatever, just as long as she was in her bathing suit and her legs were on display. In the second half of July photos appeared in the *Post* of Cannon leaning, Gloria Swanson-like, against a door frame; of her climbing the ladder of the Cape Gris-Nez lighthouse; of her playing golf; of her looking out to sea with a telescope; of her running a flag up the pole; of her taking French on the beach with Louisette, who, unlike Cannon, appeared in the photo wearing a long dress buttoned up to the neck.

The postman at Cape Gris-Nez was soon labouring under the weight of correspondence from the *Post*'s appreciative readers, and Cannon was "greatly cheered" by their number and their content. One male correspondent from Pittsburgh declared, "From the very first day I read of your undertakings I have often thought of you. I am very much interested in you and your undertakings." Although Cannon explained there were too many letters to reply to each one, she used her column to say, "I really do love to get such letters."

The longer Cannon and Ederle deferred their attempt, the more sceptical the British became. One of the Scripps-Howard reporters based in Paris, Henry Farrell, asked the opinion of an "old salt" in Dover as he waited to catch his ferry back to France after an assignment in London. The English seaman laughed at the idea of a woman conquering the Channel. "Swim 'er? 'Tis a hard job for a man to ride 'er. Look at the way she's running now. I'd call the bobbies if a girl of mine tried to swim 'er."

Meanwhile John Hayward, Channel "expert" of the London *Daily Sketch*, wrote in late July that in the past newspapers had a tendency to exaggerate attempts by women to swim the Channel in order to sell more copies; readers preferred a plucky "so-near-yet-so-far" story to one of abject failure. The fact was, wrote Hayward, "no woman has yet been anywhere near success". And neither Hayward, nor any of the other British sages, gave Cannon or Ederle much hope, according to Minott Saunders, the replacement reporter for the *Baltimore Post*'s Nelson Robins, who had returned to the States at the end of June. Saunders had gleaned from the British press that the pair were destined to fail because, first, they were speed not endurance swimmers, and second, because of their age. "Young athletes are inclined to suffer from nerves," so Saunders had been told.

Normally Ederle didn't read the British newspapers, preferring to stick to her fifty-cent novels or days-old copies of the *Daily News* sent from home. First-person news, however, was harder to avoid. It was now the height of the tourist season, and every week a fresh batch of Ederle's "Channel croakers" checked into the Hôtel du Phare and pestered her with swim talk. "It has reached a stage now," she explained, "where I bring a book to the [dining] table, and when I am not eating I sit with my fingers in my ears, impolitely burying myself away." But the British weekend holidaymakers who arrived at Cape Gris-Nez on the afternoon of Saturday, July 24, brought news that made Ederle remove her fingers. A pretty young Englishwoman called Gleitze had set out that very morning to swim the Channel, and they had seen her from their steamer several miles out from Dover, swimming strongly for France.

Chapter Twelve

SOMEHOW, SOMEWHERE, Clarabelle Barrett had got waylaid, and Jabez Wolffe was not happy. For the past fortnight he had been ensconced in the Hôtel du Phare, causing Gertrude Ederle no end of mirth as she watched him "walk up and down the unpaved roads of Cape Gris-Nez, staring at every woman he meets in the hope she may prove to be his Claribelle [*sic*]". But it was now late July, and the unmissable figure of Barrett had not yet hoved into view. Having vowed to the *Standard-Star* on July 16 that once she turned up he was going to get Barrett across the Channel with just two weeks' training, Wolffe conceded to the same newspaper a few days later that he was "beginning to believe that someone has played a joke on me". He wasn't the only one. Ederle and Cannon had both been awaiting the arrival of Barrett, not just so they could size up another rival but because a neutral third party might help repair a relationship that was every bit as poisonous as the Channel jellyfish.

They had it on good authority that Barrett had sailed from New York on July 3, yet nearly four weeks later there had been no sign of her. Minott Saunders, reporting from Lillian Cannon's camp, assumed she wasn't going to show and wrote a piece for the *Baltimore Post* on July 27 in which he talked about the three American women vying to be the first across the Channel — Ederle, Cannon and Gade — and made no mention of

Barrett. The *New York Times*, however, was fixed on getting to the bottom of the mystery and asked its London-based Channel correspondent, the Briton Alec Rutherford, to investigate Barrett's whereabouts. A six-foot-tall and 210-pound American woman couldn't have just vanished into thin air.

Rutherford caught the train to the south coast and began to make inquiries. Eventually the trail led to a grubby guesthouse on Marine Parade, not far from Mille Gade's lodgings, where Barrett and Grace Leister had taken board. He fired off a special cable to the *New York Times* to inform the paper that the "mystery" had been solved. *The Times* ran a brief story on Friday, July 30, explaining that Barrett intended to swim to France in two days' time. "Doesn't it look near!" Barrett had exclaimed to Rutherford, as they stood on the beach at Dover. "And yet how many have tried and failed! I feel in perfect condition and full of pep. I feel I could get in the water right away and swim all day."

The Times, seeing that it was one step ahead of its rivals, asked Rutherford to file some more copy for the next day's edition. Barrett had been found, but what had she been doing since her arrival in England three weeks earlier? The piece appeared on the front page on July 31 under the headline NEW ROCHELLE GIRL, WITH SCANT RESOURCES, WILL TRY ENGLISH CHANNEL SWIM TOMORROW. It was a tale of indomitable resolution in the face of relentless adversity, a story guaranteed to stir the hearts of Americans. Barrett told Rutherford that she and Leister had arrived in England on July 9, armed with a letter of introduction that a friend of Barrett's had written for Walter Brickett, a former coach to the British Olympic swimming team and one of the many trainers Jabez Wolffe had used during his crusade to beat the Channel. Brickett had agreed to meet Barrett in Brighton and watch her train, just as soon as he could arrange a day away from his job as superintendent at a London swimming pool.

Brickett was a wiry man with a diligent face and a moustache that had turned grey before his well-trimmed dark hair, perhaps

Grace Leister (left) and Clarabelle Barrett

as a result of his devotion to strenuous activity. Brickett was a
fitness fanatic and in August 1919 he had featured in the British
newspapers after completing in an afternoon a one-mile run, a
one-mile walk, a three-mile cycle, a mile of hurdles, and a one-
mile swim. He had to crane his neck to look Barrett in the eye,
but the moment she was in the water Brickett had no trouble seeing how strong she was. He asked her to swim from Brighton to
Worthing and back, a distance of eighteen miles, which Barrett
completed in eight hours. In Brickett's opinion, the American
was not only faster than Lily Smith, England's dominant pre-
war woman swimmer, but also superior to Wolffe. Brickett gave
Barrett some pointers specific to Channel swimming, warned her

of its quirks, its capriciousness and its spitefulness, then wished her the best of luck and returned to London.

Barrett and Leister moved the forty-five miles along the coast from Brighton to Dover in mid-July, reported the *New York Times*, "ambitious but without a large bank account". While Wolffe traipsed through Cape Gris-Nez searching for Barrett, she pounded the streets of Dover inquiring about the hire of a tug. Every door that opened for her soon closed when she revealed her budget. Some had demanded $2,400, while the more charitable had been willing to drop their price to $1,700, but not below, not a chance. Barrett's troubles deepened, said the *Times*, when she contacted a "well-known English swimmer, who manages Channel swims". But he, whoever he was, saw only the chance of making a quick buck and "telegraphed for $50, [and] travelling and hotel expenses when his services were sought".

Barrett returned to her dingy lodgings and contemplated her options. She could admit defeat and return on the first ship to New York, or she could give it one last shot and go right to the top.

Captain James S. Learmont had first gone to sea in 1887 when he was twelve years old. By the time he was twenty-three, the Scot had his own command, the *Brenhilda*, a full-rigged sailing ship. By the beginning of the twentieth century, however, the years of sail were coming to an end, and the only routes that paid were the most dangerous: around the snarling Cape Horn east to west with general cargo, and a return laden with nitrate from Chile. In 1908, during a voyage to Australia, his seamanship skills had saved his vessel from foundering during a storm in the Tasman Sea, for which Lloyd's of London praised his "commendable resourcefulness and splendid audacity". Two years later, Learmont joined Trinity House as a pilot. One of the four societies of mariners of England, Trinity House dated from as far back as the fourteenth century.

In the summer of 1926 Learmont was the most experienced pilot in Dover, a man who for years had been assisting ships in passing through the treacherous Strait of Dover to and from the Thames. But though he lived on the southernmost coast of Britain, Learmont still retained the gruff personality of his Scottish roots. He was a man of strong opinions and watertight integrity. Even in his fifties he was an intimidating figure, someone who with his deadpan gaze judged people not by age or gender or wealth, but by whether they looked capable of surviving the Horn at the height of its fury. The previous year Learmont had accused the mayor of Dover of accepting the bribe of a boat during the negotiation of a contract with the British Oxygen Company. The mayor had successfully sued Learmont, but he'd paid his one-hundred-pound fine with a defiant sneer and a look that intimated that in his eyes the court was as rotten as the mayor.

When Clarabelle Barrett knocked on his door pleading for assistance, he listened to what she had to say. Something about her, perhaps the fervour in her eyes, appealed to Learmont, and he agreed to help. Within a short space of time he used his contacts to obtain a rowboat and a motor boat, both from a reputable local boatbuilder called Brockmans, and all for just seventy-five dollars. As for the pilot, he told Barrett, that would be his responsibility. In addition, Alec Rutherford volunteered to accompany her on the swim as her official timekeeper and witness.

With such a distinguished support team now behind her, Barrett felt confident enough to write to Brickett to see if he was able to spare the public holiday weekend of Sunday, August 1, to join her crew. Brickett replied that he would do better than that: he would take a week's unpaid leave and arrive in Dover on Wednesday, July 28. "I cannot leave such a splendid woman in difficulty," he told the *New York Times*. "She may surprise us all.

I consider her good for twenty hours."

It was Learmont's task to ensure Barrett wouldn't have to spend twenty hours in the water by drawing on his colossal knowledge of the English Channel. Having agreed to pilot her, the Scot now had to plot the best course across the twenty-one miles that separated Shakespeare Beach from Cape Gris-Nez.

Ideally, Barrett would have swum from France to England because the tides were more favourable to the swimmer in this direction. Though Bill Burgess had swum the other way in 1911, he did so only because he wanted to replicate Captain Webb's route. But Barrett couldn't afford to take the ferry to Calais and a taxi to Cape Gris-Nez; she barely had enough money to pay her rent. Even the grease for the swim had been brought from America to save on costs.

Once Learmont had consulted Brickett and Barrett as to her intended stroke rate, he worked out a route across the Channel. Then he sat down with Barrett and explained her course. The first thing he stressed was the Strait of Dover's freakish microclimate and its wicked currents. If Barrett had a magpie memory, she might have recalled an article published eleven months earlier in the *New York Times*, just days after Ederle had failed in her first attempt. "To understand the problem which is faced in laying out plans for any Channel trial," Louis de Breda Handley wrote,

> it must be realised that the Strait of Dover, where the swim is made, is formed by two sharp promontories, on either side of which land recedes abruptly. Swift tides sweep the course laterally, running approximately eastward and westward, back and forth, for periods of about five and three-quarter hours in each direction. As a consequence, the swimmer does not go in a straight line, though he aims for a definite point. The recurring flood and ebb tides force him first one way, then the other, so that he

describes a great zigzag . . . he must approach the opposite coast within the narrow lane marked by the extreme ends of jutting promontories and on the favourite tide; otherwise, upon nearing the finish, he will be carried irresistibly outside the landing area and find it impossible to cover the final stretch.

Handley's article had been a concise explanation of the Channel's vagaries, though he was slightly wide of the mark about the changing of the tides; they shifted direction every six hours, not every five and three-quarter hours. A small error in print, but a potentially disastrous miscalculation in the water.

By the time Learmont had briefed Barrett she was able to differentiate between a flood tide, when the sea flowed to the northeast from one and a half hours before high water to four and a half hours after high water, and an ebb tide, when the sea turned 180 degrees and flowed to the southwest from four and a half hours after high water to one and a half hours before high water. She also knew the difference between the neap and spring tides, both of which lasted for seven days. The former was when the Channel's tidal movement was at its lowest, and occurred when the sun and the moon were at right angles to each other; the spring tide, on the other hand, was when the sun and the moon were aligned – in other words, when the moon was new or full. This brought with it the greater tidal movement, as well as an argument among Channel trainers that had yet to be resolved.

Some, like Wolffe, would never dare let one of their swimmers start on a spring tide, but the more adventurous – Burgess, for example – reckoned this was the best chance of success, even though he, Webb and Henry Sullivan from Massachusetts had all swum across on the neap tide. It was more stable than the spring tide, agreed, but it was slower, too. The two men who had crossed in the quickest times were Charles Toth and Enrico Tiraboschi, and both had gone on a spring tide.

Burgess had been mocked for his unorthodoxy in the past, with the *Dover Express* labelling him a man of "strange impulses" in 1922, when he'd advised a French swimmer to start his swim on a spring tide, but he remained unswayed. He proposed to get Ederle off on a spring tide, but the last series of such tides had just run from July 24 to 30, a week in which the wind had been too strong for any attempt. Thwarted once, Burgess was now waiting for the next run of spring tides that were forecast to begin on August 6.

Another factor in Channel swimming, added Learmont, was how the wind and the tide combined. If they moved in the same direction, the sea was long and flat, but if they opposed each other, the sea was short and choppy. And any strong wind in the Channel, regardless if it went with or against the tide, caused the sea to become rough.

Learmont had one last warning for Barrett about the Channel's irascible weather system: fog. He had spent years rescuing vessels disorientated by the fog that descended on the Channel on average once every fourteen days. Often it rolled in and was gone almost as quickly as it arrived, but at other times banks of fog appeared and stubbornly remained for half a day, a day, two days even.

The threat of fog was greatest at the height of summer when the warm air temperature passed over the still-cool Channel waters, and right now the sea was unusually cool, only fifty-nine degrees. The air temperature, however, was also below the seasonal average, with one fed-up London newspaper complaining on Tuesday, July 27, that it felt as "cold as Christmas". But the forecast for the holiday weekend was for a sharp increase, and by the end of the week it had warmed up enough for the citizens of Dover to begin shedding their coats. The temperature continued to rise over the weekend so that by Saturday it was eighty degrees.

But Barrett couldn't afford to be influenced by the weather.

She had made up her mind to set out from Shakespeare Beach early on Monday, August 2, and that was that. Gertrude Ederle, Lillian Cannon and Mille Gade might have had the luxury of waiting for the right conditions, but she had neither the time nor the money to dally. Barrett intended to be first across the Channel, fog or no fog.

Chapter Thirteen

EVEN BY BRITISH STANDARDS , the summer of 1926 had been dismal. June and the first half of July had felt more like March, and along the beaches of the south coast deck chairs were piled high like washed-up driftwood. When summer did finally arrive on Tuesday, July 13, the London *Star* could scarcely contain itself. HOTTEST DAY, 82 IN THE SHADE AND NO BREEZE, it screamed on its front page of July 14. But then – as if to curb its readers' excitement – a subheading cautioned: thunder likely.

Far from deterring people, the *Star*'s warning only made city dwellers more determined than ever to capitalise on the good weather before the thunder arrived. The beaches along the south coast teemed with life, and the ice cream company J. Lyons struggled to meet demand on Wednesday. The London *Daily News* divulged that Lyons had increased productivity from 30,000 gallons a day to 50,000. Why, it was so hot, panted the *Daily Sketch*, that "even an ice-cream vendor – and an Italian at that – collapsed".

For the first time that summer, British newspapers had the opportunity to assess the latest seaside fashions, and the London papers explained that the strength of the sun had failed to weaken the resolve of the English gentlemen. Despite the heat, they strolled along the seafront dressed in dark suits and collar and tie. One or two of the more effete succumbed as they roasted on the beach, guiltily rolling up a couple of inches of trouser leg to reveal a glimpse of milk-white flesh.

Their womenfolk, on the other hand, decorated the beach-front with their colourful apparel. Hats were adorned with fruits and flowers of every sort, some encircling the crown, others hanging over the brim. Those women who chose not to wear hats instead twirled a gaily-coloured Japanese parasol above their heads.

Patterned silk, muslins, and crêpes de Chine were the *en vogue* materials for summer dresses, with pink, pale biscuit, tortoiseshell brown and blues of all hues the preferred colours. The *Dover Standard* grumbled disapprovingly that "what with the new thin dresses and minus sleeves and minus any length that can be called noticeable, the fair sex is revelling" in the heat wave, and the London *Star* blushed in reporting that "legs without stockings were no longer the sign of seaside freedom. They were to be seen in most of the London parks."

For those frolicking in the water a typical bathing costume consisted of navy-blue and rose-colored crêpe marocain with a rose skirt and overblouse. A black silk monogram on a pink medallion was imprinted on the bib-shaped front of the blouse, and the crowning glory of the ensemble was a huge shawl-cape of rose-coloured duvetyn with navy lozenges and a deep navy woollen fringe. Sandals and bathing cap were of matching navy blue, but, of course, bob-haired girls were inclined to do away with caps.

The bobbed hair was just one of the fads that had arrived in Britain from the United States. More and more Englishwomen sported white belts around their bathing costumes in the style of the Mack Sennett bathing girls, and earrings, necklaces and bangles – some wood, some rubber – were just as popular. One American innovation not welcome on British beaches was the flesh-coloured bathing suits made from snug-fitting stockingette, as modelled by the more daring tourist. The Brighton town council was so ruffled by their appearance it felt moved to issue a directive on the matter: "Pretty visitors are more than welcome but they must respect the laws of Brighton and wear bathing dresses of a contrasting colour. They need not wear stockings and we don't mind the close-fitting one-piece suit but we draw the line at anything which suggests that Mademoiselle is entering the water with nothing on."

The temperature reached nearly ninety degrees on Thursday, July 15, as the crowds continued to flock to the beach. The *Daily Sketch* reported that several people were drowned near the south coast resorts, but thousands of other bathers cavorted in the Channel. Many took with them into the water an invention by Colonel McCaskill, a retired Indian army officer, whose inspiration had come from "watching natives crossing swift-flowing rivers on inflated goat skins". The colonel had set to work designing an inflatable rubber horse, four feet long and two feet wide, which after one or two modifications proved successful. By the summer of 1926 a London firm was struggling to churn out enough of the colonel's horses, tigers and elephants.

The heatwave ended on Friday, July 16, with a spectacular electric storm. A bolt of lightning hit a power station in Greenwich, south-east London, plunging much of the capital into darkness. As the rubber horses were deflated and the crêpe bathing suits folded away indefinitely, Mercedes Gleitze sat in her Hythe boarding house waiting for the storm to pass. She had scheduled to start her Channel swim on Monday, July 19, but revised her plan when she woke that morning to the sound of a thirty-mile-per-hour wind rattling her bedroom window.

Gleitze had hired as her support vessel the *Ocean King*, a lifeboat that had been converted into a pleasure boat, but the outlay had cut deeply into her finances. Drawing on her long tradition of initiative, Gleitze went to see the *Folkestone Herald* and persuaded the paper to run an article in its weekly edition of July 17 that was more of an advertisement than a piece of reportage. For only ten shillings ($2.50), the *Herald* explained, readers could book their place on the *Ocean King* and follow pretty Mercedes Gleitze as she swam from England to France. The paper also hinted that if any musicians fancied joining the party, Gleitze would be thrilled to have some musical accompaniment. No musical benefaction was forthcoming, nor was any improvement in the weather, although the forecasters predicted the wind would abate and the temperature rise on the weekend of July 24-25. Putting her faith in the experts, Gleitze rescheduled her attempt for Saturday morning, but the forecast was inaccurate. The wind had eased slightly, but when Gleitze looked out across the Channel that morning it was still strong enough to transform the sea into a mass of small, white-capped pyramids.

The decision whether to postpone for a second time rested with her. S.T. Hirst, the coach from the Amateur Swimming Club, had been forced to return home after the first delay, and the only other adviser was her part-time coach, Horace Carey, a local bus driver who had taught himself how to swim three years earlier. She waited a couple of hours on the off chance the wind might suddenly drop – which it did fractionally – and then decided to go ahead with her attempt.

Greased from head to foot, wearing a one-piece black bathing suit, and with her long dark hair squeezed under a bathing cap, Gleitze entered the water at Folkestone Beach between the lifeboat station and the red-brick Southern Railway Pier, from where a boat train could be taken to Boulogne or Calais. A couple of hundred holidaymakers lined the promenade that ran parallel to the railway pier and gave her a hearty send-off, wrote the representative of the *Folkestone Herald* aboard the *Ocean King*. He didn't disclose if anyone had parted with ten shillings for the privilege of accompanying Gleitze, but the only encouragement she received as she used the breaststroke to distance herself from the shore was the singing of the female doctor who was in the rowboat alongside Horace Carey and Mr. Harry Sharp, the pilot.

As Gleitze headed out into the open sea, the *Herald*'s reporter wrote, the "conditions were far from promising because there was a nasty lop on the water owing to a southwest wind". Worse, the direction of the wind was opposed by the easterly drift of the tide, creating a short and choppy sea. At least Gleitze had the spring tide to hasten her on her way, and at 1:00 p.m., an hour after starting, she was three miles from Folkestone and Dover was visible over her left shoulder. But not long after, the wind began to freshen and the sea became rougher. The doctor jumped into the water and swam alongside Gleitze, and together the pair sang and chatted. Despite the lumpy sea, the Englishwoman could feel herself scooting toward France on the fast-running spring tide, and two hours into the swim, according to the *Herald*, she was still "cheerful and confident." At 3:00 coach Carey told her she was twelve miles from Folkestone and six from the English coast. "Miss Gleitze found herself among the steamers passing up and down the Strait of Dover," wrote the *Herald*.

Passengers on board the steamers looked in awe at the tiny head in mid-Channel, which looked like a shuttlecock bobbing down a river, while in the rowboat Sharp's forearms were aching with the effort of trying to keep close to the swimmer in a sea that was toying with his insignificant vessel like a cat with a mouse.

At 4:00 Carey suggested Gleitze give up, but she laughed off the idea. "Tremendous seas began to roll" at this point, according to the *Herald*'s correspondent, who was drenched with the white spray that washed over the boat. At 5:00 Gleitze had been pummelled into submission, and she signalled that the game was up after five gruelling hours. She was pulled on board the *Ocean King* nine miles southeast of Dover, and for most of the one-and-a-half-hour voyage back to Folkestone she and the doctor were violently seasick.

Her colour hardly improved in the next day or two as she read the newspaper reports of her attempt, which ranged from the mocking to the indifferent. The front-page headline of the *Daily Sketch* on Monday, July 26, was TYPIST'S PLUCKY SWIM, under which was a large photo of Gleitze being taken from the water onto the *Ocean King*. Inside, however, the account of her swim ran to a mere six lines. The jeering headline in the *Dover Standard* – MISS GLEITZE FAILS AGAIN – was followed by a mean-spirited paragraph in which the writer said it was hard to imagine "how success could have been anticipated by starting so far west". The London *Daily Herald* chose to title its story about Gleitze SEASICK CHANNEL SWIMMER! and the *Dover Express* covered the five-hour swim in two paragraphs, giving far greater prominence to the news from Manchester that the first greyhound race in Britain had been run that weekend using the "electric hare" that had proved such a hit in the United States.

America heard about Gleitze's unsuccessful effort from Julia Harpman on Wednesday, July 28, in a report that had been hurriedly cobbled together from various secondhand sources. Harpman called her "Emma Gleitz" and said she had quit after four hours in the water.

She was more sure of her facts when she listed the other swimmers still waiting along with Ederle for their chance to take on the Channel. The "unfortunate Englishman" Frank Perks had already tried and failed, while Ishak Helmy's attempt had been held up by the weather. Then there were Jeanne Sion and Omer Perrault, a few miles up the coast in Dunkirk, who were waiting for better conditions before striking out.

Arthur Sorenson corralled some of the contenders on the Cape Gris-Nez beach one afternoon – Ederle, Perrault, Sion and Helmy – as well as Pop Ederle, Margaret, Bill Burgess, Henry Vincent (the trilby-wearing manager of Perrault),

Chashak (Helmy's Egyptian friend who had flown in from Paris) and Bob (Burgess's Alsatian dog). There was only one absentee from the happy photo, and that was Lillian Cannon. To the Ederle camp, she was still the leper of the Cape Gris-Nez swimming colony, to be avoided at all costs in person and in print.

Across the Strait of Dover the numbers of Channel hopefuls seemed to be swelling by the day at the start of August. The British newspapers dubbed it "Channelitis", and the *Star* reckoned that "if it goes on like this, we shall soon have to make a channel through the swimmers".

At the beginning of July there had been just Gade and Perks, with Gleitze down the road in Hythe, but by the end of the month one couldn't stroll down Marine Parade without bumping into a Channel aspirant looking dreamily out to sea. "It's becoming a joke," said Gade. "There are so many here now that we keep apart." Dr. George Brewster, originally from the Shetland Isles but now practising medicine in London, had come down to see if he could succeed where he'd first failed in 1923. Even more secretive was Colonel Freyberg, VC, DSO, who was doing his best to avoid the gaggle of reporters who trailed him and his wife wherever they went. "I would like to swim the Channel unheralded and unsung" was all he would say when asked his intentions. Another Englishman, a twenty-six-year-old bedspring manufacturer called Norman Dereham, had failed after twelve hours in the water but was training hard for a second attempt. A Norwegian policeman, Olav Farstad, was preparing to catch the ferry to Cape Gris-Nez, convinced that his daily intake of twelve eggs would compensate for his scanty knowledge of the Channel tides. An American, William Jackson from Alabama, was expected to arrive any day, bringing with him "the astonishing feat of swimming forty miles in the Gulf of Mexico in eighteen hours". Jackson never showed, but his compatriot did, Louis Timson, a thirty-six-year-old Massachusetts shoe manufacturer, who was sponsored by the American Legion. Within hours of arriving in

Dover, Timson, who looked and acted like a man at ease with the world, had won over the locals with his handsome smile. His war service, in which he had been decorated for bravery by both the American and French armies, only enhanced his appeal. The *Dover Chronicle* was sure Timson was "the only American aspirant likely to succeed" because he possessed "a particularly fine breaststroke, great buoyancy and stamina". He had many exceptional feats to his name, the paper added, the most recent being "a 14-mile swim on July 5 from Nantasket Beach to Egg Rock in 7 hours".

And, of course, there was also Clarabelle Barrett, recently unearthed by Alec Rutherford on behalf of the *New York Times* but still dismissed as a no-hoper by nearly all the British and American papers. She made it into a London newspaper only on Monday, August 2, when she was derided by the *Daily Mirror*. "Miss Claribel [*sic*] Barrett, a swimming instructress of New York, who has devoted her vacation to her attempt, [and] is 6ft tall and weighs nearly 20st, is in a dreadful hurry. She will make her attempt tomorrow morning, weather permitting. The first time she went into the water the other day, she wanted to start right away for France. Her trainer, Mr. Walter Brickett, had considerable difficulty in persuading her to 'go slow'."

The *Mirror*'s story had more holes than a Dover fisherman's net, but Barrett didn't care, for by the time the paper was printed, she was already swimming toward France.

Chapter Fourteen

FOR A WOMAN who had never been to England before, Clarabelle Barrett must have wondered in what strange land she had arrived. The furnace heat of mid-July had gone, replaced within forty-eight hours by the sort of chill wind that normally blew through New Rochelle in March. Then on Friday, July 30, as she and Captain Learmont mapped out her course, an earthquake shook the Channel Islands. The incident was widely reported in America, with the *Philadelphia Inquirer* describing how "a small tidal wave formed, driving the frightened bathers ashore before any of them were caught". English newspapers didn't dwell on the earthquake, preferring to speculate on a more alarming tremor within the England cricket team: Captain Arthur Carr was suffering from tonsillitis and looked a doubtful starter for the next match against Australia.

That was the main topic of conversation among the thousands of passengers who shoehorned themselves into the trains in London on the morning of Saturday, July 31, bound for the coast where it was rumoured the sun might reappear. At Dover, as at other southern resorts, those who arrived on Saturday found No Vacancy signs festooning the many guest houses and hotels. Undeterred, hundreds of families camped out on the beach or on the cliff tops, eating stale sandwiches and listening to Daddy reminisce about life in an army camp a decade earlier.

Walter Brickett, Barrett's trainer

When Barrett arrived at Shakespeare Beach a little before 7:00 a.m. on Monday, August 2, she found a couple of dozen campers stretching out stiff joints after an uncomfortable night on hard shingle. Slipping into one of the bathing huts at the top of the beach, underneath the railway line that ran into Dover, Barrett changed into her bathing suit. Grace Leister, wearing a navy-blue dress with a sailor's collar, smeared her from head to foot with a grease that was a mix of castor oil and lard, before Barrett pulled on a black singlet and a pair of loose shorts that flapped as she walked down the beach to where Walter Brickett was waiting to apply a second layer of grease. The Englishman had dressed up for the occasion in white slacks, cardigan and straw boater. He reached up on tiptoe and helped Barrett fit into her bathing cap and motoring goggles. Nurse Leister then circled her friend, making sure there were no small wrinkles where water might seep under the cap.

There was now a crowd of about thirty curious bystanders,

140

some campers, others locals out giving their dogs an early-morning walk. An old man in a trilby and overcoat, oblivious to the already climbing temperature, shuffled up to inspect the giant swimmer and then peered inquisitively at the lone newsreel cameraman filming the departure. The cameraman asked Barrett if she wouldn't mind returning to the bathing huts so he could get a shot of her striding down the beach with the white chalk of Shakespeare Cliff as a backdrop. Barrett did as requested, at the same time answering a couple of questions from the *Dover Standard*. "I know I have a hard job ahead," she said with a smile, "but the conditions appear as good as they ever are and I am now in splendid condition. Right now I feel confident of making the route."

A small white dog scampered down the beach in front of Barrett and halted at the water's edge to test the temperature of the water with his paw. He decided against a dip and retreated past Barrett, who was taking off her shoes and handing them to Brickett. Then she marched purposefully into the water and without a backward glance dived into the Channel. In a small rowboat a few yards offshore, Alec Rutherford made a note of the time: 7:50 a.m.

"The start was made in most favourable weather," said the representative from the *Dover Standard*, "the sea being smooth as glass and the sun shining with full power." A slight sea mist obscured the French coastline, portending another hot summer's day, and the temperature of the sea was a bearable sixty-three degrees. Captain Learmont was at the oars of the rowboat with Brickett and nurse Leister in the stern. Having started the clock on Barrett, Rutherford had then transferred to the motor boat to join the small contingent of reporters and photographers along for the ride.

Barrett soon put a good distance between herself and Shakespeare Beach, moving confidently through the water using the six-beat American crawl she had learned all those years earlier in New York. Brickett counted Barrett's speed, making sure she maintained a steady twenty-four strokes a minute, while Learmont kept one eye on the water and another on the compass that lay between his feet. On the assumption that Barrett maintained a stroke rate of twenty-four a minute for the first few hours – when she would be fresh and strong – he'd devised a route that left England on the middle of the flood tide heading east. He wanted Barrett to be northeast of Cape Gris-Nez when the ebb tide arrived at approximately 10:30 a.m. because she would then be pushed southwest for six hours. When the flood tide returned, at around 4:30 p.m., Barrett should be a few miles off the French coast, within sight of the Gris-Nez lighthouse, but the six hours that would then follow would be the hardest. Barrett would be tired and hungry and cold, and yet she would find herself being bullied east, away from her destination. Only when the tides switched at 10:30 p.m. would she be able to swim hard for the shore on the southwest ebb tide, if she had any energy left. But Brickett had said Barrett could last twenty hours in the water, so Learmont had based his assumptions on that prediction.

On board the motor boat the reporters scribbled observations in their notepads as the American swam east. They were all impressed with Barrett's powerful stroke and attributed it to her size, although unanimity was absent from their estimations as to her exact dimensions. The *Dover Express* reckoned she was six foot three and fifteen stone (210 pounds) while the *Dover Chronicle* opted for a more petite five foot ten and fourteen stone (196 pounds). The chap from the *Dover Standard* sided with his colleague from the *Express*, adding that whatever her exact measurements, "she is a woman of fine physique".

For the next two hours Barrett's hands moved through the

water with the precision timing of a wristwatch. She reached her first marker point at ten o'clock, half an hour ahead of schedule, so that for the next thirty minutes she would swim against the diminishing flood tide. As Learmont steered the boat 180 degrees, he shouted to Barrett that she was five miles out from Dover and making "capital progress".

The sea was still benign and the early morning mist had been burned off by the sun as Barrett trod water and gulped down the beef tea handed her by nurse Leister. Learmont removed his jacket, rolled up the sleeves of his white cotton shirt and pushed back his blue sailing cap. How did she feel? he inquired. Barrett said she was on top of the world and looking forward to reaching France. She even had a speech prepared, she told him, through a mouthful of sponge cake, for when she waded ashore at Cape Gris-Nez in a few hours' time.

Her metronomic advance toward France continued, and at midday the passengers on the motor boat saw in the distance the Varne buoy, a warning to vessels that the Varne Sands lay to the southwest. Barrett had another break for food, and as she ate some chocolate and bananas, the motor boat pulled up alongside. The reporter from the *Dover Standard* found her "strongly and infectiously cheerful" after nearly four hours in the water. Barrett wanted to tell the journalists all about the thrill of swimming in mid-Channel, but before she could say more than a few words, wrote the *Dover Standard*, "Pilot Learmont found it necessary to remonstrate with the swimmer for wasting her lung power in vivaciously trying to open conversation with members of the party". Then a series of loud cracks to the northeast drowned out Learmont's querulous voice as the Dover gun began firing at some targets in the Channel pulled by a naval tug.

Barrett's next distraction came shortly before 1:00 p.m. when a motor boat came out from Dover carrying Frank Perks, Mille Gade and a reporter from the Associated Press. Gade and Barrett hadn't had time to become acquainted in Dover, but now, in the middle of the English Channel, they made their introductions. Both had come to England to swim the Channel, but neither was as electrically charged with rivalry as their two compatriots training in France. Gade and Barrett were older, wiser, and, most pertinent of all, neither had the hand of a newspaper sponsor gripping their elbow. The visitors didn't stay long and soon returned to England, with the Associated Press reporter finishing the report he was going to cable to America as soon as they disembarked.

A few hours later the final editions of several newspapers carried the dispatch, including the *New York Telegram*. "At one o'clock this afternoon, five hours after entering the water, Miss Clarabelle Barrett of New York was twelve miles out, on a straight line between Dover and Calais, in her attempt to conquer the English Channel. She had thus negotiated half the distance in almost record time and was still going strong. Weather conditions were favourable, and her chances of success seemed good."

The dispatch created pandemonium in the editorial office of the New Rochelle *Standard-Star*. Its typesetters had been faithfully working on Lillian Cannon's next "How to Swim" article when the wires began to hum with a story about their own Clarabelle Barrett, the woman the paper had ignored for months. In the time it took to convene one frenetic editorial meeting, all that had changed. The evening edition on Monday, August 2, led with the front-page headline MISS BARRETT IS SWIMMING THE CHANNEL, while alongside the AP report, the paper announced it was starting a campaign to raise five hundred dollars to assist Barrett's swim. The newly appointed "Channel swim editor" of the *Standard-Star* told readers he had cabled the London *Times* to ask that paper to "communicate with her requesting her to acknowledge the cable".

The Channel swim editor then dashed over to the vine-covered cottage at 208 Young Avenue, New Rochelle, to get an exclusive with Barrett's mother, only to discover he had been beaten to it by a reporter from the *New York Sun*, who was now taking tea with the accommodating Mrs. Barrett. She provided the *Sun* with the necessary background information on her intrepid daughter, and some colourful quotes. "Clarabelle doesn't know what it is to give up," she said. "If any woman can swim the Channel, she can. My baby will do it." The reporter was amused that "the hopeful mother still calls her daughter 'baby' despite the latter's 185 pounds and 31 years".

There was one question, however, which Mrs. Barrett chose to answer with maternal discretion rather than veracity. Clarabelle was thirty-one, she told the *Sun*, knocking four years off her daughter's age in the time it took to offer the reporter another slice of cake.

At 3:30 p.m. on Monday, August 2, Clarabelle Barrett was well on her way to fulfilling her mother's prediction. She was over halfway to France, heading southwest on the ebb tide, and neither Brickett nor Learmont could detect any weakening of her stroke. Barrett had been in the water for over seven hours, three and a half hours longer than Dr. George Brewster, who had set out from just east of Dover at 11:18 a.m. on the same ebb tide. He planned to swim a less westerly zigzag, staying in line with Calais and not being propelled beyond it as Learmont intended for Barrett. But Brewster and his pilot, a man called Miller, had their calculations all wrong. Instead of heading southwest, toward the Varne sandbank that Barrett had passed several hours earlier, Brewster was being pulled west, parallel to the coastline. When he saw Folkestone seafront a few minutes before 4:00 p.m., the doctor lost heart and gave up after four hours and thirty-seven minutes. Brewster clambered aboard the boat and told the reporter from the *Dover Chronicle* that though he felt "as fresh"

as when he went in, he would conserve his energy for a second attempt later in the month. As they headed back to Dover, the *Chronicle* correspondent rued his bad luck in backing the wrong swimmer while his rivals from the *Dover Standard* and *Dover Express* were with Barrett. But as he scanned the sea to his south for any sign of the party, he whistled in surprise at what he saw coming up the Channel.

As Brewster was climbing into his support boat, Barrett's team were quietly confident that in a few hours she would be the first woman to swim the Channel. Alec Rutherford slipped some Channel statistics into the report he was writing for the *New York Times*, saying that of the two hundred people who between them had made over a thousand Channel attempts, only five had succeeded. Then he returned to the present using prose that suggested he thought success was a formality. "Miss Barrett is the giantess of Channel swimmers," he wrote, "standing 6ft tall and strongly built in proportion. She weighs nearly 210 pounds. The course was mapped by Captain J. Learmont and was adhered to very closely, as the tides were not running very heavily and Miss Barrett's drift therefore was less than on an average Channel swim."

Learmont had had little choice but to plot the course on the slower neap tide because of Barrett's determination to start on Monday. If she had gone on a spring tide, she might have been nearer to France than the eight miles she now was, but she might also have been pushed farther west by the faster sea. As it was, at 4:30 p.m., when the ebb tide gave way to the flood tide, she was on the exact course Learmont had calculated. Now she had to swim for six hours in a northeast direction, hopefully the penultimate tide of her swim.

Barrett remained in good spirits as she turned 180 degrees and drove herself forward through the docile sea. The only trouble she had encountered so far were the plate-size jellyfish which, like the bathers on Dover Beach, were basking in the hot sunshine while they could. Dense shoals of the creatures floated just below the surface, and several times Barrett swam straight into them, "causing her to shout out loudly" as she was stung on her arms, legs and face.

It was Learmont who saw first the reason for the concern of the *Dover Chronicle*'s correspondent. Minutes after the flood tide took Barrett in a northeasterly direction, Learmont looked up from his oars and saw a tidal wave of grey fog approaching. Brickett and Leister, sitting in the stern of the rowboat, caught his look of dismay and turned to watch as the fog engulfed their craft. It continued to roll across the Channel until it hit Dover with such speed, related the London *Daily Express* the following morning, that "in ten minutes the bright sunshine of the afternoon was screened by a great bank of fog". A couple of miles north of Barrett, the *Maid of Kent*, a Southern Railway steamer returning to England from Calais with five hundred day-trippers, reduced speed and had to be guided home by Dover's fog guns.

Barrett was as surprised as everyone by the sudden arrival of the fog. One minute her back and shoulders were being warmed by the sun, and the next the air felt cold and damp. She stood up in the sea, treading water, as the gray murk obscured everything but the rowboat a few yards to her right. The only evidence that the motor boat still existed was the hollering of its passengers. A few minutes of whistling by Brickett brought the motor boat to their side, and Barrett began swimming northeast, away from Cape Gris-Nez and into the path of the cross-Channel ferries.

"I didn't think much of it [the fog] at the time as I thought it would clear," Learmont admitted later to the *Dover Standard*. "But instead of that it became worse and it was difficult to give the swimmer attention. We never saw a thing. Navigation of a little boat like that by compass is very difficult in a fog and we were worrying about losing sight of the swimmer." The Scot was now relying more on his own experience than on the small circular compass at his feet. Unable even to see the beam of the Cape Gris-Nez lighthouse, he refused to allow self-doubt to worm its way into his head. He was still on course, he repeated to himself, and at 7:30 p.m., some two hours since the fog had descended, he was proved correct by the appearance of the North Ridens buoy.

The buoy had an effect like a signpost for a weary traveller tramping an endless road. Learmont shouted that Cape Gris-Nez lay southwest of their current position; Barrett raised her pace from twenty-two strokes a minute to twenty-four. Suddenly everyone in and out of the water felt less cold. Learmont joked that he'd better brush up his French so he could talk to the locals when they landed.

They were still cracking jokes a little while later when the world around them detonated in a petrifying blast of a ship's horn. Learmont's mouth dropped open as he looked up and saw the outline of a massive vessel coming through the fog. Brickett leaped to his feet, waved frantically at Barrett, and yelled, "Swim, girl, swim as hard as you can to your left!" Learmont heaved at the oars with calm desperation as the sound of the ferry's propellers churning through the water grew louder. He screamed a warning as Barrett thrashed through the water. She looked up to see, as she put it, "a great ship as high as a house suddenly looming up over me. It seemed about two yards away". Brickett later estimated that the steamer* passed by no more than ten yards from them going like a "railway train". It was close enough for those passengers leaning against the deck rail to point at the swimmer and offer cheery words of encouragement. Learmont shouted at Leister and Brickett to hold on tight as their boat was caught in the ferry's wake and pitched from side to side. Barrett gasped for air as the foaming water surged around her like a whirlpool. In less than a minute the drama was over and the only clues to their narrow escape were a slightly ruffled sea and their pounding hearts. Barrett asked for some food to steady her nerves, and everyone took a few moments to regain their composure.

Throughout the next couple of hours, Barrett began to decline. There was no longer the easy fluency to her strokes, and just as the tide was trying to drag her physically from her destination, so the fog distanced her mentally. Where were the twinkling lights on the French shore five miles away to act as welcoming beacons? There was nothing to see that indicated she was making progress, just fog. Learmont noticed that every steamer's fog horn that blasted through the murk, no matter how distant, made Barrett start.

The onset of darkness rallied her for a while as she no longer had to battle the dreary greyness of the fog. She enjoyed the sensation of swimming through patches of phosphorus and watching as they "broke up and sparkled like millions of diamonds".

On board the support vessels the clothes of the passengers were damp and heavy from the fog. Some of the journalists tried to sleep, but the cold gnawed through their light summer clothes. They veered course with the start of the ebb tide at 10:30 p.m. and headed directly south. Learmont told Barrett she would have to call upon every last ounce of strength to stop herself from being tugged past the Gris-Nez promontory. To encourage her,

* On the same foggy night a steamer heading from Boulogne to Folkestone with seven hundred passengers struck a trawler, although neither vessel sank.

he began to sing some of the old Scottish songs he had once sung to himself as Cape Horn appeared off the bow.

Barrett heard the songs, as she heard someone shout that she had now spent longer in the Channel than Jeanne Sion's previous record of fourteen hours and thirty-five minutes, but she didn't respond. Even when she stopped to shove some fruit or chocolate into her mouth, or gulp down a cup of cold beef broth, she gave the briefest of acknowledgments to those in the boat. Leister scrutinised her friend's face for signs of hypothermia, but Barrett shrugged off her anxious questions and continued swimming south, her world now condensed into the metre of water in front of her.

The first strands of dawn pierced the blackness at around 4:30 a.m., the same time the tide changed once more. It was indiscernible to Barrett, but those on the boat could see the water shift direction as the flood tide began to push her northeast. As the night receded, they suddenly caught a glimpse of something else, a weak light flashing through the swirling mist. In a moment they slipped underneath the fog, and there in the distance was the Gris-Nez lighthouse. The outline of the cliffs was also visible, as were one or two of the whitewashed houses dotted among the grass and wildflowers, and the Hôtel de la Sirène where Lillian Cannon was wrapped up warm in bed. There were triumphant cheers and excited cries from the passengers on the motor boat, but the reaction in the rowboat was more muted. She was two miles from shore, but the tide was against her. Can I do it? Barrett asked Learmont. Only she had the answer to that question, he replied.

For thirty exhausting minutes Barrett tried to break free from the tentacles of the tides that had wrapped themselves around her. The watching journalists shook their heads in astonishment and asked each other how it was possible that a woman could display such stamina and courage. But for all her tremendous pluck, Barrett was getting no closer to the shore; and even through a brain befuddled with exhaustion, she knew it. "Tell me the truth," she gasped to Learmont. "I can manage two hours more, but does it mean eight hours more before I finish it?" Learmont hid nothing from her, explaining that the tide wouldn't change for another five hours, and then she'd have a couple of hours' hard swimming after that to reach land. "If that's so," said Barrett, "I'm going to stop."

The motor boat came alongside, and as Barrett reached out for the ladder that was lowered over the side, Alec Rutherford noted the time: 5:35 a.m. on Tuesday, August 3. She had been in the water for twenty-one hours and forty-five minutes. A blanket was thrown over her shoulders, and Barrett's sang froid crumbled. "I am sorry I've failed," she sobbed.

Grace Leister had to wake Barrett when they reached Dover at eight o'clock. Almost immediately after her anguished cry, she'd fallen into a deep sleep, which had at least spared her the misery of watching the boat chug quickly over waters she had taken nearly a day to cover. Barrett insisted on stepping ashore unaided, and before she and Leister walked back to their boarding house, she shook hands with everyone who had accompanied her on the attempt.

The reporters from the *Dover Standard* and *Dover Express* expressed their admiration in words that were later reproduced in headlines on the pages of their newspapers: A SENSATIONAL PERFORMANCE and A GREAT SWIM.

It wasn't in Captain Learmont's nature to be too demonstrative; that wouldn't do for a hard-bitten Scot. "I take it you'll be back again soon for another try, Miss Barrett?" he asked. "I shall never come back again," she replied. A hint of a smile flickered across his lips. "Well, there are some blankets here which I got for this swim, and I'll keep them for you next year, OK?" Barrett grinned. "Oh no, you won't. I'll leave those for some of the rest of them."

Once Barrett was safely out of earshot, Learmont told the reporters exactly what he thought of the American's swim. "It was the fog entirely that beat Miss Barrett," he said. If they had had a clear run, he was in no doubt she would have reached France. As it was, "she must have a marvellous constitution to stand the strain of nearly 22 hours' swimming. I have seen Channel swimmers worse done up after nine or ten hours' swimming than Miss Barrett was at the end of her swim". The Dover journalists couldn't remember seeing the old sea dog quite so animated. Normally it was a struggle to extract more than a grunt out of Learmont, but now it was hard to get a word in. Nurse Leister was a "most cheery person", he said, and no friend could have been as supportive. He finished by praising Barrett one more time. "She can stand fatigue better than all the rest of the women Channel swimmers I have seen. She did all I expected her to do – in fact, more."

The *Dover Chronicle* correspondent arrived at the quayside to discover that his run of bad luck had continued. Barrett had retired to bed, and his rivals from the *Standard* and *Express* were interviewing Learmont. He got a few words from Walter Brickett, however, who told him about the incident with the steamer and estimated that Barrett had made 26,400 strokes during her twenty-one and three-quarter hours in the water.

When Barrett woke in her bed on Wednesday, August 4, she hurt all over. Jellyfish had tattooed her arms and legs with livid welts, and every joint and every tendon throbbed. But the greatest agony was the one that couldn't be healed with a balm or a massage: the pain of failure. Barrett forced herself out of bed, put on a brave face and traipsed down to breakfast. It was Grace

Leister's thirty-sixth birthday, and she didn't want to spend the day moping.

Leister was waiting at the table with a present of her own for Barrett: the morning editions of the London newspapers. SUPER-WOMAN OF THE CHANNEL was the headline in the *Daily Express*. GREAT CHANNEL FIGHT, roared the *Daily Chronicle* on its front page alongside a photo. The *Daily Sketch* described her swim as a "Splendid Attempt", the *Daily Herald* lauded her "remarkable courage", the *Daily News* her "wonderful stamina and endurance", and the *Daily Mail* thought it the "finest" swim ever accomplished by a woman, surpassing Jeanne Sion's 1922 attempt. The *Daily Mirror* reckoned that no swimmer, man or woman, had ever made such a "gallant attempt" and carried some quotes from Walter Brickett. "She is the most wonderful woman swimmer I have ever known," he exclaimed. "Altogether she must have swum nearly forty miles, an extraordinary feat of endurance." Barrett was the toast of England.

A few hours later the cables began to arrive at her guest house to inform her that back home in the States people also thought she had done something a little bit special. A telegram from the London *Times* explained that the New Rochelle *Standard-Star* had launched an appeal on her behalf. A cable from Mrs. Walter Kraslow of Brooklyn, New York, read: CONGRATULATIONS, SPLENDID HERCULEAN EFFORT. APPRECIATE YOUR TYPIFYING FINE MODERN WOMAN. WON'T YOU ACCEPT FIVE HUNDRED DOLLARS TOWARDS ANOTHER ATTEMPT. MONEY WILL BE CABLED AT YOUR REQUEST.

By the afternoon, when a reporter from the United Press knocked on the door of her guest house to ask her about the *Standard-Star* fund, Barrett had been overtaken by excitement. What America wanted to know, he asked her, was if she was going to have another crack at the Channel. A few hours after telling Learmont she never wanted to set foot in the sea again, Barrett had changed her mind. Yes, she would definitely be

PRAISES PLUCK
OF MISS BARRETT

By LILLIAN CANNON

CAP GRIS NEZ, France, Aug 4—
One swimmer after another has been
setting out these recent days to conquer the 20-mile ribbon that is the
English channel—and to learn first-
hand that beneath the water's surface
are hidden dark secrets.

Those tides. The swimmer who,
by dint of expert advice and the right
luck, hits them at just the proper
time will win. That is, if she is dur-
able enough. The one who hits them
at the wrong time loses.

Miss Clarabelle Barrett made a
splendid effort. She swam for more
than 21 hours. But the tides defeated
her. As to the rest of us—we shall
see.

Swimming in the channel is a
manyhued adventure. The other day,
as I was sweeping along, my head
bumped against something. I was
startled, and swerved aside. But it
was only a bottle, tightly corked with
a little note and a Belgian address
inside.

Other obstacles we meet in the
water aren't so innocuous. The dogfish, for instance. They never attack
human beings, I'm told, but they
have sharp, vicious-looking teeth.

One day when I was on a long
swim, accompanied by a rowboat, my
trainer calmly told me that there was
one of these dogfish playing about
near me. He didn't want me to be
alarmed, but I scampered aboard the
boat at a great pace. A moment later
I was a bit ashamed of myself, for
the fish cut away 10 times faster than
I did. He was about 10 feet long.

Experience gets a swimmer accustomed to such things, and I now
fee much more at ease in the channel
than I did at first.

One of Lillian Cannon's columns praising the pluck of
Clarabelle Barrett

having another crack, thanks to the generosity of the people
back home. She asked Brickett to change her return passage to a
later date and began to plan a second attempt.

As Barrett looked to the future, the morning editions of the
American newspapers were busy analyzing the present. An
editorial in New York's *Herald Tribune* praised her "exhibition
of pluck and endurance that must command the heartiest admiration. New York can especially take pride in the athletic feat
of . . . a young woman of Amazonian physique and lion heart,
who undertook her adventure in the best of spirit of sport". The
World also devoted an editorial to Barrett, calling the swim "a

heroic effort" and offering its commiseration: "Two more miles and she would have won. Two miles! . . . But, as it happens, there is a glamour about defeat which does not go with victory, so perhaps Miss Barrett can take consolation from the fact that she will be more loved for her failure than she would have been for success."

Across America, from Los Angeles to Dallas to Boston, newspapers joined in the adulation, even those such as the *Chicago Tribune* and New York's *Daily News*, whose loyalty lay with Gertrude Ederle. The *New York Times* carried a report on the front page and described her as "the least equipped of any woman who has made the attempt to swim the Channel".

The *Standard-Star* was less gracious in drawing comparisons with Barrett's rivals. Ignoring its own initial indifference to its "local miss", the paper crowed that "Miss Barrett did not have the help, and advise [*sic*] that the other Channel swimmers, such as Lillian Cannon and Gertrude Ederle, enjoy. Her attempt was made on her own all the way". But despite the *Standard-Star*'s self-indulgent pledge of allegiance to Barrett, its edition of August 4 still carried Cannon's latest column from Gris-Nez. Unfortunately for the Baltimore woman, she now sounded precious when she whined that "one of the most distasteful parts of Channel swimming is the greasing . . . you simply are all mucked up". People had grown tired of Ederle and Cannon's "ballyhoo", as the *Herald Tribune* called it, particularly now that America had a new heroine, a fearless woman who dodged steamers and defied jellyfish. She might not have had Cannon's wholesome appeal, but the photos of Barrett's firm jaw and broad shoulders had a strength and indomitability that resonated with Americans.

Chapter Fifteen

THERE WAS NEVER any doubt that Clarabelle Barrett would be a heroine to the British people. This was, after all, a nation who still believed it better to be a good sport than to be good at sport; that it was more honourable to lose gracefully than win ruthlessly. As the *Daily Mirror* said of her attempt, "She had no financial backing, she was merely taking a sporting chance."

But Barrett's unquenchable spirit also captured the imagination of the American public, although there were more pertinent reasons for her instant popularity. "What use is the Channel swim?" George Trevor asked his *New York Sun* readers on August 4. "Well, what use is climbing the Matterhorn or finding the North Pole? 'Is is worthwhile?' asks a contemporary. As much worthwhile, I think, as any sporting event can be. Here is the supreme event in sport – untarnished by sordid gate receipts. The Channel swim satisfies man's elemental urge to pit his puny strength against the cosmic forces of nature."

Trevor's readers knew what he meant when he talked of "tarnished gate receipts", and most shared his distaste for a generation of sports stars who appeared to have let fame and fortune go to their heads. Seven years after the Black Sox scandal had rocked the country, baseball was still making headlines for all the wrong reasons. In July Ty Cobb, the manager of the Detroit Tigers, had to be restrained by police and umpires when he jumped into a stand and attacked a spectator during a match in Washington, DC. Two days later a pitched battle erupted between the Cincinnati Reds and Boston Braves which ended with the Braves' Frank Wilson arrested for assaulting a policeman who'd tried to stop the mayhem.

Still, muttered the sportswriters, at least there was something to write about in baseball, more than could be said for the heavyweight boxing division, where the only ducking and weaving of late had come from the lawyers representing New York State's Athletic Commission and champion Jack Dempsey's manager, Tex Rickard. The latter wanted his fighter to defend his title against Gene Tunney at the new Madison Square Garden, but the Athletic Commission insisted Dempsey should fight Harry Wills, New Orleans's "Black Panther", in a bout that would have been far less lucrative for the champ. The dispute had reached an impasse on July 24, prompting the *World* to run a mocking editorial: "Apparently the preparations for a big fight involve more legal points than the launching of a bond issue for a railroad, and the amount of money involved is about as large . . . this is an intolerable state of affairs."

But hadn't greed and odium always been the corner men of boxing ever since John L. Sullivan had toured America in the 1880s offering to fight anyone for $250?

Greater dignity was expected from the world of tennis, particularly the graceful Frenchwoman Suzanne Lenglen, who had won twenty-eight Grand Slam titles in the last seven years and who moved around the court like a ballet dancer in her white accordion-pleated skirt and scarlet bandeau. But on Monday, August 2, the same day Barrett set off from Dover, she announced she was turning professional. Everyone had their price, and the legendary sports promoter C.C.Pyle had discovered Lenglen's was $100,000. The *Boston Post* lamented her decision "to forsake the simon pure ranks for money chasers" on the professional circuit, on the same page that it celebrated the courage of Clarabelle Barrett.

If Barrett was the woman of the hour, there was still enormous interest in Lillian Cannon and Gertrude Ederle, despite the ballyhoo in Cape Gris-Nez. Before Barrett, even the most fervent supporter of women swimmers had been unsure deep down if overpowering the Channel really was possible. Perhaps the Channel for a woman would remain like Everest for a man: a tantalising but impossible dream. But after Barrett's attempt, people quickly grasped that the dream could soon become reality. So America turned its gaze toward the two young women still training hard in France, both of whom, reported the *New York Sun*, were becoming "increasingly impressed with the size of the job" they had undertaken.

Ederle and Julia Harpman lunched together at the Hôtel du Phare on Tuesday, August 3, a few hours after Barrett had been dragged exhausted from the water two miles to their north. They totted up on their fingers the number of failures so far this season: Perks, Gleitze, Dereham, Helmy, Brewster, Barrett, Farstad and Freyberg. There were a lot of fingers.

Harpman had just written an article telling America that Ederle hoped to make an attempt on the Channel between the sixth and twelfth of August, when the spring tide returned. If she failed the first time, she would try again later in the month, and then a third time if necessary. But as Ederle stared out across the sea she knew she would only have a realistic chance of success on the first shot. "I have made up my mind to swim the Channel this time or sink," she said firmly to Harpman. "It wouldn't be nice to drown, but I'll feel like it if I see I'm going to fail and they will have to take me out of the water unconscious."

Ederle lapsed into silence and picked at her food. Normally she and Helmy competed at the dinner table to see who could laugh the loudest, but today for the first time Harpman found her distracted and edgy. It wasn't just the weeks of training and waiting that were weighing heavily on her shoulders, nor was it the prospect of tackling the Channel once more. What made her shudder with apprehension was the thought that another woman might bag what she had been stalking for two years, ever since she first scented the Channel during the Paris Olympics. The name Clarabelle Barrett no longer made her giggle the way it had when she first heard about the giantess being hunted by Jabez Wolffe. The previous evening she had gone down to the beach with dozens of other villagers and hotel guests when word reached them that Barrett was closing on Cape Gris-Nez. For hours the people had stood on the beach, peering into the soupy darkness in the hope they might be about to witness history being made. But not Ederle. She dreaded the prospect of hearing the distant hum of a motor boat engine above the purr of the surf and watching as another woman reeled ashore.

On the morning when she'd heard of Barrett's gallant defeat, Ederle had been effusive in her praise, telling reporters how "thrilled" she had been by her "wonderful performance". But it was easy to be magnanimous when nothing had been lost.

Even so, there were other women who wanted to rob her of her dream. Mille Gade across the Channel, who, if the rumours were to be believed, would start her swim on Saturday, August 7; Jeanne Sion in Dunkirk, whose plans were unknown but who had just announced that, as a Frenchwoman, she had no intention during her swim of feeding on cake and fruit but would dine instead on pigeons and mutton cutlets. And of course there was Ederle's *bête noire*, Lillian Cannon, the girl from Baltimore who looked as if butter wouldn't melt in her mouth.

The week before, an artist working for Scripps-Howard, Manuel Rosenberg, had visited Cape Gris-Nez to sketch Cannon in a variety of poses: Lillian swimming, Lillian climbing rocks, Lillian sharing a joke with Helmy, Lillian lying seductively on the cliff top among the buttercups and the sea pinks. The sketches had subsequently been published in a number of newspapers, along with Rosenberg's thoughts on his subject: "Another celebrity is just routine work after an artist has put in years at drawing everyone from murderesses to kings. But I'd like to say for Lillian Cannon . . . that I never sketched a celebrity who had more quiet charm than she. From the artist's point of view, I'll say further that few of the persons who have served as my models have had features of more classic beauty. The perfect development of her athletic figure is a delight to any eye and I can imagine a sculptor's particular enthusiasm over it."

What's more, added Rosenberg, Cannon was charm personified, always happy to strike whatever pose was requested. Little wonder that she was "a great favourite around Cap [sic] Gris-Nez. The other swimmers training with her, almost without exception, have made a sister of her and the townspeople give her their ardent hopes for success". The "almost" was Ederle. The Channel waters might have warmed in recent weeks, but the relationship between the two swimmers remained as chilly as ever.

Had Harpman been misguided to promulgate the fact that she would start sometime between the sixth and twelfth of August? Ederle wondered. Might not Cannon, scheming with her coach, Jack Wiedman, over a mug of hot chocolate in the Hôtel de la Sirène, launch a preemptive strike? The Associated Press reporter detected the mood of furtiveness and described it on August 5. "There is the keenest rivalry here and much uncertainty as to who will take to the water first," he wrote. "It is possible that Miss Ederle's starting time may be advanced an hour or two at the last minute or that Miss Cannon may start secretly before dawn, in which case Miss Ederle would be most certain to hurry the plunge in the fear that another of her sex may surpass her."

Bill Burgess stoked the tension by telling reporters on the morning of August 5 that he hadn't decided for certain when

Ederle would start, only that when she did it would be on the wane of the ebb tide so that for two hours she would be thrust southwest before turning on the flood tide and swimming northeast into mid-Channel. Burgess reckoned that after three hours on the flood tide, Ederle would then reach a point where she had to swim directly north, rather than northeast. "This is where I will have to call on her for four hours of hard swimming across the tides," Burgess explained. "If she is as strong and fast as I think she will be, the end of the ninth hour will find us somewhere between South Goodwin and East Goodwin lights, marking the famous Goodwin Sands, where so many ships have piled up. If she is well in toward the shoal, the next set of tides [the ebb tide] will sweep her ashore without any more struggle than just the effort to keep afloat."

Burgess was asked what would happen to Ederle if she wasn't strong enough to swim against the tide in mid-Channel. "Then the drift begins to carry her out of her way in the opposite direction – up the Channel, toward the North Sea."

Another reporter asked when the spring tide would arrive. Tomorrow morning, replied Burgess. So, in theory, Ederle may enter the water at dawn tomorrow? Burgess agreed that was a possibility but one which he was unable to confirm, not for another few hours at least, not until Julia Harpman was certain that the *Daily News* had the exclusive. While the paper's rivals speculated that Ederle would start sometime over the next few days, the *Daily News* ran Harpman's scoop in the late edition of Thursday, August 5, under the headline EDERLE SWIMS TOMORROW. "Weather permitting, Gertrude Ederle, world champion woman swimmer, will attempt to swim the English Channel from Cape Gris-Nez to Dover on Friday morning. According to present plans she will take the water at 6:45 a.m. (12:45 a.m., New York daylight saving time) to reap the benefit of a westering tide."

The story sparked a flurry of late betting, although the odds offered by the Wall Street betting commission had dropped from 5-1 to 3-1 after Clarabelle Barrett's stirring performance. Lloyd's of London had also lowered its odds from 5-1 to 4-1. Someone in New York placed $2,000 on Ederle to succeed, a hefty sum but small fry compared to the $25,000 with which Pop Ederle had originally planned to back his daughter. At the beginning of July he'd gone to London to place the bet with Lloyd's at odds he believed would be 50-1, but he was told he had been misinformed and the best it was prepared to offer were 7-1. Ederle refused to accept this offer and returned to France having decided not to place any bets. That, at least, was what he told the newspapers.

Throughout the afternoon of Thursday, August 5, Gertrude Ederle kept a low profile in the Hôtel du Phare. She whiled away the hours reading or chatting to Julia and her sister Margaret. The silk bathing suit that Margaret had designed was ready, as were Ederle's amber goggles. After the unsuccessful trial at the end of June, the goggles had been sewn with leather and chamois in a bid to plug the leak at the bridge of the nose. When that hadn't worked, they dripped molten wax around the edges and rimmed them with white lead. That had done the trick. In the afternoon of August 5, Margaret became all things to her sister: her seamstress, her confidante, her counsellor. Ederle unburdened herself of all her worries and fears, and at the same time she derived strength from her sister's unwavering belief that in a little over a day the name Gertrude Ederle would be reverberating around the world. If there was one topic that probably wouldn't have been discussed, it was the news carried in several English papers on Wednesday, August 4. The outstanding feature of the Norwegian policeman Olav Farstad's second unsuccessful Channel attempt was the twelve-foot bottle-nosed shark that had trailed him for several minutes.

In the early evening Ederle strolled along the beach with her father. He and Margaret were about to leave for Boulogne, where they would spend the evening ensuring everything on the tug *Alsace*, from the wireless to the lights to the gramophone to the first-aid kit, was in place. Then just before dawn they would accompany Captain Joe Costa and his crew on the short voyage to Cape Gris-Nez. Before they parted, Ederle asked her father to promise her something: "Don't let anybody take me out of the water unless I ask."

After supper that evening Ederle popped her head around the door of the small bar of the Hôtel du Phare to wish everyone good night. Burgess had made it public a few hours earlier that she would be embarking on her swim just before 7:00 a.m. the next morning, and now a group of reporters were firing questions at him over a round of drinks. There was no barman present; instead Monsieur Blondiau was happy to allow guests to pour their own beer and put the money in the till above which was a sign: LET CONSCIENCE BE YOUR GUIDE. Ederle went around the bar shaking hands with the journalists. Everyone was impressed with her equanimity on the eve of the biggest challenge of her life. "Feeling confident, Trudie?" one of them asked. " 'England or drown' is my motto," she said. "I could never face people at home again unless I had got across."

The reporters waited until the sound of her footsteps up the stairs had vanished before turning to Burgess. Did he really believe she could do it? All the fishermen, all the old-timers, in France and in England, reckoned she had no chance. "If she can last 14 hours," Burgess replied, "Gert will have a splendid chance of getting to England." The newspapermen stared at him in astonishment. Fourteen hours? If Ederle could last fourteen hours, she would smash the existing record for the fastest crossing.

Chapter Sixteen

A s the alsace rounded the Cape Gris-Nez promontory,
Margaret and Pop Ederle stood on deck and stared toward
the beach. They were looking for a sign; a candlelight flickering
in a window of the Hôtel de la Sirène or a flashlight beam dancing on the beach, anything that might suggest that the rumours
of Lillian Cannon's early start were true. They saw nothing.
They couldn't even distinguish where the surf of the low tide
broke against the sandy beach. The new moon had turned the
Cape as black as the mussels that lay in its waters.

The sea was running fast with the spring tide as the Ederles
were helped down into the rowboat and taken ashore. Margaret
and Pop tramped up the wet sand and past the Hôtel de la Sirène
that only now began to take shape in the dawn light. Surely
Cannon must still be tucked in bed.

By the time they had negotiated the lane that led from the village to the Hôtel du Phare, the milky orange sun was rising
above Cape Blanc-Nez to their east and the swallows in the nest
above the hotel's porch were singing. Burgess was already in the
hotel, standing over Amédée Blondiau in the kitchen as he
cooked Ederle's breakfast. Fifteen years earlier his pre-swim
breakfast had been a plate of bacon and eggs, and he wanted
Ederle to line her stomach with something more than just bread
and jam. While Pop joined the cluster of reporters fortifying

themselves with strong coffee, Margaret bounded up the stairs to the first floor. Her sister was still asleep as she knocked and entered holding a candle. "Do we go?" were her first words on awakening. Margaret nodded. Gertrude jumped out of bed and ran downstairs to the dining room still in her pyjamas. She made short work of a bowl of cornflakes and then turned her attention to half a fried chicken. "How do you feel?" Burgess asked, as he handed her a coffee. "Fine," boomed Ederle. "I feel like I could lick Jack Dempsey today!" Burgess ran through the strategy one last time, reminding Ederle of the need for patience. If she was swimming too fast, he told her, he would make a signal with his hand, as if he were patting a dog's head, and she must reduce her stroke rate. Ederle nodded and, pushing away the chicken carcass, asked for a peach. Burgess advised her not to eat fruit so close to the swim, but he was ignored.

After breakfast Ederle retired to her bedroom to be greased by Margaret and Harpman. She removed her pyjamas and lay naked on her sagging bed with the same clammy sheets that were in all the bedrooms. Harpman had recoiled in horror at the state of the hotel when she had arrived two months earlier, but now she didn't notice the dust and dirt. Gertrude shuddered at the touch of cold hands as her sister and Julia covered her in olive oil. Burgess loitered outside the door reminding them to pay particular attention to the armpits and the back of the neck, the areas most susceptible to sea-water chafing. When the greasing was done, Ederle put on her bathing suit under some warmer layers and hurried downstairs to the waiting automobile.

When they arrived at the parking lot of the Hôtel de la Sirène, Ederle was greased for a second time. This coat was lanolin, a heavy yellow-white grease that Margaret scooped from a tin and slapped across her sister's oily body until she looked like a basted chicken. Ederle squeezed into her red bathing cap, yanking it right down over her ears. She walked across the parking lot and down the short flight of narrow steps that led to the sand.

Ribbons of white seaweed were strewn across the beach, which was already patterned with the feet of scavenging seagulls. Otherwise the sand was as golden as Lillian Cannon's hair.

Ederle could see the *Alsace* anchored a couple of hundred yards from the shore, its American flag hanging lifelessly from the mast in the still morning air. Beyond the tug a sheet of soft mist lay on the water, and in the distance, just visible, was the English coastline. As Ederle walked across the beach toward Burgess, she saw Harpman and Arthur Sorenson remonstrating with some of their colleagues. Ederle recognised a few of them: Alec Rutherford, the *New York Times* correspondent, who had sided with her against Jabez Wolffe last year; a couple of Americans – Fred Abbott, the Paris-based correspondent for the International News Service; and Sid Williams, the staff correspondent in London for the United Press. Alongside Williams was thirty-six-year-old Minott Saunders, also of the United Press, and of late the unofficial manager of Lillian Cannon. There were one or two other reporters jabbing fingers and waving hands in the direction of Harpman and Sorenson, but Ederle didn't know them, nor could she hear what they were saying. But whatever it was, it was clear they weren't happy.

The reporters and photographers who had drained their black coffees in the Hôtel de la Sirène and the Hôtel du Phare made their way to the beach expecting to follow Ederle aboard the *Alsace*. They stood waiting for the swimmer's arrival, yawning in harmony and laughing at poor Olav Farstad. Not only had he been trailed by a twelve-foot shark, they told those who hadn't heard the story, but his French engineer had drunk so much wine during the crossing that he had fallen sleep and allowed the fires of his engine to be extinguished by sea spray. They looked out across the water at the *Alsace*, a sturdy vessel about seventy feet long, and hoped its engineer was a more temperate character.

When Julia Harpman appeared on the beach, she had an unpleasant surprise for her fellow journalists. The *Alsace* was Ederle's support boat, reserved for "Trudy's Gang", as they had been dubbed in certain newspapers. Apart from Harpman and Sorenson, only Margaret, Pop, Madame Costa (the captain's wife), Ishak Helmy and John Hayward of the London *Daily Sketch* would be allowed on board – and the latter was there only in his capacity as the official British witness. Rutherford, Abbott, Saunders and the other newsmen were livid. Angry words were exchanged, with the Americans accusing Harpman of some shoddy trickery. She was within her rights to protect her paper's exclusive, that they understood as fellow reporters, but she had intentionally deceived them by allowing them to believe they would be welcome on the official escort tug. Now, at the eleventh hour, she was marooning them on the beach and sailing away like some eighteenth-century pirate.

Harpman, almost certainly acting under instructions from New York, apologised but refused to listen to their impassioned entreaties. As she was rowed out to the *Alsace*, Harpman's newspaper rivals formed a council of war to discuss their next move. Suggestions were tossed from reporter to reporter: hire a local fishing boat? Too small, too dangerous. Take the ferry to Folkestone and hire a tug in England? How would they find her in mid-Channel? Then Minott Saunders hit upon an idea. Lillian Cannon had hired another Boulogne tug, *La Morinie*, the vessel which had supported Ederle in 1925. Contrary to some of the gossip the previous night, Cannon had no intention of embarking on her swim today. They could hire that boat and its skipper. It was large enough, and it had a Marconi wireless so they could transmit their reports. If they sent word to Boulogne at once, they could be under way in a couple of hours. Great plan, they all agreed. Saunders shot into the Hôtel de la Sirène, high on self-satisfaction, to effect his plan, while on the beach the rest of the abandoned press pack cursed Harpman and the *Alsace*, and all who sailed in it.

While the reporters had been feuding, Bill Burgess was busy smearing Ederle with a third and final layer of grease, this one a mixture of lard and Vaseline. "I feel just like a grease ball!" she said with a laugh, as Stroke, her small brown and white mascot dog, stuck his head in the tin in the hope it might be breakfast. Burgess rolled up the legs of his pants and knelt down on the sand, greasing Ederle's feet and the inside of her toes. "For heaven's sake," snapped Ederle, "let's get started!" Just as Burgess finished, Jack Wiedman and Lillian Cannon appeared through the crowd of villagers. Wiedman was wearing a cloth cap and a loose-fitting jacket, and a challenging grin. Although Burgess had told reporters that his conquest of the Channel was due solely to his own efforts, Wiedman knew otherwise, and so did the ten other members of Burgess's support crew who were known in Dover as the "12 Club". They remembered how Burgess had cried like a baby in mid-Channel when the tides pushed him back toward England; they recalled the songs they had sung to keep up his fraying morale; they hadn't forgotten that Wiedman had handed over his goggles when Burgess's sprang a leak after only a few hours; and etched on all their minds were the final three hours of the swim when the puffy-eyed Wiedman swam alongside Burgess encouraging and supporting him until they touched down at Cape Gris-Nez.

Like any man with a psychological hold over another, Wiedman goaded Burgess, telling him that he was surprised he was allowing Ederle to start today, what with the strong winds that were predicted for the afternoon. Didn't he think it advisable to wait a day or two? That was why he had deferred Cannon's attempt. With the scene being filmed by a movie-reel cameraman, Burgess refused to rise to the bait, replying brusquely that the Dover forecast had spoken only of a light southwesterly wind with the chance of slight local rain in the afternoon. And anyway, he added, the temperature of the sea was sixty-three degrees today, just about the warmest it had been all summer.

Cannon was uncharacteristically dressed as she stood before Ederle. Her body – even her legs – was covered by a long beige Macintosh. She extended her hand and wished her rival "good luck". Ederle's goggles were down over her eyes, but she smiled as she took Cannon's hand, grasping it for a moment before relaxing her grip and leaving Cannon to wipe away the lard, lanolin and olive oil. One of the photographers snapped the handshake, the rapprochement, while in the background Burgess and Wiedman continued to debate the merits of the weather. Arthur Sorenson had already taken several shots of Ederle, but he was still after the one that would jump off the front page the

Lillian Cannon shakes Gertrude Ederle's hand just before Ederle's swim

next day. Ripping off his shoes and socks, he waded into the Channel, wincing at the coldness of the water, and waited as Ederle said goodbye to her Gang. Margaret hugged her, then her dad, who also reminded her there would be a red roadster waiting for her in New York if – or rather when – she became the first woman to swim the Channel. Ederle walked toward the surf with Burgess shuffling alongside her. "Good luck," he said, kissing her on the cheek. Ederle smiled and shouted "Cheerio!" to the hundred or so people gathered on the sand.

She paused for a moment. "This is now or never, I am going to cross this time." Then she was splashing through the surf, laughing at the coldness of the water. Sorenson snapped a photo of her, but he knew it wouldn't be the grease or the goggles that would raise eyebrows when the photo appeared in the *Daily News* the next day; it would be the bathing suit.

Gertrude Ederle in her two-piece swimming suit and layers of grease

Male reporters were afraid to let their gaze linger too long on Ederle in case their colleagues thought them lascivious. Alec Rutherford said simply that it was "cut deeply under the arms". It was a woman who best described its innovative design. "Entering the water," wrote Harpman, "Trudie wore a red diving cap and goggles . . . [and] short, black silk trunks and a narrow brassiere of navy-blue silk on the front of which is sewn a tiny silk American flag and also the emblem of the New York Women's Swimming Association . . . the brassiere unties, and, once abreast the channel, she removed it, wearing thereafter only the trunks. If these chafed her she was resolved to undo and kick them off as she swam."

It was a first for a female swimmer, a two-piece bathing suit that exposed the midriff. But as Ederle paused waist-deep in the English Channel and looked heavenward, whispering, "Please God, help me," it was hoped that this would be a day of firsts.*

Ederle was twenty-five minutes behind schedule when she took her first stroke in the Channel at 7:09 a.m. She set off as if intent on making up the lost time, heading northwest at twenty-eight strokes per minute using her powerful overarm crawl. The rowboat carrying Burgess, her sister Margaret and her father to the *Alsace* struggled to keep up, and Burgess was soon bellowing, "Take your time, Miss Ederle!" Alec Rutherford watched from the beach and thought she looked like a "pretty, tiny atom of humanity" on the calm sea.

Ederle came level with the *Alsace* and laughed at the large

---

* Was Gertrude the inventor of the two-piece bathing suit? The man credited with giving the world the bikini was the Frenchman Louis Reard in 1946, but in 1975 Gertrude said, "I invented the two-piece bathing suit, although I didn't have the sense to patent it."

white arrow that had been attached to the black hull with the legend "This way, ole kid!" chalked below. Once the rowboat had been tied up behind the tug, and everyone was safely on board, Captain Costa pushed down the throttle and the *Alsace* began its slow voyage across the Channel with Ederle swimming a few yards away in its lee. Those passengers privileged to be on board settled down for the long day that lay ahead.

No one expected anything of interest to happen for a good few hours, but in fact within minutes of starting Ederle experienced a series of severe stomach cramps. She trod water and clasped her midriff in pain, but no one on the boat paid any attention. Perhaps they thought she was fiddling with her bathing suit and averted their gaze. As she prayed that the cramps would subside, Ederle thought of the peach she had eaten and wished she had listened to Burgess.

After several seconds the pain dissipated, and Ederle set off, increasing her rate until it was back to twenty-eight strokes a minute. Glancing at the *Alsace*, she saw Ishak Helmy leaning nonchalantly against the rail. Ederle began to sing "It's a Long Way to Tipperary", and Helmy joined in, then Sorenson and Margaret and Pop, until everyone on the tug was belting out the song at the top of their voice.

By 8:00 Ederle had covered two miles, and Burgess was telling Harpman she had started at a "remarkable" pace. Harpman could feel there was a *but* close by. What's the matter? she inquired. Ederle looks strong, after all, and the spring tide is carrying her rapidly in the right direction. With a nod of his head, Burgess indicated the gun-metal-grey clouds that had started to form over the English coast. He didn't like the look of them. But before he could elaborate on his apprehension, there was a crackle from the gramophone as Margaret placed the needle on the disc. Then "No More Worrying" began to drift across the Channel. "There won't be," yelled Ederle to her sister, "not if we get to Dover tonight."

Thousands of miles away Ederle's eldest sister, Helen, was arriving at the offices of the *Daily News* in New York. It was a little after two in the morning, and she had in tow her sixteen-year-old brother, George, and her best friend, Martha Behrens. They were handed cups of coffee and led to the paper's wire room, where Harry Bolig, the *Daily News'* chief telegrapher, explained as best he could the bewildering array of instruments. He left for last the most important: the stock ticker machine that sometime later that day would spell out either success or failure for Helen's sister. A telephone was made available to her so she could call her mother, who was on holiday in Highlands, New Jersey.

As Helen and George gawked at the complex machinery in front of them, their mother was keeping a lonely vigil on the veranda of the family's red summer house, which overlooked the Shrewsbury River in Highlands. Mrs. Gertrude Ederle's two youngest children, Henry, six, and thirteen-year-old Emma, were asleep inside, but she was determined to stay up the whole night in case of any unexpected news from France. There was no telephone in the house, but a relay system had been organised by Mrs. Ederle. If any message arrived from the *Alsace* at the *Daily News'* office, Helen was to phone the hotel that was just a few hundred yards from the summer house and pass it on to the manager, William Kruz. He would then race down the road and deliver the news.

Kruz was only too happy to oblige. Like the rest of the town, he considered Gertrude as one of their own, even though she and her family only visited the town during summer holidays. But it was in Highlands that she had learned to swim, and many people could point to the exact spot on the Patton Line Pier where her father had once lowered Gertrude into the water on the end of an old clothes line and taught her to swim.

During the summer the population of Highlands tripled as New Yorkers made the short journey south on steamboats. Earlier that evening restaurants like the white-timbered Bahrs had been packed with people enjoying the town's famous seafood, and the riverside Kruz Dance Hall had reverberated to the sounds of the Charleston and the Collegiate Shag. Now, however, the town was asleep, and Mrs. Ederle was left in silence to think of the times she had watched Trudy thrash her way across the Shrewsbury River as a little girl. "Nothing comes easy in this life," she had once told her daughter. "But however difficult the task, never quit until it's time to put it in God's hands. If it's God's will everything will be all right."

Chapter Seventeen

TWO HOURS OUT FROM CAPE GRIS-NEZ, everything was going as well as Ederle had hoped. She was four and a half miles northwest of her starting point and about to swing northeast on the flood tide toward mid-Channel. Burgess, who had removed his jacket and was dressed in a waistcoat and cloth cap, rested his hands on the *Alsace*'s rail and observed Ederle's steady rate of twenty-six strokes a minute. A while earlier he had exhorted her to drop her speed still further, but she had retorted that if she went any slower she'd sink. Margaret, meanwhile, continued as bandleader, playing records such as "Yes, We Have No Bananas", "The Sidewalks of New York", and Ederle's favourite, "Let Me Call You Sweetheart". Ederle began to set her strokes to the rhythm of the song's waltzing beat, but Burgess ordered her to stop fooling around.

The sea was as flat as it had been when they set out, and even Pop Ederle, with his thick scarf wrapped tightly around his neck, seemed to have found his sea legs as he stood ramrod straight at the ship's side, looking as if he was back behind the counter at their butcher shop on Amsterdam Avenue. "Come on, Pop," said Ederle, giggling and slapping the water. "I'm going slow enough for you to keep up now!" Pop's jowls wobbled with laughter at the teasing. Perhaps he deserved his daughter's playful taunts, her revenge for the time he'd spanked her when he caught her

Ederle swimming alongside the *Alsace* while her sister Margaret
cheers her on. Also on the boat are Ishak Helmy (far right) and
William Burgess in the waistcoat in the centre

splashing around in a water trough on Tenth Avenue and Fifty-
first Street.

It wasn't long after Ederle had picked up the flood tide that
she began to feel the sea stir. She glanced up at the tug and
noticed that the Stars and Stripes was being tousled by a stiffen-
ing breeze from the southwest. Soon Ederle's goggles were
being intermittently slapped by small waves, but on each occasion she just shook her head like a dog emerging from a river and
smiled at the efficiency of her goggles.

At 9:45 a small motor boat approached the *Alsace* from the
north. As it neared, a man stood up with one hand clamped over
his trilby and the other waving cheerfully. Mr. W. Brockman,
owner of the Brockman Boat Company, slowed down and
brought the motor boat alongside the tug. The man in the trilby
grabbed the ladder and hoisted himself up and over the side.

Introducing himself as Don Skene of the *Chicago Tribune*, he shook hands with everyone and took possession of a package from Sorenson. Inside were the plates of the photographs Sorenson had taken at Cape Gris-Nez a few hours earlier. Skene tucked the package inside his jacket, tipped his hat to the ladies and jumped back down into the motor boat. Within minutes the boat was just a speck in the distance, and it felt like they had all imagined Skene and his trilby.*

As one vessel diminished to the north of the *Alsace*, so another took shape to the south. It wasn't moving as rapidly as Skene's motor boat, but by 10:00 a.m. Burgess had recognised it as the tug *La Morinie*. The news was a jolt to Harpman, who believed she'd outmanoeuvred her rivals with her slick chicanery. She scribbled in her notes that five minutes later the tug was abreast of them, "crowded with independent, unofficial reporters, photo-graphers and moving-picture cameramen". Among the glowering expressions of the pressmen, Harpman spotted the pretty face of Lillian Cannon.

Unlike Harpman, Ederle was unconcerned with the arrival of *La Morinie*. She harboured no professional antagonism toward the other reporters, and now that she was on her way across the Channel, with her fate in her own hands, she bore Cannon no ill feelings. *La Morinie* reduced its speed and drew up alongside Ederle to allow the photographers on board to take some photos. Alec Rutherford was delighted at her progress and thought it wise she was swimming on the leeward side of the tug because the wind was beginning to make the sea a trifle "rough". Ishak Helmy "yahooed" Lillian Cannon and exploded in laughter when he noticed that Amédée Blondiau, the proprietor of the Hôtel du Phare, had come along to support Ederle.

* Once Skene and the plate arrived at Dover, he drove in a "speedy automobile" to London, where the photo was cabled to New York using a Bartlane process tape in time for Saturday's front page of the *Daily News*.

Ederle had been treading water for a minute as she welcomed *La Morinie*, but now she turned to her tug and called out, "Tell me when it's noon so I can take 12 to 2 out for luncheon." Burgess nodded, and Margaret shouted that she was putting on one of her sister's favourites: Irving Berlin's "Always". Ederle sang along as she swam:

Days may not be fair always,
That's when I'll be there always.
Not for just an hour,
Not for just a day,
Not for just a year,
But always.

As Ederle moved through the water like a well-oiled machine, her arms and legs powerful pistons, Harpman alternated her glances between Ederle, *La Morinie* and the sky, which she noted was now "a dull grey with no sun in sight or in prospect". In her notes she chose the same word as Rutherford to describe the state of the sea: *rough*. Ederle didn't drop a beat in the next hour as she drove inexorably north toward England. At 11:15 a.m. Ederle was six and a half miles north of Cape Gris-Nez and having the time of her life. She felt at one with the Channel: "The water is wonderful," she cried. "I could stay in it a week." Margaret and Helmy took turns in writing messages on a blackboard and hanging them over the side of the hull for Ederle to read. Margaret's words were ones of encouragement; Helmy preferred to pass on jokes that he'd picked up on his travels, some more risqué than others. Arthur Sorenson took off his shoes and socks and clambered over the side of the *Alsace*, perching himself on the narrow steel rim that circled the hull a foot above the water. "He clung there, like a monkey," wrote Harpman, "and as Trudy would swim opposite the fore part of the tug, Art would run on his toes to that part of the boat and, when the tug pushed forward, Art ran toward the aft, cheering Trudy on, drawing silly pictures on a small blackboard which he lowered to the tumbling water for Trudy to read."

Fifty yards away aboard *La Morinie*, Sorenson's rivals watched his antics with irritation. All they could see of Ederle was her red bathing cap bobbing up and down – hardly a photo that would please their editors. It was as if Sorenson, by running around the rail, was taunting them, driving home the fact that he had the best seat in the house.

Twelve o'clock heralded a truce as Ederle stopped for lunch and *La Morinie* steered closer so the photographers could take some pictures. Alec Rutherford said that "wild enthusiasm, to which Gertrude responded, greeted her arrival in mid-Channel just about midday". Sorenson and Harpman broke into a rendition of the "Star-Spangled Banner", and Captain Costa sounded twelve blasts on the *Alsace*'s siren. Burgess climbed nervously over the rail and dangled in front of Ederle a child's fishing net in which was a glass baby bottle filled with tepid chicken broth. Ederle took the bottle and clamped her lips around the rubber teat, all the time making sure she didn't come into contact with either Burgess's hand or the hull of the *Alsace*. To touch either would mean disqualification. She found the broth "unpalatable" but drank it anyway, and then gnawed a leg of cold fried chicken as Burgess told her she was an hour ahead of schedule, having swum eleven miles in the five hours she had been at sea. With the zigzag course Burgess had plotted, Cape Gris-Nez now lay nine miles due south and Dover was ten miles northwest. As Burgess gratefully hauled himself back onto the deck of the *Alsace*, Margaret joined her sister in the sea, wearing her light blue bathing suit. "How's the water?" she asked. "It's colder here than it was a couple of miles back," said Gertrude, picking the last strands of meat from the chicken leg.

The two sisters swam north, chattering at first but falling silent as the wind strengthened and the movement of the

Channel increased. They covered a mile in forty minutes, but by 1:00 p.m. Margaret was beginning to lag behind. Helmy swapped places with her and arrived at Gertrude's side with an almighty splash.

On the deck of the *Alsace*, Burgess was becoming ever more concerned about the worsening weather. Captain Costa shouted from the wheelhouse that the wind was now so strong he was finding it hard to keep windward of Ederle without running the risk of straying too close to her. Harpman asked Burgess if he thought Ederle was still on course to succeed. "Not if this weather continues," he replied. Even by Channel standards, what they were now experiencing was exceptional. In fact, Burgess told Harpman, "No living swimmer has ever approached Miss Ederle's performance under such conditions."

Since Ederle's break for food, Harpman had been recording the deteriorating weather in her notebook. At 12:45 p.m. she wrote that Ederle had encountered "a terrific sea, with the wind blowing a gale", and at 1:15 "a wild wind was raging, and the sea was rampant". On board *La Morinie* more seasoned Channel reporters plumped for less dramatic words, even though they, like Harpman, could taste the salt on their lips. Rutherford wrote that at 1:30 "rain started with a strong fierce wind causing a heavy swell difficult to battle against", and the correspondent for London's *Daily Telegraph* expressed his admiration for Ederle because the "sea at that time was rough, the wind breaking up the seas into little white-capped waves".

Only Minott Saunders of the United Press remained unmoved by either Ederle or the weather. In the report he wired from *La Morinie* at 1:39, he wrote that she was "within nine miles of her goal and more than half the English Channel was behind her . . . the sea was becoming calmer and smoother than during the corresponding period in last year's attempt". The wind, he added, almost as an afterthought, was "troublesome".

There was one advantage to be had from the hostile

conditions. The jellyfish, which waltzed with the water in great shoals when the weather was good, were now being hurled inelegantly by the waves. Ederle hadn't been stung once, and at 2:20, when Helmy asked Ederle if she minded his stopping, she was in good spirits. "Not at all," she replied. "I'm confident I can do it."

Helmy climbed out of the water and sat on deck shivering as blankets were thrown over his broad shoulders. Looking up, he saw that *La Morinie* was approaching off the starboard stern. He and the rest of the *Alsace*'s passengers watched with mounting alarm as *La Morinie* manoeuvred closer and closer to Ederle. Pop began to shoo it away with his hands, as if the tug was an inquisitive cow disturbing a family picnic, and Burgess yelled that the vessel's wake was unsettling Ederle. No one on *La Morinie* took any notice. The photographers' cameras were trained on the bemused figure in the water, and the reporters seemed unfazed by the irate cries from the *Alsace*. After a couple of minutes *La Morinie* veered away from Ederle, covering her in a plume of spray and black engine smoke, and resumed its position seventy-five yards to starboard.

Helmy dived into the Channel and swam after *La Morinie* to find out what the hell they thought they were doing. The reporters helped him aboard and accepted his admonishment, apologising but explaining they had needed some photos. Before he returned to the *Alsace*, Helmy asked Lillian Cannon if she would care to keep Ederle company for a while. Cannon accepted enthusiastically. Harpman was startled to see Cannon enter the water at 3:00 and swim over to Ederle. "As rivals at Gris-Nez there was not much love lost between the two swimmers," she wrote. "Together in this hour of trial, they behaved as long-separated near-kinsfolk might. Miss Cannon's splendid sporting spirit won her plaudits on every side."

Ederle was having a drink of hot chocolate when Cannon appeared. "Hello, Lillian," she said with a smile, "we're 50 miles from nowhere, aren't we?" Cannon laughed. "Why, Trudy,

181

you're almost there." She pointed beyond Gertrude's left shoulder. In the distance they could see the white cliffs of Dover. "Oh boy!" whooped Ederle, "It looks close doesn't it?" She offered Cannon some of the hot chocolate, and then the two of them started swimming northeast.

Not long after, Don Skene reappeared in Brockman's motorboat. This time he was there not to collect but to deliver. He scrambled up the ladder of the *Alsace* clutching a bunch of bananas and a bottle of brandy, and in his wake came the nimble figure of Louis Timson, who was keen to show his support for Ederle. As Timson introduced himself, Skene flopped down on a tarpaulin-covered object. There was a crack, and a curse from Margaret. He had sat down on her pile of records. Margaret shoved him to one side and inspected the damage. Several of the records were broken, including "No More Worrying" and "Valencia". Skene doffed his trilby as a mark of contrition and then launched into a tuneless rendition of "Don't Sock Your Mother, It's Mean".

Cannon and Ederle swam side by side until 4:00, when the Baltimore girl succumbed to seasickness. Sympathetic hands on board the *Alsace* pulled her onto the boat and wrapped her in blankets as a heavy rain began to fall.

If Cannon had earned the respect of her former enemies, there appeared to be no thawing in relations between the two tugs. While Cannon was sick over the port side of the tug, thoughtfully away from Ederle, *La Morinie* began to trespass once more. Sorenson knew that this time it wasn't for pictures that it was coming so close; no photographer would be able to take a decent shot in these conditions. *La Morinie* was now fifteen yards away from Ederle. Burgess gestured frantically for it to back off as it closed to ten yards. Harpman stared at the reporters, then at Ederle, who had stopped swimming and was treading water and looking confused. Suddenly the truth dawned on Harpman: the journalists on board *La Morinie* were trying to disqualify Ederle. They wanted her to reach out a defensive hand and fend off the tug. No triumph for Ederle or for the *Daily News*. Harpman screamed at *La Morinie* to back off. Pop cursed: "You damned loafers, do you want to kill the kid?" and hollered that if he had a gun he would shoot every one on that infernal boat. Then at the last minute, just as it seemed Ederle would be run down, it veered away.

Spray slapped Ederle's face as she rode the waves from the tug's wake. Startled and upset, she asked for some chocolate. Burgess held some out for her in the net and told her to forget about the tug. Anyway, he had some good news: he could see the lights of the South Goodwin lightship ahead. Ederle smiled weakly. Sensing that she needed more encouragement, Burgess unfurled the chart over the side of the boat and pointed out her position. She was south of the Goodwin Sands. "How long until I reach England?" Burgess estimated five hours. "You mean we maybe will reach it by 9 o'clock!" For a moment her shoulders seemed to slump. Then she raised her fist in defiance: "Don't let me ever give up," she yelled and launched into her six-beat crawl.

Timson leaped into the water to do his bit for Ederle, but after half an hour he confessed he could no longer last the pace. "Have I got to take you into training, too?" she said, laughing. Timson retreated to the sanctuary of the *Alsace* and told Harpman "that he had never seen a swimmer like her".

At 5:00 the weather was so aggressive that passengers on both tugs could only move securely around the deck with one hand gripped to the side rail. Don Skene, Louis Timson and Arthur Sorenson held on tight and belted out, "Yes, We Have No Bananas", and Alec Rutherford on *La Morinie* scribbled on his sodden notepad that "the wind was increasing in power and velocity and the sea was choppy and angry". Above the noise of the singing and the groan of the wind there was the constant whiplike cracking of the American flag on the mast.

Margaret had just received a message on the wireless from her mother back in Highlands and was chalking it up on the board. Ederle looked up and read it in the few seconds before it was obliterated by the rain.

Captain Costa called Burgess into the wheelhouse, and Pop Ederle followed. He wanted to be privy to any discussions that concerned his daughter. The French skipper made it clear they had to alter course. They were straying too close to the Goodwin Sands. What does that matter? demanded Pop. Costa gave a hard laugh and asked Pop if he knew what the English called the Goodwin Sands. No? "The Ship Swallower". Twelve miles long and two miles wide, the Sands had wrecked hundreds of ships over the years, and Costa didn't want to be added to their toll.

Burgess asked to see the chart of the Goodwin Sands, and he and Costa studied it as Ederle peered over their shoulders. Costa was adamant that to try and steer between the narrow strip of water that lay between the lightship and the southernmost tip of the Sands would be madness in this wind. Burgess suggested that he get in the rowboat and accompany Ederle across the Sands, meeting up with the *Alsace* on the other side. Costa wouldn't hear of it. The force of the currents around the Sands was too vicious, too unpredictable and too downright dangerous.

Eventually, Burgess and Costa agreed that the only chance Ederle had of succeeding was if they steered west by southwest, around the South Goodwin lightship and the southernmost tip of the Sands, and then made hard west for St. Margaret's Bay, two and a half miles north of Dover. Neither held out much hope for success. It would require almost Herculean strength and endurance from the nineteen-year-old. Burgess scratched his moustache, stiff with salt, and gave her odds of 100-1 against reaching England.

Margaret took the message to her sister in person and swam alongside her as they turned 180 degrees and began to swim away from England. Burgess speculated what people on shore would think if they saw them veer away from the English coast. "It must have seemed that I'd gone stark mad and was steering back to France," he said later, "but we had to do it to avoid the wrecks of Goodwin Sands."

Now that the *Alsace* was headed straight into the storm, the Channel bared its teeth in fury. Jagged white waves lashed at the vessel's bow, spewing great foaming plumes of water up and over the deck. On board Harpman recorded her impressions of the Channel in her notebook as "tumultuous seas whipped up by a gale-like wind . . . the seas soon became mountainous as she swam towards Dover".

Pop Ederle scribbled a message on the blackboard and turned it toward his daughter, hoping she would see ONE WHEEL, written in large letters. Five minutes later he scrawled TWO WHEELS and hung the blackboard over the side as the wind tried to rip it from his hands. Burgess asked what he was doing. Ederle told him he was reminding his daughter part by part of the red roadster she would win if she reached England.

Gertrude saw neither message. She could just about see the tug fifteen yards to her right through the waves and the rain driving against her goggles. She stole one or two glances toward the English coast, but it seemed if anything to be receding. "After that I felt I had better not look any more," she said later, "but just go on swimming as long as I could keep alive."

A few hours earlier Ederle had felt as if she had merged with the Channel into one entity; but now the sea was bucking and threshing, trying to shake her off. With each stroke she was forced to reach higher to clear the waves, expending vital energy. She concentrated on moving her body to the rhythm of the water, feeling the waves and judging the right moment to open her mouth to breathe in air, not water.

At 6:00 p.m. Burgess began to fret that Ederle was swimming to her death. He'd heard of climbers being gripped by some strange fever as they neared the summit of a mountain; perhaps this teenager had been similarly touched. His anxiety grew every time he lost sight of her red cap beneath another roiling mass of water, and for a couple of torturous seconds he feared she wouldn't reappear. When she did, there was a momentary surge of relief, followed by more terror as she was submerged by another wave. Finally, Burgess could bear it no longer. He confronted Gertrude's father and "insisted that she be taken from the water before the waves battered her into unconsciousness". Ederle's face darkened: "Leave your hands off her." Costa thrust his head out of the wheelhouse window to support Burgess. The wind was so violent, said Costa, that he was having "much difficulty keeping near enough to her for anyone to save her should she collapse and sink". Ederle "pointed out that Gertrude had yet to object to continuing" and in the same breath asked Costa if a further two thousand dollars would strengthen his sinews. The French skipper hesitated, looked up at the sky, and after a couple of seconds conceded that perhaps the storm would soon pass.

Burgess turned imploringly to Margaret for support, but she sided with her father, saying she had just swum with her sister for twenty minutes and Gertrude seemed in high spirits. Harpman, Sorenson, Helmy and the others were standing on the edge of the confrontation. Harpman said later that they "were all agreed that achieving her ambition on this try was humanly impossible. Finally someone, losing their head, shouted from the *Alsace*, 'Come on, girl, come out!'"

Chapter Eighteen

GERTRUDE EDERLE HADN'T noticed the showdown on the *Alsace*, but even with the water sloshing around inside her ears, she heard someone lean over the rail and shout that she should quit her swim. "I never dreamed they were worrying about me," she said later, "until someone, I don't know who, called to me loudly to board the tug. At first I thought somebody was kidding me but then I was angry. But as I knew it wasn't Pop or Burgess, I dismissed it from my mind."* Ederle didn't even miss a beat as she turned and shouted over her shoulder, "What For?!" adding, "I am going right through with it this time." It hadn't been Pop or Burgess who'd ordered her out because they had been too busy shouting at each other. Eventually, when Burgess realised he was wasting his time, he grabbed a pencil and paper, marched up to Pop Ederle, said Harpman, "and insisted he sign a paper releasing him from any claims and criticism should she be lost beneath the waves".

On board *La Morinie*, meanwhile, the previous hostility directed toward the *Alsace* had abated. No one wanted to harass

---

* It was never revealed who shouted at Ederle to leave the water, but it can't have been Burgess for Harpman or Ederle would have said so subsequently. "Come on, girl!" sounds like it would have come from an American man, perhaps Sorenson or, more likely, the brandy-guzzling Skene.

Ederle again, least of all the skipper, who was as frightened as Costa about steering west and leaving them side on to the wind. As he looked out of his wheelhouse the skipper of *La Morinie* could see the *Alsace*'s little boat, the one Burgess had wanted to row across the Goodwin Sands, rocked about like a cork despite being tied to the tug. Spray from the waves that butted the side of *La Morinie* had leaked into the wireless set, and like a swimmer who had swallowed too much water, it was spluttering and coughing.

The commotion on the *Alsace* had been witnessed by those on *La Morinie* not yet laid low with seasickness. Rutherford had seen Burgess and Ederle square up to one another, and he'd heard Gertrude scream "No!" in the general direction of the *Alsace*, "before she seemed to swim more strongly against the terrible conditions . . . on she struggled a few yards, only to fall back twice as many".

At 6:30 p.m. Ederle was a couple of hundred yards from the South Goodwin lightship, holding her own against the cross tides that were trying to drag her west, past Dover, past Folkestone, back to New York if they had their way.

Everyone on both tugs was now willing Ederle to keep going. If she could make it past the lightship, she would be clear of the treacherous currents and swells that clung around the Goodwin Sands. It might seem a strange thing to say on a day like today, reflected Rutherford, but once Ederle was past the lightship, she would be in less turbulent waters and in a position to swim with the southwest current of the ebb tide toward Dover. Ederle's body had taken a battering from the Channel, but they were the scars of battle she expected. Spasms of pain shot through her right wrist with every stroke, and her ankles were sore and puffy. Her goggles had stood up magnificently to the Channel, but the rest of her face was bruised like a bare-knuckle fighter's, and her tongue was lacerated by the salt water so that to talk or to swallow was agony.

Margaret wasn't much concerned about her sister's external state – she knew how tough she was physically – but her mental durability was an unknown quantity. She had never undergone such an endurance test before, and no one, not even Gertrude herself, knew the depths of her mental strength. Would her mind weaken with her body, or did she have the willpower to push herself beyond the limits of her physical endurance?

Ederle had already experienced the first of what she later called her "brief mental sinking spells". After several minutes of vigorous swimming against the tide she had found herself no closer to the coastline and the "sight of England became discouraging instead of encouraging". She rallied, however, and told herself to forget about what she could see in the distance and concentrate only on the small strip of water directly in front of her.

Ederle put her head down and swam. At 6:50 she passed two Calais trawlers. Their crews ran to the rail to give her a lusty cheer, but she neither heard nor acknowledged them. Ten minutes later there were hurrahs from the *Alsace*, and this time Ederle glanced up and saw the Goodwin lightship to her right. She was so close she could read the lettering on the side and see the Union Jack being run up the mast in her honour. She allowed herself a little peek in front of her and saw the sun emerge over England from behind a dark bank of cloud, just for a brief few seconds. Then it disappeared. A violent gust of wind rocked the *Alsace*, and its passengers slid across the deck. Burgess scrambled to his feet, shaking his head in happy disbelief. "God Almighty, I never saw anyone so marvellous." He leaned over the rail, cupping his hands and yelling, "It is sure, Gertie, take your time. You are in this time, certainly."

Harpman appeared alongside Burgess and shouted, "You will never miss it now!" Pop and Margaret bellowed that the worst of it was over; she was on her way to England. Gertrude thought the words were the sweetest she had ever heard.

Now Ederle changed course and began to swim toward Dover five miles to the southwest. At last the ebb tide was more friend than foe. Costa told Harpman that Ederle was a superwoman and that her success was assured. Burgess was just as bullish, noted Harpman, now that he had "recovered his poise and confidence in the girl".

And then something extraordinary happened, something that left Burgess cursing the fact that Ederle "had had the worst luck possible": the tide changed two hours early. Costa became aware that it was starting to shift at 7:15. How is it possible? groaned Harpman. "The wind is so strong," replied Burgess, "that the tide has turned two hours earlier than it should."

Burgess and Costa had another of their snatched conversations in the wheelhouse, working out a fresh strategy now that Ederle was entangled in a new current. They ran their fingers along the stretch of coastline north of Dover up toward Ramsgate, suggesting several possible landing spots. St. Margaret's Bay was three and a half miles due west, but that would entail another desperate struggle against the cross-currents. Beyond St. Margaret's there were a couple of options: Kingsdown Beach, five miles to the northwest, a hard swim against a northeast current, or Deal, seven miles north by northwest.

Ederle bore the news stoically when Burgess told her of her misfortune. "I'll do it," she shouted. "Don't be anxious." But as she turned away from the direction of Dover she had another of her brief sinking spells. "It was very difficult when I got close in to Dover and suddenly the tide changed and a strong current swept me round towards Deal," she said later. "I felt as if the sea were pulling me right away from England."

As the flood tide took Ederle northeast, she had to again fight hard to keep headed west toward St. Margaret's Bay. *La Morinie* kept a safe distance sixty yards off the stern while Costa had to

The Port Arthur News

VOL. XXV. NO. 217   PORT ARTHUR, TEXAS, FRIDAY, AUGUST 6, 1926.   PRICE FIVE CENTS

GERTRUDE MAY CONQUER CHANNEL

Only 5.5 Miles Off Dover, 45 Distant

Miss Ederle, American Ace Still Reported Strong As She Approaches Hardest Part Of Battle With Tide

Doughty American Gal Swimmer Nears British Coast

Early news of Ederle's progress on August 6, 1926

steer in different directions to give Ederle some protection from the waves. At 7:45 she could see the distinctive white lighthouse on the cliffs above St. Margaret's Bay flash its warning, and fifteen minutes later she was adjacent to Dover Patrol Monument, an eighty-three-foot granite obelisk erected five years earlier to the memory of the sailors killed during the war. She asked for some more pineapple, and as Burgess handed her a slice in the fishing net, he told her she was one mile from shore. Ederle signalled for another slice of pineapple and swilled the last dregs of its juice around her throbbing tongue. She waved at Harpman and, ignoring the excruciating pain in her mouth, asked how she was. "I'm fine," replied Harpman, "and you're glorious!" As Burgess watched Ederle recommence her crawl, he turned to Harpman and said, "No man or woman ever made such a swim. It is past human understanding."

At 8:45 Ederle was half a mile from her goal, but she didn't know if she had the strength to make one final push for the shore.

191

Her senses were dulled, her spirits depressed and her body shattered. Even though she had come so far, Ederle knew that the last mile was always the worst. She had read of Freyberg's heartbreaking collapse the year before, and she was aware that Wolffe had been beaten back by the tide almost within touching distance of the shore. And now Clarabelle Barrett had been added to the list of the broken-hearted. Ederle was on the point of no longer caring. She was cold, so cold, with her layers of grease washed away by the sea. She craved sleep. It would be so easy to climb aboard the *Alsace*, she told herself, as close to her as it was with its bright lights and warm cabin. Why not? asked a voice in her head. You have shown wonderful pluck for more than twelve hours; now you deserve a rest. Go on, hop aboard the *Alsace*. You can always try again next week, or next month, or even next year, when the weather is better.

It was so tempting, tempting enough to ask her support team what they thought. "Are you sure I can do it?" Ederle asked pitifully. As one, they roared back over the wind, "Assured!" Burgess could see Ederle was nearing the breaking point, but from some place, deep down in her soul, she had to dredge up one final supreme effort. He pointed at England, tantalisingly near, and screamed, "You are sure to make it, Gertie, if you swim." A few minutes of all-out push, and she would be across the tide sweep. Ederle knew it now. She looked for Margaret, smiled and shouted, "Won't mamma be glad?"

As Ederle prepared to launch herself against the crosscurrent, she allowed herself a glance toward England. It was an extraordinary sight. Through the darkness she could see the cliffs were illuminated by dozens of red and blue flares, and on the beach bonfires blazed for hundreds of yards. Most astonishing of all were the crowds of people jumping up and down at the water's edge, intoxicated with excitement as they realised what they were witnessing.

The excitement had been growing on the south coast of England since the afternoon when news first filtered back to Dover that a swimmer was battling against the Channel storm. At first people assumed only a fearless war hero like Colonel Freyberg would be reckless enough to be out in such weather. Two days earlier in Ramsgate, twenty miles up the coast, a teenage boy and a man had drowned after the tide had dragged them out to sea, and the report that it might be a nineteen-year-old girl swimming the Channel in such weather was greeted with widespread sceptcism.

But a radio report from *La Morinie* in the early evening, sent just after the South Goodwin Lightship had been passed, confirmed that it was indeed Gertrude Ederle. Couples in Dover undecided whether to go to the Queen's Hall cinema to watch the new Rin Tin Tin film, or the King's Hall to see the latest Jackie Coogan movie, instead dashed to the seafront to join the hundreds of others scanning the sea for a sight of Ederle. A reporter from the *Daily Telegraph* was among the crowd who learned at 8:30 p.m. that she was headed not for Dover but for St. Margaret's Bay. Within minutes the seafront emptied as people piled into automobiles, hopped on motorbikes or ran as fast as they could along the coast. The convoy paused momentarily at St. Margaret's but was soon on its way again when they discovered she was headed toward Deal.

There, too, the citizens were giddy with exhilaration, but the reports they received stated Ederle was going to land a couple of miles south, probably close to the village of Kingsdown. Shunning the band of the Royal Marines who were performing in a military torchlight tattoo that evening, Deal en masse raced south past the stately Walmer Castle and toward the unsuspecting village of Kingsdown.

Nothing much ever happened in Kingsdown. It was a tiny

village that owed its livelihood to the herrings, sprats and white-bait that were caught offshore. But on this day the Kingsdown fishermen had turned in early because of the foul weather. Now they were nice and snug in the Zetland Arms public house, drinking warm beer and discussing cricket. Hearing a commotion outside, one of the fishermen stuck his head outside and gasped in surprise as he saw his village being invaded by "cycle, motor cycle, car, taxi and private hire buses". When the vehicles arrived at the beach, their drivers shone the headlights out to sea and then began to build bonfires from driftwood. One of the drinkers, William Sutton, coxswain of the Kingsdown lifeboat, followed the invasion to the beach and asked what was going on. Hearing that Ederle was less than a quarter of a mile from shore, Sutton went to the lifeboat station and switched on its powerful searchlight, sweeping it across the waves until he caught in its beam the *Alsace*.

The people who had come from Deal and Dover and the surrounding villages gathered on the cliff tops and on the beaches, lighting flares and burning bonfires so that a nineteen-year-old from a country most of them had never visited could make her way toward them. By now there were over a thousand people on the beach, and the Zetland Arms was about to run out of beer. Police Inspector Mark Apps arrived from Deal with a couple of constables in a vain attempt to bring a semblance of order to the chaos. Newspaper reporters shoved their way to the water's edge for a better view, among them a correspondent from the *Daily Mail*. He thought that "with the tide in her favour it was clear the American girl would accomplish her task". But the *Westminster Gazette* reporter was more circumspect, aware that the Channel had only been swum when the swimmer was standing on the shore, no longer in the Channel's clutches. "Everything seemed to depend on whether she could get into a position to finish her swim before the flood tide carried her past her objective," he wrote. Such calm assessment was the exception at that moment on Kingsdown Beach. It was bedlam for the most part as people scrambled to see history being made. Car horns were blasted, more beacons were lit and hundreds of people cast off their shoes and waded into the sea as they spotted the red bathing cap coming closer and closer.

Chapter Nineteen

BILL BURGESS TOLD COSTA to untie the rowboat, he was going to accompany Ederle for every stroke of the four hundred and fifty yards that lay between the *Alsace* and the euphoric mob on the beach. Costa agreed, although he insisted one of the crew should be at the oars in such rough water. Burgess climbed gingerly down the ladder and dropped into the boat, followed by Pop Ederle. The storm had eased in the last half hour, but the seas were still running fast as the crewman pushed them away from the tug toward Ederle.

As they rowed, Burgess knew that in a few minutes Ederle would forever be remembered as the first woman to swim the English Channel. In the thirty minutes since he had asked her for one last effort, she had swum a quarter of a mile through the tide sweep without once faltering. As he had lowered himself into the rowboat, Burgess could see that the currents were diminishing. Perhaps the Channel recognized the game was up.

Watching from the deck of the *Alsace*, Harpman thought that if anything Ederle was increasing her speed. "She gave all she had for this gesture of triumph," she wrote, "and her progress through the raging water to the surf line was at an incredible rate." In the rowboat Burgess began to count down the yards with great bellows, while Pop ranted incoherently about a red roadster. All eyes on the *Alsace* and *La Morinie* were fixed on the small head silhouetted by the bonfires on the beach. Harpman suddenly lost sight of Ederle as she disappeared under a heavy roller. Where was she? Then she saw her red bathing cap emerge through the foaming surf, followed by her neck, her shoulders, her back . . .

Harpman gasped. Ederle wasn't swimming; she was standing. Margaret screamed, threw off her dressing gown and dived in after her sister. On board *La Morinie* Sidney Williams and Minott Saunders of the United Press didn't know whether to laugh or cry. They felt privileged to have seen something they would be able to tell their grandchildren about in years to come, but their more pressing concern was how to tell America about it in time for tomorrow's newspapers. *La Morinie*'s wireless had been broken for the last two hours, and they didn't hold out much hope of Harpman welcoming them on board the *Alsace*. Then it struck them: they could telephone their London office with the news from Kingsdown. Williams squawked at the brilliance of the idea, and without bothering to remove his jacket he jumped overboard and started swimming toward the nearest telephone.

Now that Ederle was standing up, she found her legs had temporarily forgotten how to move on firm ground. Her head, too, began to spin as she became vertical. For a moment she tottered about the surf, "laughing like a kid". The crowd, now somewhere between three and four thousand strong, surged toward her shouting and shrieking in delight. A hundred hands offered to help her the last few yards through the surf, but Ederle waved them away. At 9:48 p.m., fourteen hours and thirty-nine minutes*

---

* This is the official time listed by the Channel Swimming Association, although some other sources state her time as fourteen hours and thirty-one minutes. To avoid confusion, the time checks used are all French times, so in fact she landed at Kingsdown at 8:48 British summer time.

after leaving Cape Gris-Nez, she walked onto the shingle beach at Kingsdown, removed her goggles, pulled off her cap and shook the water from her hair and ears. Then she was engulfed by well-wishers. Some grabbed her hand – the painful right one – and pumped it vigorously, while others slapped her on the back and showered her with exuberant praise. Ederle was disorientated and bewildered. She searched the crowd for a familiar face but saw none. Suddenly Pop elbowed his way through the crowd and threw his coat over her shoulders. He saw the panicked look on his daughter's face and bundled her toward the beach and the rowboat. People reached out and touched her hair, her face, her arms, any bit of her, just so they could say they had touched the first woman to swim the Channel. Ederle became frightened and cried out for her sister. She wanted to get back in the water and escape all these strange people. Margaret appeared from the sea and after a quick embrace, the sisters climbed into the boat and were rowed the 220 yards to the *Alsace*. "I'm all right," she whispered to Margaret through the pain of her swollen mouth, "but I cannot realise what it's all about."

The original idea had been to return immediately to Cape Gris-Nez so that the *Daily News* could better protect its story, but the rough weather, and Ederle's fragile condition, demanded a change of plan. It was agreed to head to Dover and hole up in a hotel before departing for France the next day. As the *Alsace* chugged away from Kingsdown Beach, *La Morinie* gave chase.

In the cabin of the *Alsace* the realisation of what had just happened began to take effect. Pop danced a jig, Margaret kissed her sister, Helmy hugged everyone and Burgess cried tears of joy. The only person in control of their emotions was Ederle. She sat quietly, swaddled in Burgess's thick winter coat, grimacing as the blood returned to the tips of her fingers and toes. On the rowboat back to the tug, she had joked with her father about getting her hands on that red roadster, but now the headiness had worn off and the exhaustion had set in. She understood the excitement, but as she explained later, "[I] wanted just to be let alone to try and realise that all I had been hoping and planning and training for had materialised at last. I wanted sleep, not food; rest and quiet, not congratulations."

She tried to sleep on an old couch in the cabin, but the pain from her mouth was too great to allow her anything than a few minutes' slumber. When she woke she felt seasick. The two tugs arrived in Dover Harbour at 11:30 p.m. as a large barge was being unloaded on the pier. A small crowd was waiting to greet Ederle, among them some reporters and a by-the-book customs official who had been forewarned by the *Alsace*'s radio. He boarded the tug to inspect passports. Burgess gave one of his sheepish grins and explained the unusual circumstances behind their arrival at Dover. The customs official wasn't interested. No passport, no disembarkation. After a lengthy argument, in which the dockers unloading the barge wandered over to lend their support to Burgess, the official agreed to fetch the police to resolve the dispute.

Those British journalists on *La Morinie* who had their passports stepped queasily ashore, relieved to be on dry land at last. The tug's skipper joined his crew in bailing out fifty pails of seawater that had been washed on board during the voyage. Alec Rutherford boarded the *Alsace* at the invitation of Ederle, whose seasickness had been superseded by acute cramps in her thighs. "I just knew if it could be done," she told him, blaming her strained voice on her painful tongue, "it had to be done, and I did it." Others then talked on her behalf. Burgess confessed that twice he had wanted Ederle to leave the water because he feared for her safety, and Pop said there had been a time when he'd doubted whether his daughter would succeed. What do you intend to do now? inquired Rutherford. A hot bath, replied Ederle, then "I shall go to bed and sleep all day. I need it. I am so tired."

The police arrived an hour later and informed those without

passports that they would be free to disembark provided they gave the customs official their names, addresses and reasons for visiting England, and agreed to present themselves at the Dover passport office at ten o'clock the following morning. Ederle wasn't happy. "Gee, have I got to get up just for that?" she grumbled, adding that it felt like they were being treated as if they were criminals.

In spite of the late hour, and the drizzle that continued to fall, a knot of locals and a few dedicated journalists had maintained their watch on the quayside. Ederle was helped ashore by Helmy and her father, and the *News of the World* correspondent thought she "looked in a state of physical exhaustion . . . sick and pale and [she] showed plainly the strain put on her by the swim".

When she arrived at the Grand Hotel, Ederle requested four ham sandwiches and some fresh tomatoes. Then she hobbled upstairs to her room. It was unlike anything she had ever experienced at Cape Gris-Nez. There was a bathtub, hot running water, a well-sprung bed with fresh soft sheets, even electric lighting. If this was the reward for swimming the Channel, she thought, it had all been worthwhile.

Chapter Twenty

A T AROUND THE TIME Ederle's head hit the pillow in Dover, the evening papers hit the news-stands in America. GERTRUDE EDERLE SWIMS ENGLISH CHANNEL IN RECORD TIME was the front-page headline on Washington's *Evening Star* with a report underneath filed by Julia Harpman, "aboard the tug *Alsace* in the English Channel". It was a breathless, rambling dispatch that lurched from drama to crisis the way the tug had pitched from wave to wave, but it was largely free from intrigue. There was no mention of *La Morinie*'s treachery (or hers), and Costa's mercenary instincts had been omitted. Burgess alone came in for criticism. Harpman called his approach "ultraconservative" and described how Ederle had laughed at his command to give up.

The staff at New York's *Evening Telegram* got the news just before they went to press, and there was a frantic scramble in the newsroom as they added: EXTRA! US GIRL CUTS 60 MINUTES OFF FASTEST MAN'S MARK. There was little meat to their story, attributed to the United Press, and the "60 minutes" claim was grossly inaccurate, but that was probably because as Sidney Williams had stumbled ashore at Kingsdown, plucking seaweed from his favourite suit and asking Inspector Apps to direct him to the nearest telephone, he'd had time to send through only the barest of facts with no recourse to verification. Ederle hadn't improved

201

Enrico Tiraboschi's three-year record by one hour; she'd smashed it by two. All across America, but particularly in New York, people stopped taking an interest in Jack Dempsey and Babe Ruth, Helen Wills and Suzanne Lenglen, Gloria Swanson and Rudolph Valentino. They didn't care about the lurid murder trial in which old Mrs. Hall was accused of murdering her husband and his chorister "friend"; nor were they interested in Mexico's religious war or the leopard that was on the run from a New Jersey zoo. They just wanted to know more about Gertrude Ederle and her swim.

The *Herald Tribune* described how in New York "the exhilarating news swept through the subways and shops just at closing time, causing congestion at the news-stands and sending hot and tired women workers home in triumphant mood." The *New York Times* was surprised at the "profound stir" the news caused in the city as the nineteen-year-old became the sole subject of conversation in impromptu gatherings in the street and in nightclubs "where she has never gone". Acting Mayor Joseph McKee rushed out a statement in which he said: "We are proud of her accomplishment as a New York girl. She not only brought honour to us but to the nation."

Other dignitaries leaped on board the bandwagon and issued their own toadying congratulations, among them Congressman Jacob Ruppert, owner of the New York Yankees, Albert Goldman, commissioner of the Department of Plant and Structures, and Magistrate Charles Oberwager, president of the United German Societies, who told Ederle that she had "the best wishes of all Americans of German descent and all Germans in the United States". And there was Frank P. Burck, president of the Meat Council of New York, who was immovable in his assertion that "Miss Ederle's triumph may be attributed to the fact that she is the daughter of a butcher. Meats have always been a staple article of food in her diet. A thick, juicy steak is her favourite dish".

WEATHER
Fair and cooler today; tomorrow, fair, is the official word of the forecaster for this section of Pennsylvania.

Indiana Evening Gazette

TEDDY SAYS:
The first week of August has saved our history, B. & M. Laurin tomorrow will open the new week to join the right way.

VOLUME 22—NO. 294.   TWELVE PAGES   INDIANA, PENNSYLVANIA, SATURDAY, AUGUST 7, 1926.   TWO SECTIONS   TWO CENTS

GERTRUDE EDERLE CELEBRATES CHANNEL VICTORY BY GOING SWIMMING

American Girl Betters By Two Hours Five Previous Victories, By Male Sex

Offers Flood In By Cable

First Thing Trudie Wanted This Morning Was the Newspapers

'It Seems Like A Dream Now'

Great Point of All to Show Girl Could Do It She Says.

CAMP MAHONING A POPULAR PLACE

CAN'T LEAVE COOLIDGE ALONE

VACATION NOTES

Headlines spread across the country quickly, like this one from the *Indiana Evening Gazette* of Indiana, Pennsylvania

But American newspaper editors wanted more rousing tributes, ones that came from the heart and not an organisation's PR office. Reporters were dispatched across the country to track down those who really mattered: women. "Bully! That's great," hooted Mrs. Raymond Brown, managing director of the American suffrage journal the *Woman Citizen*, when she was told the news by the *Herald Tribune*. "It just shows the truth about the female of the species after all. The beauty of these spectacular achievements by any one woman is that they kill off a lot of bugaboos that hinder the rest of women. People still say silly things about women being weaklings . . . it takes a good drama like this to teach people a lesson!"

Another reporter telephoned the Briarcliff home of Carrie Chapman Catt, leader of the American suffragettes, for her opinion of Ederle's swim. She, too, was cock-a-hoop, reflecting that it was "a far cry from swimming the Channel to the days to which my memory goes back, when it was thought that women could not throw a ball or even walk very far down the street without feeling faint". The telephone receiver grasped excitedly in one hand, Catt told the reporter about one of the first speeches she'd heard from a suffragette, way back in the 1880s in Boston. "The speaker said that women's freedom would go hand in hand with her bodily strength. The first necessity in the battle for equal rights, she said, was equal health, and she implored women to set up a standard of health. I think that has been accomplished."

The national women's golf champion, Glenna Collett, sympathised with the opposite sex because "it just goes to show that women can even beat the men if they try hard enough . . . Miss Ederle is a great credit to all of us American women", and Ethelda Bleibtrey, the woman who seven years earlier had been arrested for removing her stockings on Manhattan Beach, sent a public message to Ederle in which she exclaimed that women swimmers "are all immeasurably proud of your courageous victory against tremendous odds".

Some reporters poked around in the nooks and crannies of Ederle's life, eliciting comment from her friends at the WSA pool on 145 West Fifty-fifth Street, although most of what they said was inaudible on account of the "tremendous splashing and high diving by way of celebration". At the Ederle meat shop on Amsterdam Avenue, Ederle's Uncle John heard the news at 5:00 p.m., and by the time the *New York Times* arrived to interview him, the street was decked out with flags and bunting. John and his twenty-seven employees were partying with their friends, handing out hunks of bologna and throwing garlands of sausages over the necks of neighbours. "We were all sure of her victory," John told *The Times*. "In spite of her first failure we knew that she would not come home again until she had made the crossing."

Dozens of journalists beat a path south to the Highlands summer house where John Ederle's sister-in-law was trying to take it all in. Throughout the day there had been a constant relay between the hotel at the top of the street and Mrs. Ederle's red house. When Helen Ederle, who had spent the day at the *Daily News* office in front of its stock ticker machine, received confirmation that her sister had done it, she shouted the news down the telephone to William Kruz, who scribbled the message on a piece of paper and hurtled out of the building, hollering, "She's done it! she's done it!" He handed the message to Mrs. Ederle, who read it calmly and smiled. "Somehow I feel she's swimming near me now." When the reporters and photographers arrived, she and her two youngest children, Henry and Emma, posed for photographs in front of the summer house, the two children clutching their mum and Mrs. Ederle waving Kruz's message in the air. She answered all their questions with courteous forbearance, pointing time and again to the Shrewsbury River and retelling how that was the spot where Gertrude used to swim. "I can't remember the first day she went swimming, as all five* of the youngsters acted more or less like little ducks." It was ten years ago, she thought, when Gertrude had first been dunked in the river, but she couldn't give an exact date.

Once or twice Mrs. Ederle interrupted a reporter's question to correct the pronunciation of the family name. It was "Ed-er-ly", she explained, "with the first 'e' short, as in 'bed,' and the final syllable clipped briefly, as in 'pretti-ly'. " The journalist who asked if Gertrude had a beau in her life received a terse response. No, she has never had a sweetheart. The mood lightened when Henry Ederle changed into his bathing suit and ran toward the Shrewsbury River, promising reporters as he went that someday he was "going to swim the Channel, too".

The only inharmonious note was struck in Lowell, Massachusetts, when a reporter from the *Boston Post* interviewed Henry Sullivan on his way home from the telegraph office from where he had just dispatched a cable to Gertrude Ederle. Sullivan

* She refers to Helen, Margaret, Gertrude, George and Emma, and not six-year-old Henry.

was a Lowell police officer, and in 1923 he had become the first American, and the third man, to swim the Channel, although his time of twenty-six hours and fifty minutes was slower than both Webb's and Burgess's. He showed the reporter a facsimile of the cable he had sent: CONGRATULATIONS, ACCEPT HEARTIEST PRAISE FOR BECOMING THE FIRST WOMAN TO SWIM THE CHANNEL, and then gave an embarrassed grin when he was reminded that the previous year he had said women were incapable of such a feat. He confessed that he had been mistaken, although he asked the reporter if he could point out a couple of facts, from the perspective of a Channel swimmer. The first was that he considered Clarabelle Barrett's swim a finer effort than Ederle's. "Any woman who stays in the water as long as Miss Barrett did, and swimming under the conditions that she did, has Miss Ederle's accomplishment eclipsed," he said. To emphasise his second point, Sullivan sketched the Channel and its coastlines on the back of his facsimile and explained that Barrett had also swum the harder route, as he had done, because "the heavy tide smashing against the coast of France makes the swim from England infinitely more difficul".* His third point was the one that surprised the reporter. " 'Sully' deduces from the press dispatches, two tug boats sheltered Trudy, one on either side, as she swam, keeping off to a degree obstructing tides and cutting down the spray. Miss Barrett . . . put out from the English shore and moreover followed all the regulations that the English Channel

* In fact the reason it was harder to swim from England to France than vice versa didn't have as much to do with tides as with land mass. If a swimmer heading to Cape Gris-Nez didn't time the tides right, he or she would be pushed past the Cape and out into mid-Channel. To make landfall would then mean a desperate struggle against the current. On the English coastline, however, as Ederle discovered, there are places to land east and west of Dover. Today swimmers don't have that dilemma as in 2000 the French coastguard banned swims from France to England, allegedly because it was fed up with having to oversee them. Every Channel swim is now the responsibility of the English coastguard.

Swimming Club of London has stipulated – that the swimmer shall have only rowboats accompanying and that the tug boat shall be at least 50 yards behind."

When Sullivan's statement appeared in the *Boston Post* the following day, few people paid much attention; this was nothing more than the jealous cavils of a man whose own Channel effort had been ridiculed by a teenage girl. Readers of the *Post* and Americans in general preferred to read of the widely reported reaction to Ederle's success from Clarabelle Barrett's mother. "It's marvellous, just marvellous," she cooed on the doorstep of her New Rochelle home. "Congratulate her for me and tell her I'm glad . . . that an American girl succeeded in doing what no woman ever did before and I certainly do extend her my heartiest congratulations."

In the eyes of America, Barrett's words encapsulated all that was noble about Channel swimming: courage in victory and dignity in defeat.

Chapter Twenty-one

GERTRUDE EDERLE WOKE at nine o'clock on Saturday, August 7, after a fitful night's rest. Even with the soft splendour of clean sheets there had been too many thoughts tumbling around her head to permit the deep sleep her body craved. Her tongue was less painful and the swelling on her face had subsided to leave her looking less like a prizefighter and more like someone who had walked into a door. She ran another hot bath and lay in the tub, luxuriating in the water and her achievement. As she savoured the sensation of hot water, Ederle had no inkling that her name was being shouted around the world.

She was on the front page of all the French papers, with *Le Figaro* describing her as "the most glorious of nymphs". Germany's *Berliner Tageblatt* likened her physique to that of a classical Greek athlete; the *Nachtausgabe* trumpeted her swim as "one of the greatest athletic achievements of all time"; the *Zeitung am Mittag* considered that Ederle had displayed "new and conclusive proof of the athletic emancipation of the once 'weaker' sex", as well as proving that the crawl stroke – the first time it had been used in a successful Channel swim – was the "only correct style of swimming".

It was in Britain, however, where Ederle's record swim was given greatest prominence. Suddenly Suzanne Lenglen's decision to turn professional no longer mattered, and even Anita

Loos, the author of *Gentlemen Prefer Blondes*, was relegated to the faraway inside pages, despite the fact she had just swept into London declaring that "fair women are usually more frivolous and less apt to hold pronounced views on things, therefore they're better company for most men". Newspapers even pruned the number of paragraphs devoted to cricket, an unprecedented decision that stunned Harpman, who was under the impression that the sport was "the last word in thrills for the average Britisher".

AMERICA HAS SURE PUT IT ACROSS THE LITTLE OLD WORLD THIS TIME was the rueful headline in the *Star*, adding that by "knocking the men's record for the Channel swim sky high, she has also given the Lords of Creation cause to think furiously". Several of the papers found it ironic that Ederle had become the first woman to beat a man's record – in any sporting event – on the same day when the International Olympic Committee had finally acquiesced to the tenacious Frenchwoman Alice Milliat and agreed that in the 1928 Olympics women would compete in the 100 metres, 800 metres, 4-x-100-metre relay, the discus and the high jump.

The London *Daily News* disapproved of the decision, commenting that "women will no doubt proceed to break records furiously at the Olympics, but it can only be women's records that they break. For even the most uncompromising champion of the rights and capacities of women must admit that in contests of physical skill, speed and endurance they must remain forever the inferior sex". On the next page the paper disclosed that Gertrude Ederle had swum the English Channel two hours faster than any man.

The British newspapers vied with one another to see who could publish the most comprehensive coverage of the swim. Photos, maps, reports, diagrams, quotes – they all flowed on the pages. I CAME AND I CONQUERED was emblazoned across the *Daily Herald*, with a photo of a smiling Gertrude, while the headline in the *Daily Sketch* was TRIUMPH WON IN BATTLE AGAINST HALF GALE OF WIND AND HEAVY SEAS. The *Daily Mirror* cleared its entire front page for Ederle, plastering it with five photos of the epic swim under the banner FIRST WOMAN TO SWIM CHANNEL. If readers looked closely at one of the five photos – the one in the bottom-right-hand corner – they might have noticed something curious. It had been taken by a photographer on board *La Morinie* and showed Ederle swimming in the lee of the *Alsace* with Bill Burgess at the rail. But Burgess wasn't looking at Ederle; he was looking at the photographer, and he didn't look very pleased.

If Ederle had intended to keep her 10:00 a.m. appointment at the passport office, the citizens of Dover had other ideas. After her rapid departure from Kingsdown Beach, rumours had flown along the coast that she had indeed returned to France. When it became known the rumours were false, and that she was in Dover, the streets echoed to the sound of running footsteps as hundreds of men, women and children streamed toward the Grand Hotel clutching American flags, autograph books and Kodak cameras, so they could see for themselves the "World's Wonder Girl", as some newspapers were already calling her.

In the hotel lobby Pop Ederle was briefing reporters on the promise he'd made to his daughter on the eve of the swim about not taking her out of the water. Then he laughed and added, "But I intended to catch her if I saw her sinking!" Someone asked if he was going to buy Gertrude a car. "Sure!" he replied. Another correspondent wanted to know how she'd learned to swim. "I taught her myself when she was nine years old at the end of a piece of rope." And what do you think of your daughter's achievement? "I don't know anything about Channel swimming," he replied, "but I've sure got the greatest little girl in the world."

Once Ederle had finished her bath, she was escorted downstairs by Julia Harpman, who described the lobby as being full with "visitors, reporters, photographers, theatrical men bearing offers – the retinue of the suddenly famous". The *News of the World* reporter, who a few hours earlier had described Ederle as "sick and pale" when she came ashore at Dover, now found her "rosy-cheeked, bobbed-haired . . . radiantly happy" and dressed in a blue bathing suit (this one more modest than the two-piece suit of the previous day) and a blue velvet wrap.

Ederle was shepherded into the dining room as hotel staff heaved the door shut behind her like soldiers in a fort closing the gates on a fanatical enemy. She caught her breath and told Harpman she felt fine. "I'm not a bit lame and none the worse for my workout but I don't know what was the matter with me last night. I thought I'd sleep soundly but I couldn't. If it was nerves or excitement, it was all new to me. I've never laid awake at night before."

She dipped into the pile of telegrams that was swaying on the table in front of her. There was the one from Henry Sullivan, and another from Lillian Harrison, an Anglo-Argentine woman who had failed to swim the Channel in 1925. There was even one from Jabez Wolffe: HEARTIEST CONGRATULATIONS ON YOUR SUCCESS. WONDERFUL SWIM. AMERICA MUST BE PROUD OF YOU. Ederle looked surprised. "Well now, a wire from Jabez. That is a fitting finish." Then she smiled and explained that she had thought of Wolffe during yesterday's swim, or rather she had thought of his statement that she couldn't last more than nine hours in the water. "I was determined for Burgess's sake as well as my own to stick it out until we got to land."

Ederle had a massage from Burgess after breakfast, while outside the crowd grew to over one thousand and bouquets appeared in such numbers it seemed certain that England would

Gertrude Ederle looks over the pile of congratulatory telegrams. Behind her (left to right) are William Burgess, "Pop" Ederle, Margaret Ederle and Ishak Helmy

soon be stripped bare of flowers. When a local band struck up to entertain the crowd, the hotel manager pleaded with Harpman to help him disperse them, and the reporters camped out in the lobby. Even though she wanted to keep Ederle to herself, Harpman knew it was unrealistic to expect to shield her from journalists' questions until they returned to New York. With the help of the police and the hotel, it was arranged that a brief press conference would be held later in the morning in the Granville Gardens' pavilion. As for the crowd, it was decided that the best thing would be for Ederle to address them from a first-floor balcony. She did as she was told – hating every minute of it – and stepped back inside with a great sigh of relief, saying, "It's a lot easier to swim the Channel than to make a speech."

To get to the Granville Gardens, Ederle had to be forcibly squeezed from the hotel like a pip from an orange. Even Ishak

Helmy and Louis Timson, who both helped force her through, were incredulous at the numbers of people. Once inside the pavilion it was at least possible to move around without having to evade a pawing hand, although it was still unsettling to look at the building's glass sides and see the scores of faces pressed up close.

Ederle sat down on a small settee while Helmy, Burgess, Margaret and Pop stood over her with their backs to the glass. She flicked through some goodwill messages on the table, while in front of her, photographers and reporters raced to secure the best vantage spot. The *News of the World* correspondent was near the front, close enough to note that as "she sat on the settee in her bathing costume, her arms and face tanned to a uniform tint, she looked the physical embodiment of young womanhood, holding an impromptu court like a veritable queen. Streams of people shook her by the hand and tendered their felicitations, and relays of messenger boys brought batches of telegrams and cablegrams from all parts of the world and soon they were piled in a great stack".

Harpman had grudgingly acceded to the press conference, but she was resolved to keep it as brief as possible to ensure the *Chicago Tribune-Daily News* syndicate could most profitably mine Ederle's rich seam of recollection. She just hoped there would be no controversial or embarrassing questions about the swim. The first one was predictably banal. You must be delighted with your accomplishment? "You can just bet I'm tickled to death to be able to take back the honours to America," replied Ederle. "The great point in my swimming at all was to show that a girl could do it, that an American girl could do it, and that I was that American girl."

And are you surprised by the reaction to your swim? "Actually, my sensation is that I don't quite know what the excitement is all about." The man from the *Sunday Times* wanted to know if there had been a time when she thought she might

fail. "No, there was not. I just went along fine the whole time."
What about your friends and family, did they ever doubt you?
"At one moment," said a smiling Ederle, "when I was going very
slowly, Billy Burgess, my trainer, and my poppa came out and
told me to stop swimming on account of the storm."

While Pop shifted uncomfortably at his daughter's reply,
Burgess beamed guiltily, revealing his jagged teeth to the
reporters. "There was one time when I would have laid 100-1
against her completing the swim, but just afterwards the tide
changed." Happily accepting that he had been a scoundrel to
doubt Ederle, Burgess called her "marvellous" and elaborated on
her performance: he estimated that with the drift she had in fact
swum between thirty and thirty-five miles, and though she started at the rate of twenty-eight strokes per minute, her battle
against the weather reduced this to an average rate of twenty-
five per minute, thereby meaning that she had swum, give or take
the odd stroke, 21,775 strokes.

Pop didn't really understand Burgess's point, but he was
eager to quash any notion that he might have lost faith in his
daughter during the swim. "I always knew she would do it. I
thought she would do it in ten hours."

Ederle was asked about the car her father had offered as her
reward. "That was my greatest ambition," she replied, giggling,
"to swim the Channel for a roadster. One time, when we had five
more hours to go, I said to myself, 'five hours are worthwhile for
a roadster.' "

Would you describe the sensation of reaching Kingsdown?
shouted a reporter. "All of a sudden I seemed to wake up with a
glow of light and to find myself within a few feet apparently of
a beach with people dancing about round bonfires and cheering.
I was still a few hundred yards off, but the tide began to run in
and I was drawn to the lighted shore very quickly. Before I knew
where I was I was standing on the beach."

What are you going to do next? someone demanded to know.

"Well, I don't think I can go any higher at present, at any rate. I guess I will just rest on my laurels." Will you swim the Channel ever again? "No, I don't fancy swimming the Channel again."

Harpman brought the press conference to a halt, and Ederle braced herself for the scramble back to the hotel. This time, however, Helmy and Timson had an idea. They hoisted her onto their shoulders and marched back to the Grand Hotel, leaving a long trail of human detritus in their wake.

As Ederle approached the hotel, she was greeted by a large smiling woman with hair as wild as the crowd that surrounded them. "You certainly did a fine swim," roared Clarabelle Barrett, hugging her warmly. "How do you feel?" Ederle told her she was fine and thanked Barrett for her generous words. As photographers hurried to snap a photo of the famous Channel swimmers side by side, Barrett told Ederle how "they will be delighted in the States", adding that she thought the teenager was "just marvellous". "And you did very well, too," replied Ederle. The reporter from the Associated Press asked Barrett for a public comment on her young usurper. "She has shown splendid courage and strength and established a record due, of course, to her ability to swim fast," Barrett said. "I know her to be one of the fastest woman swimmers the world has ever known. There is no one who has touched Miss Ederle's records at home . . . I think she has reached the pinnacle of her success because she accomplished a feat of endurance in long-distance swimming in addition to her short-distance performances. I don't think her record can be bettered by a woman."

Can we get a shot of the four of you together, please? inquired a newsreel cameraman, indicating that Timson and Helmy should stand on either side of the two women. Ederle hooked her arm through Helmy's, and Barrett enveloped Ederle in a semi-bear hug. Timson even removed his ubiquitous boater — it was that special a moment.

For the next few hours Ederle was whirled around on a carousel of acclaim. On the advice of Burgess, she took a brief dip in the Channel, "to take the stiffness out" of her body, as he explained to the reporters who followed. One, the chap from the *Sunday Times*, described how "thousands of people, cheering madly, followed her to the beach, and there was a dense throng on the shore to watch the first woman to swim the Channel indulge in a five-minute spell in the water". Photographers piled into rowboats in pursuit as she swam out fifty yards, waved and then returned. In the dining room at lunch in the Grand Hotel, she was toasted by a holidaying American, J. McAulay, from Boston, although the greater thrill for Ederle was the ice cream she had for dessert. After lunch, the mayor of Dover, Captain Thomas Bodley Scott, and his wife arrived without the livery of office to offer their congratulations. The mayor's wife presented Ederle with a bouquet of sweet peas, and the mayor invited her to accompany them to the nearby statue of Matthew Webb – the first man to swim the Channel – for a small ceremony.

Ederle changed into a fawn-coloured tweed suit, donned a tie, brushed her hair and subjected herself to another torrent of flattery at the statue. Facing the battalion of photographers, she thanked everyone for their hospitality and promised, "If I live a thousand years, I will never forget Dover." The reporters wanted another chance to interview Ederle, but Harpman and Sorenson manoeuvred her into one of a fleet of cars (provided by Gibbs' Garage in Woolcomber Street, as Gibbs pointed out to the correspondent of the *Dover Standard*) and drove to Folkestone to catch the 4:00 p.m. steamer to Boulogne.

Only when she was on board the *Biarritz* and headed to France did Ederle start to unwind. It had been an enjoyable, even an unforgettable day, she confided to Harpman, but there had been times when "she felt like running away and hiding somewhere to escape the hero worshippers" who were "besieging her" everywhere she went. For once she was looking forward to the seclusion of Cape Gris-Nez.

Ederle's flagging constitution recovered during the voyage to France, and when she arrived in Boulogne, said Harpman, "the slight reaction Miss Ederle felt this afternoon, was completely gone". Every vessel in the harbour was flying the Stars and Stripes, not just the *Alsace*, which had pulled alongside the steamer and was blasting its siren in salute, with the wealthy Captain Costa grinning out of the wheelhouse.

It appeared that the French were bent on outstripping the English in the fervour of their welcome to the world's most famous woman. Harpman estimated that "a crowd of several thousand" hailed Ederle as she stepped onto the quayside. Gaston Smith, the American consul in Calais, and William Corcoran, his counterpart in Boulogne, stepped forward holding two great bouquets, and a third was handed to Ederle by Costa's infant daughter. From the harbour the party motored to the US consulate in Boulogne for a lavish reception laid on by Corcoran. "Hurrah for Prohibition!" he exclaimed, laughing, as he toured the room filling every glass with champagne. Consul Smith proposed the official toast and invited everyone to drink to "America's wonderful mermaid". Ederle took her first ever sip of alcohol and spluttered as if she'd just swallowed another mouthful of Channel water. "Gee, it's hot, we'd better go home now or I might do something wrong!"

With the reception over, Ederle and her Gang climbed into some taxis for the return to Cape Gris-Nez. "Loud cheers greeted her all along the route," wrote Alec Rutherford in the *New York Times*. "The enthusiasm reached its highest intensity at

Gris-Nez, where Miss Ederle was overwhelmed by admirers."
The villagers' wooden clogs clattered on the road as they ran
alongside the cars waving and shouting their congratulations.
When they reached the Hôtel du Phare, Ederle leaped out. "Oh,
it's good to be back here," she cried. "Now I can get some sleep!'

Villagers, reporters, hotel guests, even Jabez Wolffe, were
invited to the Hôtel du Phare that evening for the party thrown
by Pop Ederle. In England he'd denied rumours that he'd put
$25,000 on his daughter to succeed at odds of 7-1; but now he
was telling everyone that he had indeed won a hefty amount,
though he refused to say how much he had pocketed.* He certainly had won enough to buy seventy bottles of exceptional
French champagne and a supply of fireworks that were let off
inside and outside the hotel. Cape Gris-Nez had never witnessed
a party like it as, according to Harpman, "all the irritations of the
past two months here were forgotten in the grand celebration of
the historic feat of the little maid, L'Americaine [sic], whom the
simple fisher folk hereabouts are inclined now to worship as they
might a second Joan d'Arc."

* Pop always remained coy about how much he won, only saying, "I lost
$5,000 on last year's swim, but I got it back with good interest this year. The
best odds I could get were 7-1." In an interview in 1958 Gertrude said, "He
made $25,000. At least I think he did. Pop never told me much, but I knew he
was betting."

Chapter Twenty-two

NOT EVERYONE ON CAPE GRIS-NEZ attended Pop Ederle's boisterous party. Lillian Cannon didn't, although from her room in the Hôtel de la Sirène she would have had a prime view of the fireworks. Cannon had returned to Boulogne on *La Morinie* at six o'clock on Saturday morning, when, according to Alec Rutherford, "nobody on the tug except the newspaper men seemed happy".

As Ederle made a point of thanking Cannon publicly for her support mid-Channel – telling reporters that she "proved herself a splendid sport"– so the girl from Baltimore was eloquent in defeat. "Gertrude was absolutely wonderful," she exclaimed. "She lived one of those great days that come only rarely in the lives of any us . . . Gertrude has proved she is one of the greatest swimmers ever known, and while I am disappointed that I cannot be the first woman to swim the Channel, I congratulate her with all cordiality."

The day after the party, Sunday, August 8, as a groggy Monsieur Blondiau examined the scorched walls of his hotel bar and collected the empty champagne bottles, Cannon discovered how fickle people could be. Ederle's "Channel croakers" – the locals who had spent two months predicting her demise – were now singing her praises from the cliff tops, while Cannon had been cast aside.

As Cannon moped about the village, she bumped into Julia Harpman. Harpman asked Cannon what her intentions were now that she could no longer be the first woman across the sea, and the reply was gleefully relayed to the *Daily News*. "She declared today that the lure of the Channel swim for her is now gone 'to a better swimmer than I' and she thinks she will not try the Channeling [*sic*] for which she has been in training here." As Cannon trudged off to contemplate her immediate future, Harpman waved her off in print with a stinging backhanded compliment: "Lillian, after swimming with Trudie for an hour, remained on Trudie's tug, the *Alsace*, during the latter half of the swim. When the Baltimore woman wasn't seasick she staggered to the rail to join in the singing that was kept on to occupy and entertain Trudie."

Perhaps it was Harpman's smug countenance that helped change Cannon's mind because that same day she told Alec Rutherford that she had "definitely decided not to abandon her attempt to swim the English Channel". With Ederle successful, Cannon was now able to exercise a second option on the *Alsace* – a better tug than *La Morinie* – and to also call upon the skill of its skipper, Joe Costa.

After an afternoon conference with her husband, her unofficial manager Minott Saunders, her coach Jack Wiedman and Jabez Wolffe, who, despite his lofty words for Ederle, still ached for revenge and was offering his help free of charge, Cannon emerged to tell Rutherford and the other reporters her swim was back on.

But Rutherford wasn't convinced by Cannon's bullish facade, suspecting she no longer had the stomach for the fight but was simply obliged to fulfil her contract to the newspaper syndicate that had sponsored her for the last three months. Worryingly, however, Rutherford wasn't sure Cannon was physically equipped for the challenge. He had watched her swim from the deck of *La Morinie* and found her "frail in comparison with Miss

Ederle, [she] is not over speedy and cannot stand a severe buffeting".

On Monday, August 9, Bill Burgess appeared at the Hôtel de la Sirène, his face thundery like a Channel storm. He sought out Cannon and told her that he was now at her disposal. The previous day Burgess had rhapsodised about Ederle's swim in the *Chicago Tribune*, calling it a "miraculous performance" and humbly admitting, "[I am still] wiping tears away from my old eyes at the memory of Miss Ederle's heroic struggle . . . she gave me the greatest day of my life, greater even than when I got across in 1911." It was all a bit over the top, as if Burgess hoped his noble words would be rewarded. Soon after, he sidled up to Ederle and asked for the outstanding balance of his fee, the same fee that he had doubled two months earlier as a condition for coaching her exclusively. Ederle settled the account to the last cent, but Burgess's hand remained outstretched. A bonus, perhaps, he suggested with a smile, for helping her achieve her goal. Ederle returned the smile. Sure, you can have a bonus. You can have that antique fishing boat down on the beach with its bottom stove in. Burgess's mouth dropped. He stammered something about being entitled to a "cash honorarium". Harpman later told a colleague that Ederle "gave him a look that fried him to a crackling, and walked out without even a polite farewell".*

Now Burgess shared Wolffe's desire to knock Ederle down a peg or two, while Wiedman wanted to prove he was a better coach than Burgess by guiding Cannon across in a faster time.

---

* Ederle's attitude toward Burgess underwent a radical transformation in the days after her swim. In her syndicated column on August 8 she wrote in the *Boston Sunday Post*, "the fact, too, I had such perfect faith in my trainer, Bill Burgess, also helped me succeed. Every time I looked up at him I became more confident that I could put it across." So what lay behind the change? One can only speculate but it seems probable that either Harpman or Pop Ederle turned Gertrude against Burgess. Neither liked the coach, and in the case of Pop one senses genuine animosity.

But before any of them could begin to turn their fantasies into reality, they had to make Cannon believe she was tough enough to swim the Channel.

For Mille Gade in Dover, the disconsolation of defeat was easier to bear. Her rivalry was against the Channel more than her fellow swimmers, although she knew that some of the lustre of her own bid had been dimmed. She had called on Ederle on Saturday morning at the Grand Hotel and told her, "I congratulate you with all my heart, but you naughty girl, I wanted to be the first woman to make the swim! Now I am determined to be the second."

With Ederle back in France, Gade announced that she would try to better her time the following week. In the meantime she and her husband were going to enjoy all Dover had to offer, particularly now that the town, like most of England, was in the grip of "Channelitis".

On August 12 Gade, Clarabelle Barrett and Louis Timson were persuaded to perform a series of stunts in the water for a newsreel cameraman, which, according to the *New York Times*, brought thousands of spectators to Dover Beach. The paper reported that Gade was intent on beating Ederle's record time and becoming the first mother to swim the Channel.

The demonstration was Barrett's first time back in the water since her failed attempt nine days earlier, and outwardly at least she appeared to be none the worse for her harrowing ordeal. The *New York Times* had reported on August 9, "Endeavours are now being made to persuade Miss Clare Belle Barrett [*sic*] to start at Gris-Nez, all of the swimming camp promising her free support and advice." But Barrett wasn't stupid. She knew that she didn't possess the speed to challenge Ederle's record, so all that remained was to try to become the first to swim the Channel along the harder route. "She certainly expected to be the first woman to swim from Dover to France," said the *New York Times* on August 13. "She hopes to start during the next weekend."

Three days earlier, on August 10, Barrett had cabled the *Standard-Star* to thank its staff and the people of New Rochelle for their generosity in raising over seven hundred dollars for her Channel fund. She also told the paper that despite Ederle's swim, she wanted to swim the Channel on August 15, in five days' time.

The news distressed Barrett's mother at home in New Rochelle. Initially she had been all for Clarabelle trying a second time, but that was before she had fully comprehended what her daughter had been through: the fog, the steamers, the jellyfish. The very fact that Clarabelle had spent three days in bed recovering proved how much the swim had punished her. "If she tries this again I probably will never see her again alive," she wailed to a reporter from the *Standard-Star*. "Why will she try it? Why doesn't she come home? She has made a record and she has cause to be proud of what she did. Miss Ederle swam the Channel and did a wonderful thing, so why can't my baby let it go at that?"

The answer to Mrs. Barrett's plea could be found at the offices of the newspaper that carried her comments. Since her gallant effort on August 2, Barrett had been adopted by the *Standard-Star* as a homegrown hero. The paper had been helpful in establishing a fund but less so in running ill-informed progress reports on its front page day after day. On Thursday, August 12, the *Standard-Star* reported that "it is confidently predicted that she will exceed even Miss Ederle's time in making her second try", and two days later it was adamant that "success will crown her second effort". If Barrett wished for a more honest appraisal of her chances, she might have received one from her friend and nurse, Grace Leister, but perhaps Barrett didn't want to hear the truth. August 15 was not only her scheduled start date but also her thirty-fifth birthday, another unwelcome reminder that the sands of time were running down.

Chapter Twenty-three

W HAT CAN ALL THESE SWIMMERS hope to acquire now that the blue ribbon has been secured by a 19-year-old American girl?" asked Alec Rutherford in the *New York Times* on August 8. "It must be that they will swim for the honour of their countries." As he wrote his dispatch from Cape Gris-Nez, several of the people he had in mind milled aimlessly around the beach: Ishak Helmy, Colonel Freyberg, VC, DSO, Omer Perrault, Jeanne Sion and Georges Michel, a Frenchman who had just arrived for his eighth attempt on the Channel.

A few hours after Rutherford cabled his copy to New York, Freyberg struck off from the Cape Gris-Nez beach, followed shortly by Perrault. The latter lasted just two hours, while the colonel dogged it out for eight hours before he quit six miles from the South Goodwin lightship that forty-eight hours earlier had run up the Union Jack in salute to Ederle's courage. As Freyberg was rowed back to England, he vowed that it was the end of his Channel obsession.

The following evening, August 9, a large crowd gathered on the beach to wave off Helmy and Michel. Among their number was Gertrude Ederle, who came to wish them luck. She gave Helmy a farewell hug and turned to embrace the Frenchman, only to recoil in embarrassment when she saw that under his grease he was swimming au naturel. The two swimmers started off at 9:30 p.m., and after three hours they were five miles north-east of Gris-Nez and looking strong as they swam alongside the *Alsace*. Not long after, according to Alec Rutherford's account in the *New York Times* on August 11, "Helmy became excited, shouting out when an enormous fish passed close to him in the beam of the searchlight. We could easily distinguish the sharks, twelve to fifteen feet long and about twenty in number ... we all shouted, pelted the water with pieces of coal and, launching small boats, beat the water with the oars."

The sharks vanished, but Helmy's nerve was gone. "I am not afraid," he told the people on board the *Alsace*, "but I do not like them [sharks]." He quit a short while later, and although Michel kept going until 10:40 a.m., he was forced by rough seas to abandon his attempt three miles from Dover.

The next day Jeanne Sion and Omer Perrault trudged down to the beach at Cape Gris-Nez as Gertrude Ederle, Lillian Cannon and Ishak Helmy sang a chorus of "Hail! Hail! the Gang's All Here!" The pair entered the water at 10·00 p.m., but both swam like people who no longer believed there was a point to all the hardship. Perrault surrendered after five hours and Sion an hour later. At one moment Sion had screamed in terror as a creature – she estimated it to be several feet long – brushed past her leg in the black water. "I will never again try to swim the Channel," she told reporters on arriving back at Calais. "I am down-hearted and have finished with it."

With each fresh Channel failure the magnitude of Gertrude Ederle's exploit increased. As one British newspaper, the *News of the World*, announced a prize of five thousand dollars for the first British-born swimmer to beat the American's time (Britain had suddenly ceased to regard Channel swimming solely as an arbi-trator of human endeavour), Dr. Hugh Cumming, America's surgeon general, honoured Ederle's swim as "probably the most remarkable feat of human endurance in modern history". Some began to wonder if the Channel would ever be crossed in a time faster than Ederle's fourteen hours and thirty-nine minutes.

In its editorial of August 9 the *Los Angeles Times* stated that "she set a mark for the crossing that veteran swimmers agree may quite possibly stand for all time". Other editorials refrained from making such rash predictions and instead pondered the implications of the swim. "Miss Ederle's feat is a surpassing achievement," said the *New York Herald Tribune* on Saturday, August 7. "For the first time in the history of athletics it places a woman's record above the best man's. Here is surely a significant crossing, the end of which is not at Dover." The next day the *Tribune* theorised that Ederle's swim should signal for American women "but one feature in a broad advance that touches education and careers, minds as well as bodies". The socialist writer Heywood Broun used his column in the *World* to forecast that "epoch-making things might come of her achievement. If there are women capable of swimming the Channel it would not be illogical to draft them as shock troops in the next war. When Gertrude Ederle struck out from France she left behind her a world which has believed for a great many centuries that woman is the weaker vessel. Much of government, most of law and practically all of morality is based upon this assumption. And when her toes touched the sands of England, she stepped out of the water into a brand-new world. It may be that she will turn out to be an even greater discoverer than Columbus. It was only a continent which he found".

Broun's was not a lone voice in warning that some men might find it hard to accept that women had now proved they were equal in every way. Cartoonists lampooned the male fuddy-duddies, with one sketch in the *Boston Post* showing a man in a top hat and tails glumly tiptoeing past a sign saying THIS WAY OUT and underneath the caption "The guy who was about to write another book on the weaker sex".

Many of the newspapers carried an anonymous quote from a leading Hollywood actress who, on hearing the news that Ederle had swum the Channel faster than any man, smirked, drew on her cigarette, and said, "It will give the effete young man of today a nasty jolt." It was the second nasty jolt in rapid succession for the generation of American men whose fathers and uncles had fought in France a decade earlier. In July the *Chicago Tribune* had boiled in indignation at the news that a new public ballroom in the city contained a powder vending machine in the men's washroom. "In a men's washroom." The paper could scarely believe it. " 'Homo Americanus!' Why didn't someone quietly drown Rudolph Guglielmi, alias Valentino, years ago?" The *Tribune* knew that pinning the blame for what they viewed as the decline in American masculinity solely on Valentino was unjust; after all, no one was forcing thousands of these "lounge lizards" to buy pomades, to wear baggy trousers, to slick down their hair with Stacomb. Adopting a more serious tone, the paper speculated that perhaps "this degeneration into effeminacy [is] a cognate reaction with pacifism to the virilities and realities of the war?"

If America's men expected sympathy from their women, they didn't get much. Writing in her weekly syndicated column, Nancy Barr Mavity lectured women not to allow themselves to be patronised by men, and that they "needn't accept without question the idea of having nervous prostration because of eight hours a day in school or store or office". In a letter headlined on YOUR TOES, MEN, published in the *Daily News*, the writer gloated that the once stronger sex was being "thrown back by more venturesome women." The *Daily News* also ran another of its straw polls, this time asking four women and two men walking between East Fourteenth Street and Broadway what effect Ederle would have on the average American female. Miss Edith Nelson reckoned that women would "become much stronger and self-reliant"; Miss McKay predicted more girls would take up sport in light of Ederle's success.* Mr. Josephs said it would have a "wonderful effect", and he was particularly excited at the prospect of women becoming "better physical specimens".

If Gertrude Ederle wasn't privy to the hysteria that her achievement had generated back home, she was getting a taste of it from the British newspapers that arrived daily on the Channel ferries. An editorial in the *Morning Post* suggested that another star be added to the American flag in recognition of what she had accomplished, and an argument was raging in many papers over the location of the Gertrude Ederle statue. The French authorities insisted it should be erected at Cape Gris-Nez, with Joe Costa promising to "seek government permission", but the British were unshakable in their belief that Kingsdown was more logical.

It wasn't only the press and the public who were proclaiming Ederle queen of the Channel. Politicians of all persuasions were eager to use her to curry favour with the female electorate.† Nicholas Grattan-Doyle, the Conservative Member of Parliament, asserted in the *Weekly Despatch* that the myth of the weak woman was "shattered and shattered forever", while on the other side of the political divide the socialist writer Robert Blandford wrote that while "men aspire, women set the pace".

On Monday, August 9, the cross-Channel ferry from

---

* It was later reported that over sixty thousand women awarded American Red Cross swimming certificates in the 1920s singled out Ederle as their sole motivation.
† Female suffrage in Britain was still very much a burning issue in 1926. Women over thirty had been given the right to vote in 1918, but it wasn't until 1928 that this right was extended to women over eighteen.

Folkestone brought more than just the daily newspapers. Two rival London theatrical agents stepped off the boat with contracts for a vaudeville tour tucked in their pockets, and hotfooted it over to Cape Gris-Nez. A French agent came from Paris with a similar proposition, but Ederle rejected all three.

Cables arrived hourly from America offering her vast sums of money to endorse everything from soup to chewing gum to chocolate, and one theatre offered to pay her $8,500 if she signed up for a twenty-five-week run throughout the States. William Randolph Hearst's New York *Daily Mirror* ran a piece in which it said that all the offers arriving in France from the States had put Pop Ederle "in the best of spirits" ,and he was telling one and all, "We can sell the butcher shop now."

His daughter was less captivated by the prospect of fame and fortune. Of course, she admitted in her column to the *Daily News* on the Monday, "I have had my share of day dreams of wealth and luxury. I like nice things as well as the next person ...[but] I'm not going to accept any of the many and varied offers of large sums of money that are coming to me now unless I can do so with a clear conscience. I'm not going to endorse things that I don't know anything about." As for any public appearances, explained Ederle, the first one would be in New York, "the most glorious city in the best land on earth."

For the time being she wanted to be left in peace, free from nosy locals, pestering reporters and pushy theatrical agents. She had no wish to be held up as a feminist icon or as a role model for the flapper generation; she was still the same teenager as the one who had waded into the Gris-Nez surf a few days earlier, the one who adored eating ice cream and reading badly written fifty-cent novels. "The congratulations and the celebrations in my honour are mighty fine," she wrote on August 8, "but the hubbub and the obligations on me are so trying that I have to fight off the question that now and again vaguely forms in my mind – the question whether in the end, success in a great endeavour is worth quite all the grief." But others held an opposite view, not least her chaperone, Julia Harpman. As a journalist, she knew better than most that few things excited the world as much as a great endeavour. Perhaps its only rival was a great tragedy.

Certainly the *Daily News* had wasted no time in trumpeting the fact that Ederle's "remarkable feat was made possible" by the financial and personal support of the *Chicago Tribune-Daily News* syndicate. The paper also stressed that America's most precious commodity was its exclusive possession. In a story headlined FAKE ARTICLE IRKS GERTRUDE, which appeared on August 8, the *Daily News* said that Ederle repudiated the statements attributed to her that had appeared in another New York paper the previous day. The guilty party wasn't named, but it was probably an allusion to Alec Rutherford's report that had adorned the front page of Saturday's *New York Times*. Ederle swore blind, "I have talked to no newspaperman or newspaperwoman, nor to anyone else for that matter, except my father, sister and trainer, and my chaperone, Julia Harpman, representing the *News*, *Chicago Tribune* and associated newspapers, since I swam the Channel." She might have forgotten her brief exchange with Rutherford at Dover Harbour, exhausted as she was, or perhaps she hadn't thought an English gentleman, even a reporter, could be guilty of such skullduggery as to report what she assumed was a chat between old acquaintances. Nonetheless, tutted the *Daily News*, "Trudie was indignant at the sharp practices in some newspaper circles thus revealed to her for the first time."

Harpman also confided to her readers the actions of the journalists on board *La Morinie* during Ederle's swim, accusing them of unsportsmanlike behaviour when they "appeared to be intentionally coming too close, dangerously close to the swimmer. If it touched her she would be automatically disqualified, and Trudie circled to avoid it several times".

Ederle was powerless to prevent herself being used as a pawn in a rancorous game between rival newspapers, their representatives still encamped on opposite sides of Cape Gris-Nez. The *Daily News* ran a series of intimate articles, delving into Ederle's background, publishing photos of her as a baby and charting her progress from toddler to champion. Ederle had also to overcome her embarrassment and answer questions about her love life. "I have never been petted and I don't believe in petting," she said. "I prefer reading an adventure story to being bothered by boys." This contradicated a report in a British newspaper, however, that quoted Ederle as saying one of the good things about her triumph was she might fall for somebody – "now that I'll have more time to fall in love." Ignoring her sensitivity and shyness, the *Daily News* portrayed her as feisty and confrontational in words they claimed were hers, but which seemed secondhand to those who knew her best. "Who says woman is the weaker sex? Better not say it to me!" Captain Patterson loved it. This was the sort of rallying cry that sold newspapers.

Reporters who arrived from England expecting to interview Ederle had the door slammed in their faces. Gertrude needed rest, Harpman told them, although some journalists grumbled that she appeared in good spirits when she came down to the beach on successive nights to wave off Helmy and the other Channel aspirants.

As the resentment against Ederle's handlers took root in Britain, so the swimmer's homesickness deepened. It was two months since she'd last seen her family and her two dogs, and she longed to be back on Amsterdam Avenue telling her mother all about the swim. As it was, forty-eight hours after wading ashore at Kingsdown, Ederle hadn't been allowed the time to wire a message home. "I've honestly been trying a dozen times a day to squeeze in time to write and dispatch it," she complained to the *Daily News*.

Eventually, on Sunday afternoon, after the reporters had filed their copy and met their deadlines, Ederle cabled her mum.

WE DID IT, MOTHER! WE DID IT! THE TRICK IS TURNED
AND AREN'T YOU JUST SO PROUD? WE ARE ALL SO HAPPY.
ENGLAND AND FRANCE ARE REJOICING IN THE GLORY. OH,
WHAT CROWDS FOLLOW US HERE AND THERE! THE PAPER
PEOPLE ARE JUST IMPOSSIBLE, BUT GRAND. MOM, I HAD
THAT FEELING OF SURE SUCCESS — JUST WOULDN'T GIVE
UP. NOT ONCE WAS I ON THE POINT OF ABANDONING THE
SWIM. THE GOOD GOD LED ME ON SAFELY.

The short sentences bursting with exhilaration continued in
the rest of the cable as Ederle praised Artie Sorenson, her sister
and her father. The cable contained no criticism — Burgess's
name wasn't mentioned — and apart from the early jocular reference to the "impossible" press, Ederle didn't moan about the
reporters who buzzed around her hotel like mosquitoes on a
summer evening. It was a simple and excited girlish cable from a
daughter to a mother. But it would be another three weeks before
they were reunited in New York. First Ederle was going to spend
a few days with her paternal grandmother in Germany before
sailing from Cherbourg on August 21 aboard the *Berengaria*.

The last time Gertrude and Margaret had stayed with their
grandmother had been in the gloriously hot summer of 1914, as
around them all Europe blundered into war. The sisters were
excited at the prospect of returning, although both knew to get
there would mean another bout of public hysteria as they travelled by train from Calais to Paris to Stuttgart. Trudy's Gang left
Cape Gris-Nez on Wednesday, August 11, with Harpman
reporting that Ederle bade the villagers "a fond farewell" and
promised to visit them again someday. Helmy smothered her in
his tree-trunk arms and joked he would see her in New York
when he was heavyweight boxing champion of the world. There
was no mention if either Lillian Cannon or Bill Burgess came to
wave her "bon voyage".

From the Cape, Ederle went to Calais and a lunch at the

Foundation Company of America, which ordered its eighteen hundred employees to put down their tools and wait outside the factory gates to cheer her arrival. From there she was driven to the city hall and introduced to the mayor, Leon Vincent, and a flock of other dignitaries. She was presented with a silver medal and informed that moves were afoot to erect a statue of her in Cape Gris-Nez. The final engagement of the day was at the US consulate in Calais, where Consul Gaston Smith wanted to surpass the warmth of the welcome Ederle had received at the US consulate in Boulogne four days earlier. She arrived at 5:00 p.m. for a champagne reception and another presentation, though this one wasn't of the kind that could be displayed in a trophy cabinet. It was Monsieur Peumery, editor of the *Phare du Calais* (the Calais Lighthouse), the local newspaper which a day after her swim had published an article expressing its "vague incredulity" at her crossing, particularly as the *Alsace* contained no independent witnesses.

On Wednesday, August 11, the *Phare* had returned to the attack and stated that "proper procedure after such a swim is to publish a list of the persons who had supervision of the swim, and to submit for competent examination an exact chart of the itinerary taken in going from Cape Gris-Nez to Kingsdown". Consul Smith had been affronted at the insinuation and considered that the reception would provide an opportune moment for Monsieur Peumery to meet Ederle and the witnesses, to which end he had also invited some of the reporters from *La Morinie*.

Before the bottles of champagne had even been unsheathed from the ice buckets, Harpman was on the attack. On what grounds did Peumery believe the swim had not been authenticated? He replied that in his opinion it would have been wise to invite a local French reporter to witness the swim. Perhaps it was Alec Rutherford, well versed in the protocol of Channel swimming, who pointed out that none of the five men who preceded Ederle had been asked for such corroboration, for Peumery soon adopted a more conciliatory tone. "We are not adversaries and stubborn," he said with an ingratiating smile, "and I am willing to believe you, provided that you make me an affirmation that Miss Ederle has made the crossing in the short time stated, in spite of her youth. But as it is a fact of vital importance for our local history, give me a collective affirmation, signed, and we will publish the victorious result."

On the spot, Harpman drafted an affidavit in which she and the other signatories certified that Ederle had swum the Channel in the time stated and "received no aid in her swimming, and that she abided faithfully by all the rules of Channel swimming and international sportsmanship". Harpman and all the "Gang" signed the document; so did Rutherford and Monsieur Amédée Blondiau, who had left his wife in charge of the Hôtel du Phare to attend the reception. Even Minott Saunders put his name to the affidavit, an irony that was probably lost on the editor of the *Phare du Calais*. Arthur Sorenson produced a photo of the swim, which Monsieur Peumery studied along with the document. At length he asked to be presented to Ederle. "Mademoiselle," he purred, "permit me to congratulate you on your success. On the *Phare* we are, believe me, without party feeling against anyone. On the contrary, we prize veracity with the greatest care. As a result of these gentlemen, and the photograph, and also by reason of your fine physique, we accept the evidence. Tomorrow, in the *Phare du Calais*, we will affirm your very real victory, which we are happy to publish."

Ederle accepted his apology with a shake of the hand, related a reporter present, and as her Gang cheered in triumph, "the glasses of champagne were again filled and emptied in honour of the victory of the beautiful American champion".

Chapter Twenty-four

LILLIAN CANNON HAD still been deeply in love with Cape Gris-Nez the day before Gertrude Ederle embarked on her swim. She was charmed by the rugged coastline in the way travellers to the desert were bewitched by its harsh beauty. "Whether I succeed in swimming the Channel or not," she wrote, "I am sure I always shall look upon the experience as the happiest of my life."

Eight days later the love affair was over, and Cannon wanted to walk out on the Cape. "Gee, I never want to see Gris-Nez again if it means waiting all this time," she told Alec Rutherford. Not only was the ultimate prize gone, but her own humiliation during Ederle's swim – overawed by the Channel's power in and out of the water – had killed off her passion for the challenge she had yet to confront. Earlier in the summer Cannon had enjoyed sitting on the terrace of the Hôtel de la Sirène, tucking into a chocolate pancake fried in liqueur, and answering the questions of inquisitive guests about her task, but now she found it tiresome. She complained to Rutherford that most people "think it is only a strip of water [and] it's not until they repeatedly are told that they realise it is no kid's game". Nor did Cannon derive any pleasure from watching the sorry procession of beaten swimmers return to the Cape with tales of heavy seas and prying sharks. What with the indiscreet hotel guests who sat on the terrace exclaiming loudly that nothing would induce them to try and swim across the Channel if they ran the risk of being attacked by a shark, Cannon had reached her wits' end.

She told Rutherford that her triumvirate of trainers – Wiedman, Burgess and Wolffe – were agreed that a favourable spell of weather was forecast to begin on Sunday, August 15, which couldn't come soon enough.

"How I wish I was in the water now!" she said. "But I must wait until the weather is finer." With her rival now in Germany, Cannon was open in discussing her plans: if indeed the weather did permit her to leave on Sunday, she would set off two hours before dawn. She had chartered *La Morinie* and hired Captain Joe Costa as her pilot. Her husband and Burgess would row alongside to give her encouragement and keep an eye out for sharks. Alec Rutherford asked Cannon if she was confident. "I am told I want pluck, endurance and luck," she replied. "I know I have the pluck and endurance, but shall I have the luck?"

Despite the departure of Ederle's retinue, Cape Gris-Nez was still congested with Channel swimmers. Undeterred by his earlier defeat, Helmy was determined to try again at the end of August, and two German swimmers, Otto Kemmerich and Ernst Vierkoetter, had recently arrived with a supporting cast financed by Crown Prince Wilhelm, the eldest son of Kaiser Wilhelm II. It included a manager, a physician, a reporter and a naval officer called Lieutenant Ahrens who would act as their pilot.

The scowling British newspapers reported that Ahrens had acquired his knowledge of the Channel during the war when he had prowled its waters in a U-boat. The German camp even received daily weather forecasts from their national meteorological office. All in all, harrumphed Rutherford, the expedition had been assembled with "typical German organisation with nothing forgotten to ensure success".

Despite their meticulous preparation and evident desire to succeed, the German swimmers had no qualms about cooperating with the other Channel hopefuls. They shared their weather reports with Cannon's camp, and as a result of one such forecast, Jack Wiedman decided to postpone her departure date from Sunday, August 15, to Monday evening.

While Cannon rested on Monday afternoon, Baltimore woke up to read Minott Saunders's eve-of-swim report in the *Post*. He promised that her effort would be "on a grand scale hitherto unapproached, and her purpose [would] be to better the record of Gertrude Ederle". To ensure that there would be no unsavoury accusations, similar to those directed at Ederle by the *Phare du Calais* newspaper, Saunders explained that more than a dozen witnesses and correspondents, including representatives of French, British and American papers, would accompany her on *La Morinie*.

As the countdown entered its final phase, Cannon changed into her bathing suit, a similar design to the one pioneered by Ederle a week earlier, consisting of silk shorts and a silk slip supported by shoulder straps. Wishing to be known as a girl every bit as patriotic as her rival, Cannon had also attached a small American flag to her slip. The first two layers of grease were applied in the Hôtel de la Sirène, and the third was slapped on by Burgess as she stood on the shore. "The beach at Gris-Nez was lined with villagers and French and English vacationists," wrote Alec Rutherford, "who gave Miss Cannon a stirring send-off." She walked toward the surf as fellow swimmers and local villagers formed a guard of honour and illuminated her path with handheld flares. After a final kiss from her husband, she plunged into the motionless sea at 12:55 a.m., Tuesday, the seventeenth, an hour behind schedule.

On board *La Morinie* everyone settled down in anticipation of a far smoother crossing than the one they'd experienced eleven days earlier. Ishak Helmy roared with laughter as he gave Jeanne

Sion a detailed account of his seasickness, and Eddie Day, Lillian's husband, hectored others to sing with him. With the tug's wireless in full working order again, and Cannon swimming strongly with the crawl stroke through a Channel turned fluorescent green by the boat's lights, everything seemed ideal.

Cannon settled into a steady rhythm and commented to her trainers on the temperature of the water. She had never known it so warm. At 2:15 a.m. Wiedman told her she was three miles northeast of Cape Gris-Nez and on course for eclipsing Ederle's record. "I feel like I could swim to Marseille," she joked. Alec Rutherford grudgingly conceded that German thoroughness did have its advantages as Cannon headed on a direct course to England "in a perfectly peaceful sea and in excellent weather which promised to last for more than the time necessary to cross the Channel".

Cannon's progress was also being followed by campers on top of Dover's cliffs. Not only could they see the lights of *La Morinie*, but they could even make out the entrance to Boulogne Harbour several miles to the west. It was, they all agreed, a night not just of exceptional clarity but one also of absolute calm.

When the storm hit the southeast corner of England, it did so with such force that centuries-old oak trees were ripped from the earth. The storm first made landfall on the Isle of Thanet, the tip of east Kent, before it smashed into Ramsgate, causing a landslide that buried a large section of the tramway under two hundred tons of debris. A travelling amusement park was wrecked, its stalls and rides scattered over a wide distance, and scores of buildings were evacuated. Deal was next to be pummelled as the storm gathered momentum and hit Dover and Folkestone with its full fury. *The Times* related how at Dover "after a perfectly calm night, the wind suddenly sprang up and reached 46 miles an hour". At the town's Granville dock, the foreman suffered terrible injuries as he tried to open the harbour gates. The power of the surging Channel snapped a winch handle and sent it thumping into the foreman's chest. The usually phlegmatic *Daily Telegraph* reported that "the rain was so heavy that boats along the beach were almost filled with water, and the boatmen were busy later bailing out their waterlogged craft. Men with half a century's experience of the district and the Channel state that they have never previously known such extraordinary storm conditions".

In Folkestone trees were uprooted, roads flooded and the roof on one house collapsed under the weight of water onto a sleeping couple. Several cows in fields between the two towns were killed by lightning, and the eeriest sound of all, said many people the next day, was the screeching of terrified seagulls.

The *Telegraph* correspondent in Dover had probably come to town to report on the success or otherwise of Lillian Cannon's swim. Instead he found himself trapped in his seafront guest house – with Clarabelle Barrett and Mille Gade in a similar predicament not far away – as the storm rampaged along the coast. "Dover and the Channel were illuminated by continuous vivid lightning," he wrote, adding for the benefit of storm connoisseurs that "the lightning was mainly sheet with forked flashes between and the effect over the sea was wonderfully picturesque."

Cannon's world burst into hysterics just before 2:30 a.m. She and everyone on *La Morinie* had watched in disbelief as the English coastline was turned within minutes into a kaleidoscope of vivid yellows and whites. Fat raindrops began to dimple the sea, and then, said Rutherford, "with the suddenness of a hurricane, the storm came up and transformed the Channel into something resembling a cubistic painting". Jagged streaks of lightning tore open the velvet-black sky, and Wiedman ordered Cannon to "get out of the water, now!" She refused.

Bill Burgess needed no one to tell him to abandon his rowboat. It was already beginning to sag as waves crashed over, and he gratefully accepted the hands that heaved him back on board *La Morinie*. He joined Wiedman, Wolffe and Eddie Day in demanding that Cannon leave the water, but again she shook her head, unable to bear the thought of giving up after just two hours. Rutherford wrote that for a few minutes they allowed her to continue, even though everyone "on the tug kept their eyes on the swimmer, fearful that they might lose her in the choppy seas". A wave hit the boat with such force that the passengers were skittled across the deck like ninepins. For a moment Minott Saunders was sure they were going to capsize. Captain Costa picked himself up and screamed for Wiedman to come to the wheelhouse, where he shouted that he was not prepared to continue-the wind was too strong, the sea too fierce, and they were side on to the storm. He was going to hove to and turn the vessel face on to the storm.

Cannon heard the engine stop and began to panic. "What's wrong with the tug?" she shouted. "It's all right, dear," replied her husband, who gave a cheery wave from the rail and reassured her that *La Morinie* was going to sit out the storm for a brief while. As Cannon began to tread water in the lee of the tug, Jack Wiedman confessed to Saunders that they were endangering Cannon if they left her alone in the water. "I've been on many a swim but I have never seen a more wicked thing happen. The poor girl is likely to freeze because of this enforced inactivity."

Jabez Wolffe confronted Burgess and Wiedman and demanded that they do something – either continue with the swim or forcibly take Cannon from the water. If they didn't, she would drown. The three men marched into the wheelhouse to see if they could persuade Costa to restart his engine. But his nerve had gone, Rutherford was told later, "and he refused to go on". Four days earlier a 3,500-ton Italian steamer had run aground on the Goodwin Sands, and Costa now took it as an omen: he had dared the Channel once already this month and won; to do so again would be foolhardy. Nothing could induce him to continue.

Burgess came out of the wheelhouse and bellowed at Cannon to come on board. "I'm all right and I don't want to come out," she replied, only just able to hear Burgess over the wind. Burgess pointed out that the gale was now pushing the tug back toward France. "It's impossible to go on," he shouted. Cannon felt herself wanting to cry as she swam toward *La Morinie*. "Oh dear," she said, grimacing, "may I have another try?"

By the time *La Morinie* limped into Boulogne, the correspondents had already radioed the dramatic accounts of Cannon's swim to their newsrooms. A few hours later Britons sat at their breakfast tables drinking their tea and digesting news of the American's perilous adventure. The London *Star* correspondent described the experience as "startling" but said Cannon was set on having another try. *The Times* and the *Telegraph* appended a brief paragraph about the swim to extensive reports of the storm damage that now defaced much of southern England.

Minott Saunders's narrative made the front page of the *Baltimore Post* under the headline BALTIMORE GIRL PUTS UP PLUCKY FIGHT IN GALE. Inside the paper was Cannon's recollection of her nightmare: "The experience of being tossed about in a raging storm, with lightning flashing in my eyes, thunder crashing and my accompanying tug out of control, was terrible," she said. Then she bemoaned her bad luck and vowed that she wasn't yet finished with the Channel. Ederle's record was still in her sights. "I hope that on the first favourable day this week, I will be ready to start again."

As Cannon slid into bed at the Hôtel de la Sirène on Tuesday morning, she nursed nothing more painful than a bruised ego. Despite the wrath of the storm, and its graphic coverage in the newspapers, she knew that the one fact that would stick in people's mind above all the others was the length of time she'd spent in the Channel: two and a half hours. It was a risible effort compared to Clarabelle Barrett and Gertrude Ederle. And what would the Scripps-Howard newspapers think? They had invested time and money in backing her; they had publicised and promoted her. And what had she given them in return? Two and a half hours. For how long would their interest continue?

Cannon found out the next day when she learned that Wednesday's front-page headline in the *Baltimore Post* was $20,000 CANNON-EDERLE RACE. Far from ditching Cannon, Fred Ferguson, the spat-wearing and cane-carrying president of the Scripps-Howard group of newspapers, wanted to arrange an international free-for-all race across the English Channel. According to the *Post*'s story, Gertrude Ederle has "announced that she would be willing to engage in such a race for a $20,000 purse against any swimmer in the world". Ferguson was ready to contribute $5,000 on behalf of the *Post*'s own Lillian Cannon – so impressed was he with her pluck – and he'd cabled two prominent British newspapers to see if they would be prepared to put up a similar amount for Mercedes Gleitze and Lillian Harrison. "If the backers of Miss Ederle then care to contribute to the purse she suggests, it would seem the swim might be possible," said Ferguson. Initial noises from the *Daily News* were encouraging, the *Post* continued, and Captain Patterson had asked for time to consider the "interesting" proposal.

If Cannon liked the sound of the idea, she might also have pondered the timing of its announcement and the motive of Gertrude Ederle in accepting such a proposition. She had just swum the Channel in the fastest time ever recorded, so what incentive was there for her? The money was a fraction of what she could expect to make when she returned to New York and signed all the contracts waiting for her. The clue lay in Ferguson's final remark. In proposing the race, he wished to make it clear, absolutely clear, that his organisation suggested "nothing in the way of criticism of Miss Ederle's recent swim". But by the time the story went to press, America was talking about little else than the brickbats with which the British press were attacking Ederle. Having lionised her at first, now they were claiming she had cheated.

Chapter Twenty-five

ONCE THE EDITOR OF THE *Phare du Calais* had finished grov-elling at the US consulate in Calais, Gertrude Ederle left for the station and a train to Stuggart. She and her retinue enjoyed the tranquillity of their own compartment as the train took them east. As they crossed the border, Ederle experienced the upside of celebrity. The customs official who entered the compartment, accompanied by an armed guard, took one look at Ederle's passport and clucked with surprise. "Oh, you're the lady who crossed the Channel!" He congratulated her and left without inquiring about her intentions and without bothering to look inside her suitcases.

As they sped through Germany, dusk drew a veil over their view of the countryside. Ederle and her Gang slumbered in their seats and reminisced on the good and the bad moments of the last few days. But whatever awaited them in Germany, nothing sure-ly could be worse than the mania of the past week.

⚑

The inhabitants of Stuttgart had begun pouring into the city's railway station hours in advance of the scheduled arrival of Ederle's train. By early evening police reinforcements had been

244

drafted in to control the huge crowds. As a detachment of mounted officers kept the road clear outside the station, inside a phalanx of police linked arms to keep the army of spectators away from the platform on which the Calais train was expected any minute. The mayor of Stuttgart arrived, accompanied by the American consul and representatives from the city's Sports Association, to give the official welcome, but the flustered police commissioner explained that it would have to be conducted in a waiting room; even with all the reinforcements at his disposal, the commissioner didn't think it possible to control the crowd if he welcomed her on the concourse as originally planned. The mayor scanned the vast ocean of excitement. Including the people he had seen outside the station, he estimated there must have been around thirty thousand people at Stuttgart Station.

The mayor agreed to the police commissioner's suggestion but insisted he must escort Ederle from her compartment once the train had arrived. The police had just finished forcing a way through for the mayor when they heard the train's whistle. The crowd surged forward, breaking through the police chain, and began to bang their fists against the train carriages. The mayor eventually made it into Ederle's compartment, where he welcomed her to Stuttgart and explained the situation. She was told the safest way through the mass was on the shoulders of some of the city's burliest policemen. Harpman watched agog as "scores of Stuttgart police in their pretty green uniforms fought hard to hold back the mob".

From the waiting room Ederle and her troupe were bundled into a motor car for the twenty-mile journey to her grandma's village of Bissingen, southeast of Stuttgart. There was a delay as mounted policemen drove back the crowds so that the cavalcade could depart. Every now and then there was a thud, said Harpman, as a "shrieking worshipper" broke through the police cordon and hurled himself against the vehicle. "Many clung to the running board until forced by the increasing speed of the car to drop off."

It was dark when they arrived at Bissingen, but the route into the small village was illuminated by scores of people holding torches. A deputation of village elders in ceremonial top hats welcomed Ederle as she stepped out of the car, while a band began to play and the thousand inhabitants cheered. Pop Ederle recognised one or two of the older villagers, wrinkled friends from his far-off childhood. Garlands were thrown around the necks of Gertrude and her sister and father, and the mayor, bristling with self-importance, strode forward to make a lengthy speech. It was all too much for Gertrude. She slipped away through the crowd in the dark, to a cowshed, where she was found a few minutes later "very overwrought . . . with her arms round a cow's neck".

Once his daughter had regained her composure, Pop led her to his mother's house, where Grandma Ederle was waiting at the door of her two-hundred-year-old white plaster guest house called the Zum Lamm (Lamb's Inn), a headscarf wrapped around her seventy-seven-year-old head. Gertrude rushed forward and smothered her in kisses. "I never dreamed the name Ederle would achieve such fame," sobbed the old woman. The rest of the family were waiting inside the inn, including most of Grandma's other twenty sons and daughters, fifty grandchildren and seven great-grandchildren. There was a brief press conference for the scores of reporters who had tailed them from the station, during which Ederle recalled the time in 1914 when she and Margaret had fallen in the village lake. "I nearly drowned then!" she said, laughing. Grandma declared that she knew Gertrude would swim the Channel, but even so she'd been worried about the "sharks". The photographers wanted to take pictures, but Harpman and Sorenson refused: reunion photos were the sole preserve of their newspaper syndicate. With the press conference over, the Ederle family filed into the cottage to celebrate, and the door of the Lamb's Inn was closed in the face of the reporters.

Harpman and Sorenson spent most of the evening gazing in wonderment at the interior of Grandma Ederle's home. All the rooms were low-ceilinged and floored with heavy wide planks, except the kitchen and hallways which had flagstones. Harpman counted thirteen rooms, four cellars and five barns for Grandma Ederle's cows, sheep, horses, chickens and geese. From what Harpman could gather, "almost the entire village [was] owned by members of the Ederle family", with Grandma inheriting over half a million square metres of land from her late husband. Most astonishing of all, particularly for Prohibition America, was the discovery that everyone in the village drank "either wine or cider with water being used only for bathing purposes".*

Ederle woke the next morning with a clear head and peered out of the window. The Lamb's Inn was under siege. Reporters, photographers, villagers and representatives of various organisations from miles around all wanted a sight of her. Throughout the morning bouquets of flowers arrived, and telegrams were delivered to the door to the point where a report circulated that the lone official of the local post office was "near a nervous breakdown."

In the afternoon Ederle emerged to fulfil a promise made the previous evening to review a parade of village schoolchildren. She smiled and clapped and retreated to her grandmother's house as soon as possible, declining, as she went, numerous requests for interviews and public appearances.

Among those she refused was the correspondent for the *Berliner Tageblatt* newspaper, who, in a fit of pique, stormed back

---

* During the party a relative blurted out that one of Gertrude's aunts in New York had died at the end of June. Her father had concealed the news during her training, intending to tell her on the boat home. Harpman said Gertrude was very upset when she found out.

to his office to vent his fury on those he held responsible for Ederle's muteness. "Numerous villagers from Bissingen spent hours waiting in front of the house to see Gertrude Ederle, who is confined to the house like a prisoner," he wrote. "She is being kept in the house because of an exclusive contract she signed with the *Chicago Tribune* newspapers. This contract forbids Gertrude Ederle to be photographed by a third party — but several unauthorised photographers and film crews are lying in wait outside the house and the *Tribune*'s correspondent [Harpman] has her eagle eye permanently cast on Gertrude. The contract means that she cannot even show herself at the window . . . this has made the villagers very bitter."

Even when Ederle did appear briefly, the reporter raged to his readers, she was shielded by Harpman and Sorenson, "thus preventing the photographers and film people from Berlin from getting any shots". The ire of the press had intensified when a *Chicago Tribune* representative (probably the trilby-wearing Don Skene again) arrived at the Lamb's Inn on the Friday, having flown overnight in a private aeroplane from London to Stuttgart. He didn't linger long in Bissingen, just the time to collect from Arthur Sorenson the photo plates he'd taken in the last twenty-four hours, and then he was heading back to the airfield.

Harpman had a different interpretation for her readers. She described how Ederle's dream of spending a few peaceful days in the bosom of her family had been "shattered" by the huge crowd that hounded her every minute of the day. Contrary to what the reporter from *Berliner Tageblatt* claimed, most of the people demanding a piece of Ederle weren't from Bissingen but were "delegations from swimming clubs and other organisations in Stuttgart, Esslingen and many other towns". Harpman reiterated what she had repeatedly told the people banging on the door of the Lamb's Inn: Ederle's first public appearance would be in New York.

There was another reason, too, why Ederle wanted to keep a

low profile; a few days after her swim, she, Margaret, Sorenson and Harpman had woken up to find their bodies covered in an angry red rash. It was an allergic reaction to something they had eaten, the physician told them. Don't worry, it will be gone in a few days. But to the self-conscious Ederle, the rash was upsetting and embarrassing.

Ederle rose early on Saturday morning and was relieved to see that the weekend seemed to have dispersed the throng. She tiptoed out of the house and began to walk down the road to the post office, past fruit trees heavy with pears and plums. The Associated Press reporter who was still skulking around Bissingen likened what happened next to a kidnapping. "She was seized by a delegation of members of the swimming society of Goettingen,* hustled into an automobile and carried off."

Ederle was returned to Bissingen in the early afternoon, having been given her freedom, and was immediately "mobbed by several hundred school children who vociferously demanded to see her in action". Ederle had taken a quick dip in the same lake into which she'd fallen twelve years earlier. Back in the Lamb's Inn that evening, she pored over some of the hundreds of letters that had been delivered to her grandma's house. A few were simple messages of congratulations from people who wanted nothing more than to express their admiration, but scores, said Harpman, were from "cranks who believe the world owes them a living". A man wrote asking Ederle to pay his fare to Berlin so he could watch a championship boxing match; another wanted Ederle to help him emigrate to America so he could escape his nagging wife; dozens of young German women sent photographs of themselves pleading with her to find them a job in show business; letters poured in from limbless ex-soldiers wondering if, in the spirit of German-American friendship,

* This was a mistake. He confused Göttingen, which is several hundred miles north of Bissingen, with Göppingen, which is just ten miles north.

Ederle could spare them some money.

A few beggars managed to gain entry to the Lamb's Inn, reported Harpman, either climbing through windows or finding a passage through one of the adjoining barns. One or two even made it as far as Ederle's bedroom "before they were expelled . . . these latter met with a lively reception. Mrs. Margaret Deuschle, Trudy's sister, expressed her opinions to the intruders in terms that must have made their ears sting".

Sunday morning offered a brief respite for Ederle as the crowds flocked to church. She and her family visited Margaret's in-laws, who lived in Notzingen, a hillside village a few miles north of Bissingen. Even there, however, Sunday lunch was interrupted by a steady procession of neighbours all desperate to share in the moment. But despite all the harassments, and regardless of what some disgruntled reporters thought, Ederle's visit to Germany had been a resounding success. The Berlin correspondent for Britain's *Observer* newspaper wrote on Sunday, "Gertrude Ederle has unconsciously done more to consolidate German-American relationships by her reception in the old home of her forefathers, and to convince those of German descent born on American soil that there exists another Germany apart from that of the war years."

One or two British newspapers disclosed that some of their German counterparts were trying to claim her as one of their own; Ederle had been born not in New York, but in Germany, and had emigrated to America as a young child. The Ederles were quick to quash the calumnies.

The *Dover Express* carried the German paper's mischievous claims in its weekly edition of Friday, August 13, but it was only a small paragraph. On this day the paper was more concerned not with Gertrude Ederle's birthplace but with whether she had actually swum the English Channel.

The *Express* liked to think of itself as the doyen of Dover newspapers, more highbrow and less populist than the *Standard* and *Chronicle*. Since Ederle's spat with Jabez Wolffe in 1925, the *Dover Express* had regarded her as rather uncouth, something of an upstart who didn't know her place. In its edition of August 6 it had pointedly drawn its readers' attention to the fact that Clarabelle Barrett's swim was remarkable in many ways, not least because she had tried to swim the harder route from England to France.

The *Dover Express* had been out to get Ederle almost from the moment she landed at Kingsdown. First, she wasn't British; second, she hadn't trained at Dover, which annoyed the parochial editor; third, the *Express* hadn't forgiven her for insulting Jabez Wolffe a year earlier and fourth, the business with the *Alsace* at Cape Gris-Nez rankled. The gravest charge against Ederle, however, in the eyes of the *Express* was her refusal to grant the publication an exclusive interview. For a newspaper that prided itself as the organ of the Channel, this was a humiliating snub.

The fact that the *Express* hadn't got close to Ederle was evident in the first few lines of its story on August 13. It erroneously described her as twenty years old and five feet tall. After a brief description of Ederle's feat, the paper pompously stated that the swim could not be compared to those of Captain Webb, Bill Burgess or Henry Sullivan, because they had set out from England. Ederle had started from Gris-Nez and therefore enjoyed the benefit of the more favourable currents, which swept her toward England without the need for much swimming. If she had left from Dover, the paper reckoned, then "at least eight hours would have to be added to the time . . . as it is a pure swimming feat every inch of the way".

But even having made the swim the easy way, the *Express* continued, there were still many aspects of Ederle's swim that didn't add up, "the most extraordinary thing about it being that she made no westward drift with the ebb tide". And that wasn't all. "Her craft never came in front of Dover, and she seems to have kept, according to what details have been published of the swim, in sight of the South Goodwins [Sands] all this period." The third fact troubling the *Express* was "that she swam in a very rough sea . . . [yet] throughout the swim Miss Ederle never showed the slightest sign of fatigue or distress". In its editorial the *Dover Express* asked why it was that "although records are claimed, no independent witnesses or members of recognised swimming clubs are taken to verify the bona fides of attempts". The innuendo was unmistakable. The paper didn't believe that Gertrude Ederle had swum the Channel at all.

Now that one newspaper had broken cover, others followed, only too ready to belabour the girl who had been steadily making enemies since she landed on Kingsdown Beach. In their view Britain had extended the hand of friendship to Ederle, but she had given it the briefest of shakes before fleeing to her little corner of France. The crowning indignity was her trip to Germany, the country Britain blamed for its current economic woes and which was responsible for the hundreds of war memorials still being erected in every village and every town.

The editor of London's *Westminster Gazette* read the report in the *Dover Express* and immediately sent a reporter south with instructions to unearth fresh controversy. The journalist told his readers on Monday, August 16, he had discovered that "the merits of Miss Ederle's swim are being freely discussed along the coast". In Folkestone he chatted with a local sailor who claimed to have witnessed some of the swim from his boat. "Ederle swam under the lee of one of the accompanying boats," said the sailor, "while the other boat was navigated in such a manner as to keep the heavy seas which were running, and the tides, off her." The *Westminster Gazette* set the next paragraph in bold type, so its readers could better grasp the implications of what the sailor was saying: "The girl was swimming in calm water and getting along at about twice the speed she could ever have hoped to swim at under ordinary circumstances. By keeping close up to one boat, she was also drawn along by the suction of the vessel."*

Were it not for the two tugs, concluded the sailor, Ederle would have been swept east by the currents, past the Goodwin Sands, past Ramsgate and out into the North Sea. He'd heard that the American was a strong swimmer, but "no swimmer, however powerful, could have stayed in the sea so long on that day".

The reporter found no one willing to articulate the insinuation made by the *Dover Express* that Ederle must have made part of the crossing on a tug, so fresh had she been when she reached Kingsdown, but one Dover fisherman, a forty-year veteran of the Dover Straits, declared that "Miss Ederle swam the water she was actually in, and I do not call that swimming the Channel".

Horace Carey, one of Mercedes Gleitze's trainers, agreed that Ederle had broken Channel protocol by swimming between two tugs, and he told the *Westminster Gazette* that any woman using the same method would be able to make a successful crossing. Gleitze herself remained silent, but other Channel swimmers didn't. Frank Perks said that swimming between two tugs had allowed Ederle "far better water to swim in," echoing the comments of Henry Sullivan a week earlier when he had been interviewed by the *Boston Post*.

In its Tuesday edition the *Westminster Gazette* carried the views of more sceptics, including the Folkestone bathing inspector, who was sure "the American girl never felt the tides at all" because of the tug's protection, but the paper also noted pompously that its report on Ederle's swim had raised

---

* Such criticism from the British ignored the fact that when Captain Webb swam the Channel in 1875, a second large rowboat was dispatched during a spell of bad weather with the sole aim of giving him additional protection from the wind and waves.

extraordinary interest along the southeast coast, and it hoped, as a consequence, that an official body might be established to referee all future Channel attempts.

Not all British newspapers, however, shared the *Westminster Gazette*'s cynicism. The *Daily Sketch*'s swimming expert, John Hayward, was astonished to receive an anonymous phone call telling him that Ederle "had been towed part of the way across the Channel by a rope attached to the tug". Hayward was intrigued by the call, particularly as he had been on the *Alsace*. Far from sheltering Ederle, he explained, this boat "came close enough to set up a backwash which nearly swamped Miss Ederle". The memory most impressed on Hayward's mind from that day was the sight of Pop Ederle jumping up and down on deck demanding a gun with which to shoot everyone on *La Morinie*. Hayward added that nearly all Channel swimmers swam on the lee side of a tug, and if anyone still doubted the veracity of the accomplishment, he wanted to put it on record: "Miss Ederle's swim was the most fully attested and authenticated Channel swim I have ever seen – and I have seen many."

By midweek the British press was split into the sceptics and the believers, as was the public, many of whom were embarrassed by the narrow minds of the newspapers that claimed to represent them. But some, such as the man whose letter was published in the *Daily Sketch* on August 21, had worked themselves up into a state of high dudgeon. It was "not a fair swim and should not be allowed to stand as a record", he wrote, adding that only Webb, Burgess and Sullivan were real Channel conquerors.

The sceptics relied on quotes – often anonymous – from sailors, fishermen or jealous rivals with a vested interest in impugning Ederle. The believers asked the opinion of those who had been in the Channel with her. The reporter who had the temerity to ask Louis Timson if the swim was bona fide, received a curt response. "Take it from me that the swim was done fair

and square." Others were just as forthright, among them Mr.
Brockman, who had piloted Timson and Skene to the *Alsace*
from Dover, and Captain Costa. Yes, the Frenchman told
reporters, he had changed course twelve times to give Ederle
some protection, something he had been doing for Channel
swimmers since his first escort in 1902. "I did no more for Miss
Ederle than I have done for any of the other aspirants," Costa
added.

⚑

The American press was flabbergasted by the accusations, nearly as much as they had been by the initial magnanimity of the
British newspapers in the days following Ederle's record swim.
Then, editors the US had hardly been able to believe their eyes
when informed of the British reaction. "If Gertrude Ederle were
an English instead of an American girl she could not have
received a more enthusiastic ovation than that given her by the
London press," the *New York Herald Tribune* reported on August
9, a sentiment repeated in the *Washington Post*, whose headline
was "GERTRUDE OF AMERICA" WINS PLAUDITS OF BRITISH PAPERS.
Perhaps, a nineteen-year-old American was defrosting the icy
relationship that had existed between the two countries in recent
months – something no politician had been able to achieve.

The roots of the transatlantic animosity originated in Britain,
where consternation ran deep at America's refusal to forgive or
even reduce the size of its war debt. The bitterness felt by the
British hadn't reached the depths of that of the French, whose
citizens had started to physically attack American tourists in
Paris,* but it was viperous nonetheless. Uncle Sam was given a

---

* On July 24, a 3000-strong mob of Parisians attacked several tourist buses
and beat up a number of Americans. Next, the American war volunteers monument in the city was desecrated. As assaults continued, President Coolidge
called for restraint on all sides, asking Americans to respect France and its
people, while calling on the French government to control the rabble-rousers.

new name – Uncle Shylock – and Winston Churchill, the chancellor of the exchequer, was one of the most vociferous critics of the American intransigence, never missing an opportunity in Parliament or in the newspapers to berate America as rapacious and ungracious. Churchill, in turn, was criticised by Senator William Borah, chairman of the Senate Committee on Foreign Relations, who accused him of portraying American people as "void of high ideals or honourable purposes", while in fact they "understand how a debtor acts when he does not want to pay what he owes". In reality the war debt was just a symptom of British enmity. The underlying cause was the realisation that Britain had been usurped by America as the global superpower. During the Victorian Age the imperialists had liked to boast that "the sun never sets on the British Empire", but now it had, and as the shadows lengthened so the resentment deepened. The *Baltimore Post* announced in July that "British people hate American films as an institution, particularly because they frequently distort British life . . . newspapers viciously attacked the 'Big Parade' [a 1925 Hollywood film starring John Gilbert] because it showed the American army and didn't mention the British army's part in the war."

It outraged Britons that when they arrived in the United States on holiday they were subjected to the same customs procedure as semi-illiterate immigrants from southern Europe. Three weeks before Ederle's swim, the *Westminster Gazette* carried a story headlined US INSULT TO BRITISH WOMEN TOURISTS. It described how at Ellis Island a group of thirteen English women, all teachers and businesswomen, were "forced to strip to the waist in the presence of a roomful of immigrant women".

The British responded by lampooning what they saw as the stupidity and vulgarity of visiting Americans. In late July, as the number of attacks on American – and British tourists – in Paris rose, the *Daily Sketch* published an etiquette guide for travellers to the French capital and advised against mocking the weakness of the franc, not that a Briton would because "the worst offenders come mainly from the young and arrogant countries – America, Canada and Australia. It takes one thousand years to make a gentleman". A week later the smirking London *Daily News* told the story of an American tourist in Oxford who "refused to get out of the car ... she said Oxford bored her and she sat in the car for three hours and read a magazine". Could it have been Anita Loos's Lorelei Lee come to life?

It had even been reported that a party of American tourists on a tour of the Houses of Parliament had made mock speeches in the debating chamber, "to the cries of 'Atta-boy' and the like ... hitherto visitors to the House of Commons have observed decorum and have not used the place as a playground".

The American press chose to ignore the taunts most of the time, but when the wires began to whine with news of Ederle's traducement they went on the offensive. At first they just related the bare facts of the British papers' accusations without passing comment, but by Tuesday, August 17, America's cartoonists, columnists and editorial writers had been mobilised. In a front-page cartoon the *World* depicted Ederle being towed across the Channel by a string of her father's sausages attached to the back of the *Alsace*. Writing in the *Boston Post*, Bill Cunningham described the British reaction as a "very aggravated case of poor losing", and a headline in the *Chicago Tribune* chortled: TRUDIE DID JOLLY WELL, BUT JOVE, HOW IT IRKS THE ENGLISH. The *New York Herald Tribune* lamented in an editorial that "the grapes seem to be very sour in the neighbourhood of Dover", while the *Philadelphia Inquirer* carried the comment by Mercedes Gleitze's trainer that other women could repeat Ederle's feat if they too swam in the lee of a tug. "Well, why don't they?" it challenged.

Many reporters returned to the Women's Swimming Association pool at 145 West Fifty-fifth Street to find everyone in a far darker mood than that of ten days earlier. Charlotte Epstein, the manager of the WSA team, said she could "only attribute the attempted aspersions to jealousy", and Louis de Breda Handley dismissed the stories as "ridiculous". Not that there was unanimity among American newspapers in defending Ederle. The *New York Evening Post*, a rival of the *Daily News*, admitted in an editorial on August 17 that it found the photographs of Ederle taking a third coat of grease before her swim displeasing. "They chime in with the questions raised by the English newspapers as to possible need for regularising and equalising conditions under which the great feat is performed," explained the paper, which thought that greasing ran counter to the spirit of Channel swimming.

But the British accusations of cheating were blown out of the water once and for all when, as the *Daily News* reported on Wednesday, August 18, "the silver screen last night pointed a silent finger of scorn at those who would discredit Gertrude Ederle's feat of swimming the English Channel. One view of the motion pictures of Trudy's battle with the whirling, churning waters is sufficient to erase any doubt of her victory. Three times during one showing of the pictures the spectators at the Rivoli Theatre yesterday, numbering many thousands, rose to their feet cheering. No view of the tug *La Morinie* is shown, due to the fact that the pictures were taken from this boat. Several scenes of the tug *Alsace*, on which Trudy's trainer, her father and sister and Julia Harpman of THE NEWS rode, showed them motioning the *La Morinie* away from the swimmer in order not to interfere with her."

A week after publishing its original accusatory article, the *Dover Express* backed down. It didn't retract the story, or issue an apology, but the paper conceded that it had been inaccurate to say that swimming between two tugs would be of assistance to a Channel swimmer.

Ironically, the paper's hand had been forced by the man it had hoped would be her executioner: Bill Burgess. Having got wind of the "bonus" he had been given by Ederle, the *Express* asked

Burgess for an interview in the hope he would take his revenge by admitting either that she cheated or, at the very least, that she hadn't abided by the unwritten rules of Channel swimming. But Burgess let them down. "It was a good clean swim," he told the paper, "and I will take an oath on it. I will admit that I would not have believed the feat possible if I had not been present, so I can understand the scepticism of others. I have got my pay but no bonus, only an old rowboat, unusable anyway, so I have no further interest."

Chapter Twenty-six

A FEATURE OF THE CONTROVERSY surrounding Ederle and the
two tugs was the absence of opinion from the four people
with the most to gain. Mercedes Gleitze's trainer, Horace Carey,
had voiced his disapproval, but from the swimmer herself there
was no comment. Ederle's three American rivals were equally
tight-lipped when they were confronted, as they must have been,
by a posse of pencil-toting reporters.

Lillian Cannon wasn't in a position to criticise, however, as
she prepared to attempt to swim the Channel with *La Morinie*
close at hand,* but Barrett and Gade might have been able to
profit if they had tried to discredit Ederle. Neither did. They
might have regarded the criticism with the same level of contempt as the majority of Americans, but they might also have
realised that the best response was with deeds not words. If they
could swim the Channel without a tug, as Barrett had nearly
done on her first attempt, then they could claim that their swim

---

* On August 29 a local paper, *Le Grand Echo du Nord de la France*, published
a statement from Cannon's husband, Eddie Day, in which he said: "Miss
Cannon has authorised me to repeat the following to you: that she had never
seen anything as good [as Ederle's swim] her whole life and the only thing she
wanted was to have done as well herself. She adds that the dispute is ludicrous."

was more "sporting". The British would agree, no doubt, and with the help of a quick-witted manager, the American public might too.

With this in mind, the husband of Mille Gade, Clemington Corson, agreed to speak to the *Westminster Gazette* when its reporter knocked on the door of their Dover boarding house. Of course, he told the paper, neither he nor his wife believed for one minute that Ederle hadn't swum the Channel, but that wasn't the issue.

The question was about the assistance she had received. "With the tugs it would be possible to give shelter and to keep the swimmer in the sea when it would be impossible to do so with only a small motorboat," said Corson. "I consider that any swimmer who gets across accompanied only by a motorboat does a greater feat than one who is accompanied by tugs." He pointedly didn't mention what his wife thought, but it had already been publicised that Gade had chartered a small motorboat under the pilotage of Harry Pearson, once a coxswain of the Walmer lifeboat and the man who had guided Bill Burgess during his successful swim in 1911. Pearson and Gade's trainer, Billy Kellingley, were the men who so far had held her back from launching her attempt across the Strait of Dover.

It had been one of the most inconsistent Channel summers for years, they told her, spells of warm, clear weather disrupted by sudden cold squalls that lingered for days and took the temperature of the water down by a degree or two. Already they had postponed one start date, August 10, because the conditions had deteriorated overnight, and now that they were in the second half of August the weather was not going to get any better. The Englishmen drummed it into Gade that patience was key; it was now so late in the season that she would only get one crack at swimming the Channel this year. If she failed the first time, she would have to come back in 1927. Gade didn't have the impetuosity of youth to dispute their advice, but every day that she waited for the right weather was another day away from her two children.

During her weeks of training at Dover, Gade had trimmed her weight from 170 pounds to 158. She was now in the best shape of her life and confident of success. When she wasn't training in the water, Gade and her husband would take off on a cliff-top hike, exploring the sleepy villages that lay inland or admiring the views across the Channel. Yapping at their heels was the mascot dog she had been given, a black Chihuahua called Tiny. Gade had also become a common sight on the nearby golf course, dressed in a thick white sweater and an alarmingly loud pair of checked plus fours, loaned to her by a local with an impish sense of humour.

Lillian Cannon's enthusiasm for playing golf on the Cape Gris-Nez beach had dwindled in recent days. After her first failure to swim the Channel on August 17, she longed to get back in the water and show the world what she was really capable of. But on Friday, August 20, Alec Rutherford found Cannon in sombre mood at the Hôtel de la Sirène. Like everyone else, she had been upset by the events of the previous day. Four young Englishwomen, bathing on a beach three miles west of Gris-Nez, had been caught by the current and swept out to sea. Two of the women were rescued by a lifeboat, but their two friends drowned, one of whom had been the reigning world tango champion. Cannon and her husband and Rutherford sat chatting on the hotel terrace. She read out some of the telegrams she had received in recent days, all of which told her not to be downhearted. She gave a weak laugh and told Rutherford that the first swim had merely been a dress rehearsal for the real thing.

Cannon had no further news about the putative "Channel race". The last she had heard had been the comments attributed

Mille Gade golfing in her plus fours

to Ederle when she arrived in Paris from Stuttgart on Thursday evening. "It's all nonsense," she reputedly told reporters. "I swam the Channel once. That ought to be enough to satisfy everybody . . . I only desire to go home immediately and to sleep and rest."

Cannon had hoped to enter the water early on Saturday morning, the twenty-first, the day Ederle sailed for New York. But like dozens of Channel swimmers before her, Cannon woke to find the weather uncooperative. Her three wise men, Burgess, Wolffe and Wiedman, stood on the beach and shook their heads glumly. The wait continued.

On the other side of the Channel, Clarabelle Barrett was starting to enjoy her newfound fame. On August 15 – her thirty-fifth birthday (although her mother still swore blind she was thirty-one) – Barrett's photograph appeared in the Sunday editions of the *Boston Post* and the *Washington Post*. Because of the respect in which she was now held, neither paper made gratuitous reference to her physique, one small victory Barrett had extracted from her battle with the Channel. It was still the *Standard-Star*, however, which was acting as her unofficial cheerleader and declaring that the outcome of her second attempt would be a formality.

Barrett had altered her training schedule in light of her first swim, she told reporters; now she swam mostly at night so she would be better equipped, mentally and physically, to deal with the nocturnal sensations of the Channel on her second crossing.

On August 16 the *Standard-Star* noted with disappointment that she'd abandoned the bid to cross on her birthday because of unfavourable tides, and its front page two days later carried news of another postponement. When, on August 20, Barrett was held up by rough water for a third time, the *Standard-Star* grumbled that "a sharp wind stirred up the sea to a prohibitive extent". Despite the frustration, however, Barrett was reported to be in rude health and so eager to swim to France that Walter Brickett was practically having to lock her in her room. "I don't care for perfect conditions," she said, "but my trainer advises me there is no use entering a Channel as rough and foggy as it has been all this week." Barrett added that she felt no ill effects as a result of her first arduous attempt; in fact, far from it, she was now more determined to succeed the second time around. "I am not going home until I swim the Channel.

When I get into the water the next time no one will pull me out until over on the other side."

With Ederle already across the Channel, and a shoal of other contenders waiting their turn, swimming had captured the British imagination. In Folkestone, two hundred army officers were preparing to stage a Channel carnival, which involved the well-known swimmers Barribel Claret, Colonel Slyberg Helmee and Nahin the Hawaiian pearl diver waving to the crowds from a cavalcade of a hundred automobiles. The highlight of the festival would be a speech by the mayor and mayoress of "Clotheshanger" to the victorious woman swimmer Pansy Buckle and the intervention of a bumptious policeman demanding to see her passport and that of coach "Sturgess".

Others, however, didn't find the preponderance of women swimmers crowding the Channel so amusing. On August 20, the same day that Clarabelle Barrett was promising to be successful come what may, one of Britain's best-known stage performers, Robert Hale, wrote a guest column in the *Daily Express* in which his incandescence almost set the paper alight. "I am appalled by the present 'prowess' of women in some sports. Their participation in masculine matters is to me positively repulsive . . . women's participation in all masculine sports should be banned by law . . . girls go cross-country running, plunging in shorts through water in wintry weather. There is nothing womanly or admirable in that." Hale then warned men the world over that if they were not careful, "it will not be long, at the present rate, before the ugly, muscular mother says, as she dons her shorts: 'George, when you've tidied the house, you might bring the children down: I'm pole-jumping and putting the weight this afternoon.' That may sound ludicrous, but let me remind you of parents today who profess to be proud of their daughters horse-racing, or glad when, begreased and goggled, women are dragged from the Channel . . . why these mad women must emulate men I cannot conceive. One can only assume that they are chiefly those who normally command no attention and who seek notoriety at all costs."

The day that looked to promise the best chance of "notoriety" for the swimmers lined up on both sides of the Channel was Monday, August 23. The forecast wasn't ideal, but it was the best they could hope for, a mix of light winds and warm temperatures. Barrett, Cannon, Gade and the two German swimmers, Otto Kemmerich and Ernst Vierkoetter, all announced they would enter the water. But once again the day that dawned had a different complexion from the one predicted. The southwesterly wind was strong, not light, with a chill that mocked the month of August. Barrett had been hoping to start in the morning, but Captain Learmont cautioned against that idea. Wait at least until lunchtime to see if the wind drops, he advised. By midday the breeze had shifted direction; it was now a westerly wind, but its strength was undiminished. Barrett decided to go. She changed into her bathing suit in one of the huts at the top of Shakespeare Beach, emerging to find a crowd far greater than the one that had watched her depart three weeks earlier. Several reporters hovered with their notebooks as Brickett covered her in grease. "I am sure I can make it this time," said a grinning Barrett. "The experiences I gained the last time will be very valuable to me." One of the correspondents asked if she thought she would post a faster time than Ederle's. "I may not break Miss Ederle's record," replied Barrett, "but I want to be the first woman to swim from England to France." The reporter filing copy for the *Standard-Star* added that "if she makes the swim, [she] will not be subjected to criticism and charges that she was protected from the Channel by a tug, for she is accompanied only by a motor boat."

Barrett skipped down to the water's edge accompanied by

Kathleen Huntley, the twelve-year-old daughter of the superintendent of the Dover Sea Baths, who had asked to swim the first few hundred yards with the American. The crowd tittered at the disparity in size as the pair dived into the sea and began swimming north toward Deal on the flood tide. Grace Leister and Walter Brickett jumped into a rowboat to join Captain Learmont in the motor boat, but a wave hit them and capsized their small vessel. By the time they had all changed and relaunched the boat, Barrett was swimming twenty-three strokes to the minute and looking strong. She covered three miles in the first hour, said the *Dover Standard* reporter, who, even as he jotted the fact down, heard a cry from Captain Learmont. The Ostend steamer *Stad Antwerpen* had ignored a signal to alter its course and was now

Walter Brickett readies Clarabelle Barrett for her second attempt

uncomfortably close. It veered away in time, but the churning sea made for a "very unpleasant experience" for everyone and left Barrett with a nasty sense of déjà vu.

An hour later Barrett was sipping some lukewarm chicken broth while Brickett told her she was doing wonderfully well, and Learmont pointed out St. Margaret's Bay to their west and the edge of the Goodwin Sands to their north. Barrett tossed away the broth container and began swimming toward mid-Channel. The farther she pulled away from the English coast, the more she was jostled by the currents. She threw up her broth and wondered how it could be that her limbs already felt heavy in the water. Soon after, she began to question what she was doing in the middle of such a bad-natured sea. When she couldn't find the answer, Barrett waved over the motorboat. "I'm not going to continue the swim," she told Learmont. He was as surprised as everyone else. She had looked so spry and eager on the beach. Barrett shrugged. "I don't feel like it." Grace Leister urged her friend to continue, and Learmont produced a flask from his jacket pocket and proposed a cup of tea to reinvigorate her. "You're doing well," he said. Barrett agreed to keep going, but five minutes later she stopped again. "No, I don't feel like it, I feel awfully cold and sick." Her team tried to cajole her along, saying that she was just going through a bad spell, a spot of seasickness that would soon disappear, and then she could go full steam ahead for France. When humour failed to put a smile on Barrett's face, Learmont implored her to persevere one last time. "Don't come out like this, Clarabelle, you're doing so well." Barrett responded to Learmont's plea with a few more minutes of swimming, but at 5:20 p.m. she had exhausted her reserves of endurance. With a pitiful moan of "I can't do it now", she reached out and touched the side of the motor boat. She was lifted on board, and for several minutes all Barrett could do was vomit over the side of the boat. Then she slid disconsolately to the deck, mumbling, "I give her [Ederle] credit for swimming across . . . I will leave all the joys of Channel swimming to Miss Cannon and Mrs Corson for this year. I've had enough."

As Barrett headed back to England, Gade was on her way to Cape Gris-Nez from where she hoped to set off in a few hours' time. She had left Dover at 4:00 p.m. on board her motor boat, *Viking*, just as the wind picked up in strength from the southwest. Nonetheless, Harry Pearson was optimistic that conditions would improve after sunset. As they scudded over the water, the banter on board the motor boat was nearly as lively as the breeze. Pearson had a fund of anecdotes collected from his many years at sea, as had Clemington Corson, and neither Louis Timson nor Billy Kellingley were short of a song or a story.

But as the English coastline receded behind them, so Harry Pearson became less hopeful that weather would be kind to Gade. They arrived at Gris-Nez at 7:30 p.m. to find that if anything the sea was more agitated than on the English side of the Channel. The *Dover Standard* correspondent described conditions as "very rough" and no one on the *Viking* showed any inclination to press on with the attempt even though the beach was crowded with holidaymakers waiting to wave off Lillian Cannon and the others. Gade had been a little seasick on the voyage over, and she readily heeded the advice of Kellingley and Pearson, who told her it was folly to think the Channel could be swum on such a night. Without even stepping ashore to have a pick-me-up in the Hôtel de la Sirène, Gade and her party returned to Dover.

The Sirène was full of bustle as Gade turned tail. Lillian Cannon saw her compatriot as she prepared herself, and, according to Alec Rutherford, "the sight of Mrs. Corson's boat determined Miss Cannon to make her start, as a keen rivalry exists between the two women".

Rutherford was fond of Cannon and her equally effervescent husband, even though, as a connoisseur of Channel swims, he had rarely met a swimmer as laid-back as the blonde American. Her gloomy mood of a few days earlier had soon flown, and of late she had been her usual self, "a cheery party romping on the sands". After lunching with Cannon that day, Rutherford had expected her to retire to her room, but "she said she did not wish to bury herself in her bedroom to sleep; it was too glorious a day. Consequently, she leisurely climbed the cliffs near the lighthouse".

Nonetheless, in Rutherford's view Mille Gade had been right to abort her plan to swim the Channel on this evening. "I cannot help feeling," he wrote in his notebook, "that Miss Cannon was very ill-advised . . . as late tonight the weather was freshening." But none of her three trainers agreed with Rutherford. They mingled with the entourage of the two German swimmers, while Jeanne Sion chatted to a Frenchman, François Le Driant, who had finished second in the recent Paris marathon swim and was going to now have a go at beating the Channel.

Otto Kemmerich headed to the beach first, making no attempt, as he went, to hide his webbed gloves. The British reporters protested that they gave the German an unfair advantage in the water, but Kemmerich just shrugged and pointed out that there was nothing in the rules of Channel swimming to prohibit them. Kemmerich entered the sea at 7:48 p.m., followed twenty-two minutes later by Cannon. The Frenchman, Le Driant, began swimming at 8:30, and Ernst Vierkoetter set off last at 9:15.

Two hours out from Cape Gris-Nez, Cannon told her support team on *La Morinie* she was suffering from acute stomach cramps. Perhaps, she wondered aloud, it was a recurrence of an appendicitis problem she had had two years earlier. Cannon battled on for another thirty minutes, a half-hearted show of defiance, then left the water. There were no tears this time, just a look of weary resignation on her pretty face.

An hour later Kemmerich swam smack into a large dogfish and was hauled semiconscious from the water. The British reporters grinned from ear to ear and suggested that perhaps the dogfish had mistaken the German's webbed gloves for a duck. Le Driant's attempt was almost as brief as Cannon's, but Vierkoetter, the last of the quartet to quit, survived nine hours, although he was still a long way short of success when he gave up on Tuesday morning.

Later that day the *Baltimore Post* ran what would be the last of Lillian Cannon's columns. She began by admitting, "The game is up for this year so far as I am concerned." What then followed was a sad litany of excuses, an attempt to explain to Baltimoreans why after weeks of training she had nothing to show but two short-lived dips. "It was my big chance and I did not intend to let it slip, but it was no use." Aware of how some might view her efforts when set alongside those of her rivals, Cannon finished with a plea. "I want these friends everywhere to believe I gave the best I had. And I still believe I could swim this Channel – which has been such a jinx to me." But on the same page there was a photo of another young smiling female swimmer: fourteen-year-old Laura Louise Calligan. The previous day she had smashed Cannon's Chesapeake Bay record by a full hour, and overnight Baltimore had a new darling.

Chapter Twenty-seven

As CANNON AND BARRETT LAY in their bedrooms drying their eyes and their bathing suits, Gertrude Ederle was halfway across the Atlantic Ocean. Before sailing from France, she and her entourage had enjoyed a day's shopping in Paris, prospering from the strength of the dollar and ignoring the sullen stares from the Parisians who resented Americans and their overweight wallets. Ederle bought a powder-blue hat for herself, and a host of presents for her family, and according to the Associated Press correspondent who trailed her down the boulevards, she "gave the impression that she knew the sun was shining for her and that she intended to make hay while the sun was shining". The reporters stuck close to her throughout the shopping spree, hanging around the stores like dutiful husbands as Ederle tried on garments and picked up bargains, among them a pair of driving gloves to go with her new roadster. As she exited each shop the pursuit recommenced, but Ederle refused all requests for an interview. Exasperated, the reporters asked Margaret to intercede, but she shook her head. "Papa told Gertrude not to talk to reporters anymore," she explained. If they wanted answers to their questions, they would get them in New York, not before. Margaret didn't have much to say for herself either, except to one French newspaper on the rumbling tug controversy. "The *Chicago Tribune* acquired all the rights for Gertrude's story, as well as for everything else related to it, so they didn't allow many people on the official boat following her. You can understand that they weren't going to make life easy for their competitors. The only officials on board were, for England, Haywood [*sic*], from the London *Daily Sketch* and, for France, the popular Burgess. They had no need of any others ... but that wasn't to the liking of their news competitors who wanted to follow the attempt more closely. So what did they do? They filmed our departure and then jumped into another boat." Ah! The French reporter at last began to understand what all the fuss was about, asking, "And that was the famous second boat?" Margaret nodded. "Exactly! Far from protecting my sister from the currents, it was there to keep a close eye on her and on the authenticity of the swim." So, wondered the journalist, *La Morinie* never in fact sheltered Ederle from the elements? "That is a myth!" snorted Margaret. "On the contrary, the sea was whipped up to the point where it interrupted her rhythm."

The next day, Saturday, August 21, Ederle boarded the 9:30 a.m. train to Cherbourg with the rousing good cheer of a demobilised soldier. On the way north through the flat French countryside, she entertained her family and friends by playing the ukulele, finishing with a jubilant rendition of "Show Me the Way to Go Home". Perhaps Ederle dedicated the song to Jabez Wolffe.

There was a steady flow of visitors to her first-class compartment; some of them just gawked through the glass at the first woman to swim the Channel. The more self-assured forced open the doors and congratulated Ederle with words or a handshake. But for once she didn't mind the intruders. In a few more hours she would have left this miserable and mean-spirited part of the world behind her.

Ederle's European ordeal wasn't quite over, however, for the mayor of Cherbourg was waiting at the port. Having seen his colleagues in Calais and Boulogne shower praise on the young American, he now seized his opportunity. Several hundred people were standing on tiptoe behind a cordon of police, hoping for a final sighting of Ederle before she boarded the SS *Berengaria*. There was a small ripple of applause for Jean Borotra, France's most popular tennis player, as he strolled past to catch the boat that would take him to a Davis Cup clash with America's great Bill Tilden, and one or two people pointed at the small, sharp-eyed blonde balancing on her high heels and commented that she bore an uncanny resemblance to the Hollywood actress Peggy Hopkins Joyce. But then they reverted their gaze toward Ederle.

She grinned at the crowd as her father and sister escorted her toward the *Berengaria*, even agreeing to answer a couple of questions from the gallery of journalists – just so long as they weren't about the swim. Ederle remarked how much she enjoyed her trip to Germany, as well as her shopping extravaganza in Paris. One of the correspondents, defying Harpman's strict instruction not to ask questions about Ederle's future, did just that. Ederle glanced at her chaperone, laughed, and said, "I am going to train my sister to be a swimmer, too, and big old Papa also." It was the perfect adieu, a joke to brighten the reporters' copy and repair some of the ill feeling of the past fortnight. The newsmen laughed and wished her luck.

Dinner was served not long after the *Berengaria* departed Cherbourg, and Ederle was thrilled to find she had the same steward as on her eastward voyage, Jack Chorley, a New Yorker who sympathised with her gripes about the standard of European cuisine. He emerged from the kitchen with Ederle's special request, a plate of celery. She crunched into a stick, her eyes shut tight in rapture. "I didn't know how much I missed celery until now," she moaned. "Oh, it's good to be returning to God's country."

But it wasn't long before Ederle felt as hunted as she had done in the Grand Hotel in Dover and the Lamb's Inn in Bissingen. Every minute of every hour she was harassed by her fellow first-class passengers, who shoved autograph books under her nose or badgered her with questions about the swim. In the report that Julia Harpman radioed to New York from the *Berengaria* on Sunday, August 22, she used the word *besieged* to describe Ederle's predicament.

Ederle was further alarmed by the comments of Leopold Prince, a municipal judge in New York who, attempting to engage her in conversation on deck, said he had little doubt she would be accorded the greatest ever welcome in New York. Judge Prince was only half joking when he said the fanfare would be bigger than that for any Hollywood star, politician or European royalty. Ederle retreated ashen-faced to her cabin, telling Harpman, "I am so afraid. I'll think I'll jump off at Sandy Hook and swim to the Atlantic Highlands." Harpman tried to comfort her, but there was little she could say to assuage Ederle's fears because she shared them.

Even Harpman hadn't foreseen that a swim could generate such global hysteria. Initially her protectiveness toward Ederle sprang from professional obligations, but lately it was derived from the same concern that a big sister might exhibit for her younger, more naive sibling. Since their first meeting nearly three months earlier, Harpman had been surprised by Ederle's artless nature. She found her "wholesome, unspoiled and thoroughly natural", a young woman without side to her and totally lacking in conceit. But Harpman feared that the nineteen-year-old still hadn't realised that her life had changed irrevocably. On board the *Berengaria*, Ederle asked Harpman a rhetorical question. "What am I living for now? You swim the Channel and you die. Well, I guess I'll go to work for two or three years, and after that I can have a good time. I'd like to spend some time with my friends when I get home but I guess I'll have to start work the very next day after my arrival."

The next day, Monday, the twenty-third, Ederle remained in the cabin reading a paperback mystery called *The Black Orchid*. When she didn't show for dinner, Harpman and Margaret made light of her absence to other passengers; she is such a down-to-earth girl, she feels uncomfortable in formal evening attire and prefers to stay in her cabin eating chicken sandwiches and ice cream. They also explained that she still carried the remnants of a rash from an allergic reaction to something she had eaten in France. They thought it better to lie than to be honest and say Ederle just couldn't face the thought of another inquisition.

Fortunately for Ederle, her nonappearance at dinner coincided with some shocking news from New York that came over the ship's wireless: Rudolph Valentino was dead. The death of Hollywood's most glamorous male star dominated the dining room conversation, for a night at least, as people puzzled how it was possible that such a young and virile actor could be gone, just like that. Everyone on board was aware that Valentino had undergone an operation for a perforated ulcer eight days earlier, but the newspaper reports had said he was making a good recovery. They even reported that he was sitting up in bed joking with the doctors and asking if they, too, thought he was a "pink puff", as the *Chicago Tribune* did.

Ederle maintained her seclusion the following two days but on Thursday, August 26, with the help of some gentle persuasion from the ship's captain, she agreed to give a brief talk that evening about her swim for the benefit of an impoverished seaman's fund. That the captain of the *Berengaria* should have won over Ederle to his wishes was no surprise, for he alone of the ship's crew and passengers knew what it felt like to be worshipped by the world. Fourteen years earlier, as captain of the *Carpathia*, Sir Harry Rostron had displayed exemplary seamanship skills in rescuing 712 survivors from the *Titanic*. Later he was invited to America to receive the Congressional Gold Medal from President Taft. He also became the first Englishman to have had a plaque of his head placed in New York's Hall of Fame, all terribly embarrassing for a Victorian Englishman who told everyone he had simply done his job.

Sir Harry now empathised with Ederle and invited her and her family to tea in his cabin, one place she wouldn't be pestered by other passengers. Then he escorted her to the first-class salon and introduced her as the first woman to have swum the Channel. "Overwhelming applause greeted her appearance before the big crowd," said Harpman. "Her modest account of her feat, which tale required many promptings and leading questions, made a tremendous hit with all her hearers."

Sir Harry hid from Ederle the news he received from New York on the ship's wireless, which suggested more than one million people would be there to welcome her home. Harpman found out, however, and wrote on August 25 that Ederle had "no knowledge of the tremendous reception planned for her upon her arrival".

On Thursday, August 26, the *Daily News* told its readers that the *Berengaria* was expected to arrive in New York in the early afternoon the following day. It advised New Yorkers to go to Pier A at the Battery, no later than noon, if they wanted to have the best chance of seeing their heroine. Failing that, the paper suggested waiting outside City Hall, where she would be formally welcomed by Mayor Jimmy Walker.

Twenty-four hours later an article in the morning edition of the *Daily News* captured the mood of New Yorkers. "The day of days has finally arrived," it cried with feverish excitement. "The *Berengaria* is steaming full speed ahead with its precious burden and Gertrude Ederle, the darling of America, will set foot on her country's soil soon after noon. Europe acclaimed her, but it is the privilege of New York to extend to its own wonder swimmer a welcome unparalleled in the city's history." A map underneath the article showed Ederle's route from Pier A to City Hall, and then on to her home on Amsterdam Avenue.

As the *Berengaria* neared New York, the south of the city was already bulging with people as hundreds of thousands skipped work and headed toward the Battery, leaving behind them thin trails of confetti from their overflowing pockets. Aileen Riggin, Helen Wainwright, Elsie Viets and Charlotte Epstein were among a large group of representatives from the Women's Swimming Association who rode a packed subway south. Members of the United German Societies were at the quayside well in advance, impatient to let Gertrude know they were proud of her, and forty-two Ederles of varying shapes and sizes and ages were driven to the pier by officials from the mayor's office. Mrs. Ederle and her children were invited to join Grover Whalen, the dapper chairman of the welcoming committee sporting his trademark white boutonniere, on board the city's cutter, *Macom* (a derivative of Mayor's Committee), to go out and meet the liner. A collection of reporters and Dudley Field Malone, Ederle's silver-tongued manager, were also on the *Macom* as it headed into the morning mist. It was accompanied by another vessel, *Riverside*, which contained the Fire Department band and the rest of the Ederle clan. A little later they spotted the vast shape of the *Berengaria* approaching Ellis Island. As the sun burned away the mist, two airplanes hired by the *Daily News* swooped down and showered the liner's deck in thousands of flower petals. A hydroplane buzzed overhead and dipped its wings. On either side of the *Berengaria*'s three-storey-high hull, vessels of every conceivable type – tugs, cutters, sailing boats, motor boats – sounded their horns in salutation. A fireboat pumped out plumes of water, and a party of girl swimmers from the Highlands waved from the deck of a specially chartered boat.

Captain Rostron's response was a series of blasts on the

liner's horn that some thought startled the Statue of Liberty. From a porthole window Gertrude hailed her mother – who was nervously chewing some gum – while Pop waved a small American flag. It was all just too exciting for one of her uncles, who, on seeing Gertrude, began leaping around the deck of the *Macom*. Unfortunately, said a bemused Grover Whalen, "he jumped a little too far forward and fell right through a skylight into the tug's lower deck", where he lay groaning and cheering in the same breath.

A few minutes later, after the quarantine authorities had inspected the ship, mother and daughter were reunited on board the *Berengaria*. "Gee, it's good to have you again, mom," cried Ederle. They were allowed a brief moment together before Whalen and Malone hustled Gertrude down the gangway and onto the *Macom* for the press conference. It was now 12:05 p.m., and Whalen was anxious not to keep Mayor Walker waiting too long at City Hall. A man famous for his wisecracks, if not his morality, the mayor preferred to spend his mornings in bed with one of his mistresses than on official business.

Chapter Twenty-eight

A S EDERLE ENTERED THE SALOON of the *Macom* clutching "Channel Sheik", the French doll she had bought in Paris, she saw Westbrook Pegler among the throng of reporters waiting to question her. "Hello, pal!" she cried, throwing her arms around his neck. Whalen pulled her off and drew Ederle to one side, admonishing her with words that Pegler overheard: "Come on, none of that sort of stuff now." Charles Oberwager, president of the United German Societies, took advantage of the diversion to come forward and present his congratulations to Ederle. The previous year Oberwager had been one of the few people to welcome her home after her failed attempt to swim the Channel. "It is a matter of particular pride to the German-speaking people of this country," he announced, "that you, a child of German parents, have accomplished this great feat." Malone stormed forward, wagging his finger at Oberwager. "Cut that out!" Oberwager refused and continued his speech, praising her "German courage" but also acknowledging she was very much a New York girl. "You bet!" said a smiling Ederle, defusing Malone's temper.

Ederle had to shout to make herself heard above the cacophony of sirens, whistles and shouts. Frequently, she dabbed her forehead with a handkerchief held in her gray-gloved hand as reporters fired questions at her. She contemptuously dismissed the tug controversy and described how much stormier the sea had been compared to last year. Bill Burgess's role, she said, amounted to little more than telling her to quit as she neared England. She knew nothing about contracts or stage appearances; that was all in the hands of Mr. Malone. She had no intention of marrying, for the time being at least. She was asked if she had achieved her life's ambition at the age of nineteen. "What more is there?" she replied.

Once the press conference was over, Ederle left the saloon in the grasp of Whalen, while Malone and Oberwager squared up to each other again and traded insults, which neither could fully understand because of the din outside.

Ederle stared in stunned disbelief as the *Macom* reached Pier A just after 12:30. There were people as far as the eye could see. The Whitehall Building wriggled with humanity as people waved and cheered from its windows; the "El" station teemed with life, too, and along the ledges of the Custom House people scampered for a better view. Atop every inch of iron fencing men and women perched like blackbirds, craning their necks for just a brief sight of Ederle. The police were struggling to control the torrent as they surged toward their idol. As the official car pulled up to take Ederle, Whalen and Malone to City Hall, several dozen people stormed the police lines. There was a flurry of punches and kicks, and then some broke through and charged toward the car. The reporters and the rest of Gertrude's family watched in horror as the mob swarmed over the automobile. "Men's hands caught the edge of her blue serge coat suit and threatened to drag her backwards off the folded top where she sat," said the *Herald Tribune*'s correspondent, "and then others caught at her sleeves, at the lapels of her coat, at her hands, until four mounted policemen drove in, laying about furiously with clenched fists. Gertrude Ederle half fell back into the car, frightened and angry."

Whalen waited impatiently as the police beat back the crowd

so that the procession could begin its drive to City Hall. In the back of the car Ederle sat shaking, barely able to comprehend that one of the mob had just ripped off her bracelet and knocked off her powder-blue hat.

As she moved slowly up Broadway, four policemen rode in pairs on the car's running boards, sending out a series of well-aimed kicks at anyone who came too close and ignoring the fact Ederle was breaking one of the city's more arcane laws in not wearing a hat on Broadway. She stood on the back seat, Whalen sitting to her left and Malone to her right, his hands on her hips to steady her, and waved in all directions as a blizzard of confetti – coloured streamers, typewriter ribbons, shredded newspaper and brokers' sheets – swirled around her.

People hung from windows, appearing to defy gravity, and mothers and fathers hoisted their young children into the air so they might be able to see the most famous woman in the world. Amid the sea of straw hats, pickpockets prowled the pavements, watching and waiting for the right moment to pounce.*

Occasionally, Ederle turned and shook her head in disbelief at her parents and sisters travelling in the following cars. The sound of two million voices hemmed in by the office blocks and skyscrapers was indescribable, and it took her several minutes to understand that the strange howl she could hear was the crowd chanting, "Tr-r-r-r-u-u-u-d-d-d-d-y-y-y-y". Once or twice she caught a yell of "What For!" – America's newest and most popular catchphrase.

As they neared City Hall Park, a brass band struck up and a detachment of soldiers stood at attention. Mayor Walker

---

* Other criminal elements in New York capitalised on Ederle's swim, most notably Thomas Reefe. When the bodies of two of his acquaintances were fished out of the East River, Reefe told police the pair had drowned after trying to demonstrate "how Gertrude Ederle swims". Reefe was charged with murder.

Gertrude Ederle returns home. Her mother is shown to her right,
Dudley Field Malone to her left and "Pop" Ederle stands far left
holding an American flag

appeared at the top of the steps and nodded approvingly as a
procession of Boy Scouts, brass bands and city organisations and
institutions marched past. Bringing up the rear was the cavalcade
from the Battery. Whalen helped Ederle from the car as the
crowd pelted forward, breaking down a section of iron fencing.
Those at the front were trampled underfoot as dozens of policemen formed a barrier between the onrushers and Ederle. A
young woman fell under the hooves of a terrified police horse.
As ambulances were summoned to transport the injured to the
hospital, Ederle was led through the rotunda of City Hall by
Grover Whalen. In all his years of welcoming the great and the
good of the world to New York, he told her, he'd never known
a reception quite so enthusiastic; not two months ago for
Commander Richard Byrd upon his return from being the first

Gertrude Ederle is greeted like a conquering heroine during the parade in her honour through Manhattan

explorer to fly over the North Pole, not for Field Marshal Joffre, not for General Pershing, not for the Prince of Wales, not even for the doughboys returning from the war. They paused halfway up the twisting staircase and admired one of Arthur Sorenson's photographs of her being greased on the Gris-Nez beach. Inside the aldermanic chamber Ederle was formally presented to Mayor Walker, and he handed her a congratulatory telegram from President Coolidge.

The mayor then presented Ederle with a scroll of honour before saying a few words on behalf of the city. "When history records the great crossings, they will speak of Moses crossing the Red Sea, Caesar crossing the Rubicon, and Washington crossing the Delaware, but frankly, your crossing of the British Channel must take its place alongside of these." Ederle was invited to respond and did so, according to the *Herald Tribune*, with the speech "of a young girl, dazed and nervous and bewildered". Everything was *wonderful*, she said, a word she repeated several times as she stumbled incoherently through a list of thank-yous.

With the reception mercifully short, Ederle skipped downstairs desperate to reach the sanctuary of Amsterdam Avenue. She arrived at the front entrance of City Hall at the moment the police cordon at the front of the building burst under the weight of the crowd. Dozens of people stampeded up the steps as police reinforcements rushed from inside the building and formed a protective wall. The first man up the steps lunged toward Ederle but was wrestled to the ground by a policeman. Ederle caught a glancing blow in the melee and squealed in fright. Patrolman John Donovan gathered her in his arms and retreated into City Hall as another police officer shoved the mayor back through the doors and slammed them shut.

For the next half an hour Ederle and her family and the mayor remained trapped inside City Hall as the police struggled with the mob. The arrival of a further hundred reinforcements turned the battle the police's way, and eventually Ederle was allowed to continue her procession.

There was pandemonium all the way up Lafayette Street and at Ninth Street, too, where they turned onto Fifth Avenue. As the cars crawled past the entrance to the Union League Club, grey-haired gentlemen leaned on their sticks and waved. Every few yards shopkeepers tossed gifts in Ederle's direction. Some she caught, some landed in the car, but most ended up in the road to be fought over by demented New Yorkers.

At Fifty-seventh Street the parade turned west onto Amsterdam Avenue, where people swarmed out of hot brownstone tenements and small dingy stores. One reporter likened the scene to the Pied Piper leading away the children of Hamelin. Red, white and blue bunting hung from every building on the avenue, and neighbours dangled from the fire escapes that fretted the tenement blocks, waving flags and placards. Ederle looked up, squinting into the bright sunshine, and read some of the messages: AMERICANS CAN DO ANYTHING! THE FIRST WOMAN IN THE WORLD and the one that made her smile the most, WELCOME HOME, TRUDY!

Young men Ederle had grown up with rushed alongside the cavalcade, ringing cowbells and yelling, "What For!" Their fathers sat on chairs outside their front doors swigging beer from a growler and telling anyone who cared to listen that they had known the Ederle girl since she was knee-high to a grasshopper.

One hundred and fifty policemen encircled Ederle's car as it drew up alongside 108 Amsterdam Avenue. They linked arms and stood with feet apart and knees bent, bracing themselves for the inevitable surge. Suddenly a small girl darted between the legs of one of the policemen, a gilt crown she had made for the "Queen of the Waves" held in her hands. Ederle was still waving to the crowd in a manner that the correspondent from the *World* described as "curiously artificial", as if she had remembered it from dim memory of the vaudeville stage. The little girl thrust her gift toward Ederle, who accepted it with a smile. Aren't you going to put it on? she asked. "I'm tired," Ederle pleaded. The little girl scowled, so Ederle put on the crown.

Ederle was swept toward her front door by her police escort as their colleagues set about the more persistent members of the crowd with their batons. Paul Berlenbach, the recently deposed light heavyweight boxing champion of the world, and a near neighbour of the Ederles, acted as her bodyguard, as a

Crowned "Queen of the Waves"

representative of the *Daily News* presented Ederle with the keys to a gleaming red roadster.

Then Gertrude was bundled into the house by her little aunt Schwartz, still wearing a white apron over her best frock. Then came Grover Whalen, Dudley Malone, her mother and sisters, and finally Pop, who lingered in the doorway, still waving his flag and revelling in the mayhem. "My Heavens!" panted Mrs. Ederle, still chomping on some gum, "Did you ever?" She glanced at Gertrude and saw that she was slumped over the table, her body shuddering with heavy sobs. "You just lie down and get rested," she told her. "It's been a hard day for all of us."

Outside, the crowd took up a chant which soon spread the length of Amsterdam Avenue: "We want Trudy! We Want Trudy!" The officer in charge of the police guard dashed inside and asked Gertrude if she could wave from a window for a few minutes; perhaps that would satisfy them and send them home.

Ederle propped herself against the window and moved her hand mechanically up and down a few times. The chanting turned into a giant roar. The *World*'s correspondent found it ironic, as he stood at the periphery of the crowd, that the Ederle home was "little more than a block away from the Campbell Funeral Parlors on Broadway, where forty-eight hours before, similar crowds, in a different humour, pressed against police lines for the chance to look at the face of Rudolph Valentino, dead movie star".

Gertrude appeared three times at the window until she could stand it no more. Her father and his flag took her place, and eventually the crowd began to disperse. An hour later, Grover Whalen departed, reminding Gertrude before he left that he would return at 7:30 p.m. to escort her to the Roosevelt Hotel for the official welcome-home dinner.

The crowd hadn't abandoned their siege; they had just made a tactical withdrawal when they learned Ederle would be leaving her home to go to a dinner that evening. The instant the mayor's official automobile appeared on Amsterdam Avenue at 7:00 p.m., it was surrounded by a sweaty, swirling crowd of 4000. People leaped on the running boards and peered inside but could see no one but the chauffeur. Grover Whalen showed up in another car at the stroke of 7:30 p.m., striding up to the front door of the Ederle house wearing a "topper" with a spray of white carnations sprouting from his buttonhole. He stopped and played to the crowd for a few moments, twirling his topper in the air, once, twice, each time to a great roar of approval. He then went inside and emerged a few minutes later with Malone, Gertrude and her parents in tow. Everyone was smiling, except Gertrude, as the police used their batons to scythe a path for them to the car. "The sight of Mr. Whalen's top hat, and the air of distinction with which he manipulated it, appeared to set the crowd wild," said the *New York Herald Tribune*'s reporter, "and hundreds surged around the machine [car] and made frantic efforts to touch it with their fingers. One man became so excited that he ran round screaming 'That's the guy who owns the Channel!' "

As they arrived at the Roosevelt Hotel on Madison Avenue and Forty-fifth Street, another battalion of policemen fought with ten thousand stargazers in front of the hotel's Italian Renaissance facade. The Roosevelt had opened two years earlier, and with its spa and pet hotel, among other luxuries, had already gained a reputation as one of the city's most opulent hotels. The guest list for Ederle's official welcoming dinner was almost as exclusive. The dining room was packed with dozens of well-connected New Yorkers, all swollen with self-importance, but as Ederle was guided to her seat she couldn't see any familiar faces. Not Julia Harpman or Westbrook Pegler; not Charlotte Epstein or Elsie Viets; not even her old friends Helen Wainwright or Aileen Riggin had been considered worthy of an invitation.

At the time Gertrude Ederle sat down to dinner, a mad-as-hell Pegler was at his desk composing his piece for the next day's edition of the *Chicago Tribune*. Pegler hadn't been too bothered by the incident on the *Macom* earlier in the day, when Grover Whalen had scolded Ederle for giving him a hello hug. He'd suffered worse put-downs in his time. What had enraged him more, and what was now sharpening his tongue as well as his pen, was the treatment meted out to his wife. Harpman had sacrificed three months of her life for Gertrude, enduring a spartan existence in a hotel without a hot tub, and helping her practically, financially and emotionally. Now that they were back home, she had been tossed aside like a candy wrapper. Pegler did not hold

Gertrude responsible, but rather Whalen and, more to the point, Dudley Field Malone.

Malone had the look of a man in love with the sound of his own voice. He had established his reputation as an outstanding lawyer and skilled orator the previous year during the Scopes Trial.* "There is never a duel with truth," he had cried at one point in the courtroom, "the truth always wins, and we are not afraid of it!" But in Pegler's view, Malone wouldn't have known the truth if it punched him on the nose. He was all bluff and blarney, a shyster who had long since run out of Irish heritage. Pegler had been appalled by the gold vanity case that Malone had made a great show of presenting to Ederle on the *Macom*. On it was inscribed: TO GERTRUDE EDERLE, "MY INFANT", AS A SOUVENIR OF HER SUPERB COURAGE. But above all he hated the way Malone had taken control of the girl.

Pegler thought it disgraceful that Malone was now the dominant figure in Ederle's life when throughout June and July, Malone and his wife, Doris Stevens, the former vice president of the National Women's Party, had been in Paris (from where Malone ran his law firm, which specialised in international divorce). Only 150 miles separated Cape Gris-Nez from Paris, but in all those weeks Malone hadn't found the time to pay his "infant" a morale-boosting visit, not even when he sailed from Le Havre on August 4. But by the time Malone arrived back in New York, Ederle had reached England, and he strutted down the gangway "declaring to the host of reporters that swarmed about him" that it was he who had given her $5,000 back in

---

* In 1925 in Tennessee, high school teacher John Scopes was arrested for teaching Darwin's Theory of Evolution in class after the state had passed a law making it an offence to teach "any theory that denies the story of the Divine Creation of man as taught in the Bible". Malone was on the defence team that failed to win a case that attracted worldwide publicity and came to be known as the "Monkey Trial". Scopes was found guilty and ordered to pay a one-hundred-dollar fine.

February when no one else would. But Pegler knew that to be untrue. Malone had given Ederle only $2,500; the other half came from her father – and both expected to be repaid. Neither had Malone let on to the newspapers that in return for his munificence he was entitled to one sixth of all her net earnings.*

Pegler began his article with a thunderous description of Ederle's arrival home, and then he went for Malone. The only sour note in the rip-roaring hullabaloo, he wrote, was the ringing of Malone's cash register every time Ederle so much as breathed. She nearly never got her red roadster, explained Pegler, because the automobile company that gave it as a gift was also asked to pay $50,000, in return for a signed testimonial from Ederle. Malone laughed in the face of the company's representatives when they offered $1,000. Luckily, the *Daily News* bought the car from the company and presented it to Ederle. There were other incidents, related Pegler; "When Trudy opened a New York newspaper to a full-page photograph of herself and exclaimed, 'Gee, that's a peach!' Mr. Malone reached over her shoulder and took it out of her hands. The cameramen were shooting at the time and the proprietors of the paper hadn't paid him anything for such a testimonial."

It wasn't just Malone whom Pegler blamed for the wanton greed. "The peculiarities of the age put a cash value on the voluntary cheers of the crowd for a heroine," he wrote, aware that most other managers would have been just as grasping. But what infuriated Pegler as far as Malone was concerned was his

---

* In fact, when Malone returned to New York from France on August 12, he told reporters that Ederle had been forced to turn professional because the Women's Swimming Association (WSA) had refused to finance her second Channel attempt. The WSA issued a statement, published in the *World* on August 13, refuting Malone's claim, and Ederle put her side of the story to the *Daily News* when she heard of the row eight days later. "That is absolutely untrue," she said of Malone's claim. "The club has always been wonderful to me . . . I had reached the age where I thought I ought to be self-supporting. That was why I became a professional."

pretence that he had her best interests at heart, when all the time he was feathering his nest.

Pegler preferred the brutal honesty of a man like C. C. Pyle, known to his friends and enemies as "Cash and Carry Pyle". He was considered the sharpest, most ruthless showbiz manager in America, and Pegler had interviewed him three days earlier as he sat being shaved in a Broadway barbershop. Pyle was aghast at the way Ederle was being handled, but then, laughing, he pointed out that Malone was a lawyer, not a manager. If Pyle had been in charge of Ederle, as he had offered in a cable he sent hours after her arrival in Dover, she would have been back in New York a fortnight earlier. "It really is a shame that that poor girl went to visit her grandmother in Germany," he said, puffing out flecks of foam as he spoke. "I would have had Trudy write her grandmother a nice souvenir postcard, or even a nice long night letter. But here this girl wastes two weeks . . . You can't get a good manager for 12½ per cent."

In his opinion, the delay in returning to New York had cost Ederle at least $100,000, or put it another way, for every hour that she had dawdled in Europe, she had lost $200. That wasn't Ederle's fault, Pyle said, talking at the mirror, it was Malone's. The key was to get contracts signed as soon as possible, or else companies would start to lose interest, or worse, some other woman would go and swim the Channel.

Chapter Twenty-nine

A T THE VERY MOMENT Gertrude Ederle had been making painfully slow progress down Broadway toward City Hall, Mille Gade was setting out once more from Dover for Cape Gris-Nez. This time the weather was ideal and the water as flat as the Hudson River on a warm August afternoon. Kellingley and Pearson had scrutinised the Dover coastguard weather reports and agreed that the evening of Friday, August 27, offered the best chance of success.

Including Gade, there were twenty people on the motor boat, *Viking*, piloted by Harry Pearson, as it crossed the Channel with the sun dipping to the west. They arrived off Cape Gris-Nez at 9:53 p.m. with neither Gade nor Louis Timson having suffered any ill effects from the two-hour voyage. Clem Corson woke his wife from a nap and helped her and Billy and Ethel Kellingley into the rowboat; then he slid in alongside and rowed them ashore.

As the party walked up the steps that led from the beach to the terrace of the Hôtel de la Sirène, Lillian Cannon and her husband rose to greet Gade. It was the first time the two swimmers had met. Cannon smiled and wished her better luck than she had had.

Helmy was wandering around the hotel in his bathing suit trying to avoid the physician who had instructed him to abandon

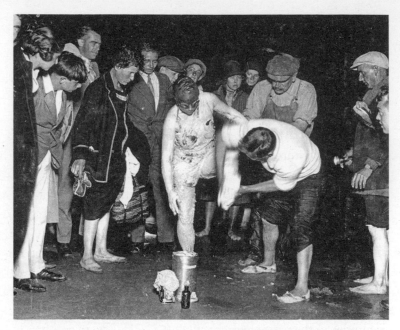

Billy Kellingley gets Mille Gade ready to make her Channel swim

his latest attempt across the Channel because of poor health. Helmy had told the doctor he'd never felt better; that the reason for his recent failures had been poor advice from his trainer, Bill Burgess. But seeing as he had fired Burgess and hired Wolffe, he would be successful next time around. He boomed a good-luck message across the lobby as Gade went to one of the garages at the back of the hotel to be greased.

Helmy had already struck off for England by the time Gade appeared on the beach greased and ready. Frank Perks was just about to enter the water for his second attempt, and as Billy Kellingley briefed him for a final time on his route, Gade spoke to some reporters. The previous night, she told them, she had dreamed that she'd landed at St. Margaret's Bay. When she woke there were tears streaming down her cheeks. So you believe you can do it? one asked. "I'm very hopeful of success," replied

Gade with her characteristic confidence. "I think of my two children always and that encourages me to keep up."

Gade walked up to Perks and shook his hand. "Good luck," she said. "You too," he replied. "Let's swim for our children." A couple of minutes later he was swimming away from the beach alongside his small support vessel, a motor boat with two English reporters and a Dover pilot. Even though Kellingley had coached Perks throughout the summer, he would be accompanying Gade across the Channel.

Ten minutes later, at 11:32, Gade pulled down her goggles and waded into the Channel as a wag on the beach yelled, "Watch out for the dogfish, they're 12ft long, I hear." Clem Corson, who had pledged to row alongside his wife until they reached England, was at the oars, and Kellingley sat in the bow measuring her stroke rate with his bright blue eyes: nineteen to the minute as she came level with the *Viking*. Gade shouted a reminder to the passengers that if they felt they were going to be seasick, would they please do it over the other side of the boat, out of her view; otherwise she might start feeling queasy herself. As Pearson started the engine, the American correspondent from the *World*, John Mitchell, asked Leslie Duncan from the *Dover Standard* what he thought of the conditions. "Perfect," he said. "The sea's smooth, there's practically no breeze and the sky is clear."

For the first hour Gade swam on the ebb tide, as Ederle had done, and then turned north as the flood tide took control. Duncan suggested to Mitchell that it might be an idea if he kept a log of the swim, so his readers could better understand Gade's progress; it was something the *Dover Standard* routinely did during a Channel swim. All it involved was noting down the time and adding any comments one considered relevant.

An hour into the swim Mitchell logged his first comment: "12.32am: two miles northwest of Cape Gris-Nez." Then:

1.33am: An illuminated clock was hung up for her to see. The moon was shining brightly and Mrs. Corson was four miles out.
1.40am: Cheers and songs from the *Viking*.
2am: Everyone sang "For She's a Jolly Good Fellow." In response to an inquiry, Mrs Corson said she was feeling fine.
2.05am: Mrs. Corson was using seventeen strokes to the minute and was five miles from the French coast.
2.25am: The Dover lights appeared and cheered Mrs. Corson greatly.

A few minutes later Gade's party passed the *Alsace* on its way back to Gris-Nez with a dejected Helmy on board, and at 2:50 a.m. they saw Frank Perks off the starboard side moving steadily through the inky water.

On board the *Viking* Mitchell was beginning to run out of incidents to log. Everything was going so well that short of commenting on the stars and the quality of Timson's singing, there was little of interest to note. At 3:00 a.m. he jotted down that Gade was still using the same crawl stroke she had from the start, and five minutes later he added that Kellingley had suddenly turned and shouted at the *Viking*, "Keep up with the boat." Unbeknownst to all but Kellingley, Gade was in trouble. A slight cramp that had started in her right leg had moved slowly up through her buttocks and along her spine and was now causing her pain around the heart. Gade grimaced with every stroke and then dropped her pace so she could talk to Kellingley in the stern of the rowboat out of earshot of her husband. "Get the life belt ready," she gasped. "I feel queer, but don't attempt to pull me out unless you see me go flat on the water." Kellingley leaned over the side of the boat and asked what exactly was wrong. Gade could see her husband straining to hear her words, so she whispered, "I leave it to your judgement whether you must take me out or not," and carried on swimming.

The life belt was attached to the side of the motor boat so Kellingley ordered the vessel to come closer without revealing why. He said nothing to Clem Corson, still tugging at the oars, but Kellingley watched Gade closely as she laboured through the water.

For the next hour Gade's stroke rate became erratic as she tried to shut out the pain. She thought of Sonny and Marjorie thousands of miles away in Virginia and then closed her eyes and said a little prayer at 4:00 a.m.: "Make the pain go away, please." As Gade prayed, Timson decided it was time for another sing-along, not just for Gade but for passengers on the *Viking*, who were feeling the chill night air. He picked up a large gramophone horn he'd brought along and started belting out the words to "Annie Laurie". Everyone joined in, stamping their feet and clapping their hands, and then they moved on to "Rosary" and another chorus of "For She's a Jolly Good Fellow".

Above the racket, Kellingley told Gade she was nine and a half miles from France. How do you feel? he asked as nonchalantly as possible. Gade suddenly noticed the pain had subsided. She'd been so busy listening to the singing she hadn't realised. As her spirits lifted, so did the sun, and the Americans on the *Viking* celebrated by running up the Stars and Stripes alongside the Union Jack. Someone produced some bunting, which they hung along the length of the boat. Everyone seemed buoyed by the sight of the salmon-pink sky away to their east, even Captain Pearson, who welcomed it with a selection of ribald jokes.

At 6:15 a.m. the white cliffs of Dover were visible straight ahead. "There's old England!" Gade shouted to her husband, "I'll do it now." Timson asked Captain Pearson if he wouldn't mind taking the *Viking* in a touch closer to Gade; he had something important to say. "Mille," he hollered, through the gramophone horn, "I've written a song for you, it's called 'O Mille, How You Can Swim!' " OK, shouted Gade, let's hear it.

O Mille! O Mille! How you can swim
O Mille! O Mille! Earnest and grim

You're making miles and miles go by
You're making hours and minutes fly
O Mille! O Mille! Please don't be blue
We'll all be cheering here for you
So for the red, white and blue
And 'cause we're cheering for you
Go Mille! Go Mille! Go!

At 7:00 a.m. the ebb tide returned and tried to push Gade west. To counter its effect, she increased her stroke rate to eighteen a minute and continued swimming toward the Goodwin Sands. The sea was smooth, commented Leslie Duncan of the *Dover Standard*, and there was still no breeze. Except for the slight haze, which indicated they were in for a warm day, the Dover Straits were being uncommonly kind. Gade had some cocoa and a couple of sugar lumps as her friends pointed out the East Goodwin lightship a couple of miles ahead.

For the next five hours Gade swam on soporifically, alternating between seventeen and eighteen strokes per minute, her mind taken over by the easy rhythm of her movements. The passengers on the motor boat dozed or chatted languidly on top of a flat sun-spangled sea. Only Timson appeared unaffected by the boredom. With every mile Gade swam, he picked up the gramophone horn and bellowed, "Another mile for Sonny, another mile for Sister." Gade's husband, meanwhile, sat implacably at the oars refusing all offers of assistance.

A succession of morning steamers passed by within two or three hundred yards – the American *Jabirn*, the Belgian *Luvia*, the Dutch *Ulysees*, the Japanese *Oregon Maru*, the British *Thorpe Grange* – and all sounded their sirens in salute.

Twelve hours after leaving Gris-Nez, Gade was three miles from Dover. She ate a couple of small cupcakes and a lump of chocolate as Kellingley told her that Ederle's record was well within her grasp. She was three miles southwest from Dover, and inside the line of the South Goodwin Lightship, near the spot where Ederle had battled so hard to keep within its sights three weeks earlier. Now was the critical moment. She had to swim hard with the ebb tide toward the coast before turning with the northeast-pushing flood tide for the final sprint on to St. Margaret's Beach when it returned at 1:00 p.m. If she landed before 2:10, the record would be hers. There was a clap of applause from the *Viking*, and Timson embarked on a soliloquy: "You are doing a marvellous swim. What will New York say of Mille Gade? I guess they'll be right pleased, for you are swimming as all Americans do, keeping right there at it all the time. But there is just this one difference – you are swimming alone and with only an open boat." A hurrah went up, and Gade waved a hand: "I'll do this swim right sure!" In the next hour Gade swam another mile nearer to England. Captain Pearson pointed out Shakespeare Cliff to the west, from where Clarabelle Barrett had started her two attempts, and told her she was nearly there, "just keep on swimming". By now another small motor boat had joined the party, much to Timson's delight, because the reporters and photographers on board had with them an orchestra of trumpets, whistles and rattles. For the next half-hour the Channel reverberated to the sounds of ragtime as Timson took on the role of band conductor.

Then at just before 1:00, Gade suffered her first misfortune of the swim. The gentle southeast breeze turned and began to blow with greater force from the northeast. Gade felt herself being dragged west, away from St. Margaret's Bay, where she had dreamed of landing two nights earlier, and toward Dover. Pearson cursed a few minutes later when he discerned that the shift of wind direction had also prolonged the ebb tide; both were combining to push Gade west, not only away from St. Margaret's but also, potentially, right past Dover.

Pearson and Kellingley discussed the conditions and concluded that as they had no idea how long the wind would delay the onset of the flood tide, it would be advisable for Gade to swim toward the nearest viable landing spot, which was Western Beach, one and a half miles to the southwest. Gade asked for the time. Her husband told her it was 1:15 p.m. She had been swimming for thirteen hours and forty-three minutes.

Chapter Thirty

FRANK PERKS WAS HALF A MILE EAST of Gade and slightly behind her when the Channel weather played its trick. During the night his inexperienced pilot had steered him too far north so that at first light it hadn't been the South Goodwin lightship that Perks had seen, but the East Goodwin Lightship. Having turned and swum strongly southwest with the ebb tide, however, he was now three miles south of St. Margaret's Bay, but the extra three miles he had swum to correct his course had depleted his energy reserves. So when the wind changed direction and held up the flood tide, Perks knew he had to take a chance if he wasn't to be swept west beyond Dover. He had to use what little strength he had left to swim across the tide and reach St. Margaret's. He thought of the financial prize on offer, the five thousand dollars offered by British newspaper the *News of the World* for the first homegrown swimmer – male or female – to beat Ederle's record, and swam directly north. For the next hour he fought a tenacious battle against the wind and the current, but the Channel finally broke Perks at 1:50, when he looked up and saw that he was being carried west past Dover toward Folkestone.

Mille Gade was as shattered as Perks by this time. In the forty-five minutes since she'd altered course for the Western Beach, she had swum just half a mile nearer to the shore. The sea was getting "lumpy", according to John Mitchell of the *World*. "Large crowds were seen gathered on the beach," he wrote in his log at 1:55 p.m., "by which time the swimmer was making very slow progress in a continual fight against the tide." Gade gritted her teeth and thought of everyone who mattered to her: her children, her husband and her mother back in Denmark, who for years had pleaded with her daughter to end her obsession with the sea. Then, earlier in the month, she had sent Mille a letter full of praise for what she was about to attempt. "You must do it," she told her.

At 2:10 Ederle's record slipped out of Gade's reach, but her team told her to forget about that. Just keep swimming. People began streaming out of the town centre onto the beach in anticipation of her arrival, but Pearson was still a worried man. If the flood tide decided to arrive, it would be the end for Gade. She didn't have the strength to launch another counter-attack if the sea began to force her east again.

Gade could see the hundreds of people splashing about in the surf; she was desperate to meet them, but her limbs felt like "lead". Suddenly an image flashed into her mind of the old woman who'd witnessed her car crash the previous year. "Whoever you are," she had told Gade, "you've been saved for something important." Gade surged forward and in a moment she became aware of feverish shouts from her boat. Pearson was telling her she was through the tide. She didn't understand what he meant. It doesn't matter what the tide does now, he yelled, you're going to do it. Timson, Mitchell, Ethel Kellingley and everyone else on the two motor boats began leaping about in delight.

Leslie Duncan reckoned there were now two thousand people on the beach, and they too were "frantic with excitement". For the first time since leaving Gris-Nez over fifteen hours earlier, Clem Corson rowed away from his wife and toward the shingle beach. Some of the crowd waded into the surf and helped pull the small boat ashore. Corson and Kellingley didn't even wait until it had run aground, but leaped into the water and stood chest-high in the surf as Gade approached. Her arms came slowly, painfully slowly over her head, and her legs searched desperately for the seabed. Gade felt her toes scrape against something hard, and she propelled her other foot forward and it landed on some shingle. In a moment she was standing. She tried to raise her hands in the air, but she was too tired and a wave almost knocked her off balance. Her husband and Kellingley came forward to grab her, but she shooed them away. Leslie Duncan of the *Dover Standard* watched spellbound from the *Viking* as Gade, looking like a ghostly apparition with the thick white grease, took her leave of the English Channel. "Staggering about from side to side she walked a few paces forward and then raised her goggles from her eyes. On her face was an expression of grim determination mixed with utter weariness. She continued to try and walk ashore and once staggered right round and faced France again. Apparently attracted by the shouts of the crowd she turned again and waved aside any help from Mr. Kellingley. . . . [and] resolutely walked ashore. She then collapsed on the beach."

There was no Grand Hotel waiting for Mille Gade at the end of her swim, which had lasted for fifteen hours and twenty-nine minutes. Once she had had a hot bath at the Dover Sea Baths — and a swig from a bottle of rum that Kellingley claimed was a hundred years old — she and her husband returned to their boarding house in Liverpool Street, where Clem cooked up a treat for her: beefsteak and macaroni. John Mitchell visited her in the evening and was startled to find that their lodgings had no electric light, no gas, no hot water, and the wallpaper was horrendous. Over a couple of flickering candles, Gade told the reporter what she remembered of the swim. "The whole story," Mitchell later related to the *World* readers, "dwarfs into insignificance beside this wonderful woman herself, her iron will, and her triumph over inconceivable difficulties in the task she set herself." Then he asked Gade some other questions, about how she'd financed the swim, and how she had trained for it. They started talking about her children, and "she broke down and wept".

The next day, Sunday, August 29, Gade was up and out of her house early to have a gentle swim at the bathing station, followed by another hot bath. But a dozen or so people were already waiting for her outside the station in Waterloo Crescent, and the first who got her autograph raced away to brag to their friends. Before long more than two hundred people had surrounded Gade, and instead of the swim she had planned she spent an hour signing autographs, shaking hands and thanking people for their messages of congratulations.

Later in the morning she and Clem, together with Louis Timson, Billy Kellingley and Captain Pearson went to the pavilion in Granville Gardens to read some of the telegrams that had arrived and answer questions from reporters. As with Ederle's appearance at the pavilion, the public stared through the large French windows as Gade, her blond hair plastered down on the sides and parted in the middle, sat flanked by her crew. One or two of the British press corps noted that unlike Ederle, who turned up in a bathing suit and a blue wrap, Gade was wearing a sensible long white dress. Unable to stop himself, Timson led everyone in one final rousing chorus of "For She's a Jolly Good Fellow", and then the questions started. She answered everything that was put to her, admitting that on two or three occasions she had nearly quit because of the pain in her right leg and spine; however, "whenever I got downhearted, I thought of 'Sonny' and his sister. Those two dear little faces were always in front of me . . . it would have broken my heart, if after all that striving and sacrifice, I had not succeeded."

She laughed when someone asked her if she still intended to come back in 1927, as she had stated previously, to swim from England to France. "I would not do it again for a million pounds. I came over to swim the Channel, and now I have done it I am satisfied." Sure, Gade said in response to another question, she would like to have been the first woman to conquer the Channel, but she was "proud to be the first mother to do so". Then her husband butted in with a reminder for everyone: "Mrs. Corson holds the record for an open sea swim," he said. "There is no reason whatever why Miss Ederle shouldn't do what she did. But we are entitled to point out that she had two tugs while Mrs. Corson had no tug at all. The *Viking* is merely a converted lifeboat with two motors, and apart from that there was a rowboat, which I rowed. Of the seven successful Channel swimmers, only three have been real open sea swimmers – Webb in 1875, Sullivan three years ago and my wife yesterday. There was, of course, no assistance to Mrs. Corson from any shelter."

John Hayward, the Channel correspondent of the *Daily Sketch*, asked Gade if she could explain why the only two people to have beaten the Channel this summer were women. "We trained hard for it," she replied. "Most of the men played at it." Clemington added his thoughts: "My wife and Miss Ederle both came all the way from America to swim this Channel of yours. When they started they both of them said it was now or never. When they felt dead beat they kept on because they knew they would never have another chance. When the men feel dead beat they say to themselves 'I can't do it this time, but I will do it next week', and they give up."

Gade began to open some of the telegrams on the table. One was from the ship's company of the USS *Illinois*, telling her how

proud they were, another from Lillian Cannon, which ran: CON-
GRATULATIONS. THESE KIDDIES MUST ALWAYS BE PROUD OF YOU.
Thomas A. Williams of the Democratic Organisation in New
York cabled: YOUR MARVELLOUS ACHIEVEMENT HAS BROUGHT
DISTINCTION TO THE MOTHERS OF AMERICA. The message that
caused the biggest cheer from the press corps came from
Gertrude Ederle: MY HEARTIEST CONGRATULATIONS ON ANOTH-
ER AMERICAN WOMAN GETTING ACROSS. An American reporter
informed Gade that Ederle had told the crowds in New York that
she had swum the Channel "for America"; had Gade done likewise? "I didn't swim for America," she replied, smiling. "I swam
for my two children and their future."

The *Herald Tribune*, *The Times*, the *Sun*, the *World*, even the
Daily News, all New York's major newspapers, printed a photograph of Mille Gade and her two children to celebrate the news
of her crossing. The front-page headline in the *Tribune* said it all:
MOTHER SWIMS CHANNEL.

Others, like the *Baltimore Post*, took a different line: FIRST
WOMAN TO CROSS IN "OPEN CHANNEL" WITHOUT TUGS was its
headline. The *Boston Post* was even more specific in its headline:
ONLY ROWBOAT AND LAUNCH GO ACROSS WITH HER — USE OF
TUGS IS BANNED. The *Chicago Tribune*, which disliked flappers as
much as it did "pink powder puffs" like Valentino, was pleased to
inform its readers that Gade was "an unbobbed blonde". This
point was picked up on by the *World*, which said the reason
Walter Lissberger had offered her financial support to swim the
Channel was that she was a mother, not a flapper, and she didn't
bob her hair.

For the next two days Gade "shook hands with anyone and
everyone", according to London's *Daily Mirror*. On Sunday
afternoon she and her husband fulfilled a pledge to have tea with

Mille Gade with Sonny (bottom) and Marjorie

Harry Pearson and his wife, and in the evening she sat in her room signing five hundred photographs of herself, which were to be sold for a shilling each to raise money for a local orphanage. On Monday morning she went to Dover Station to wave off Frank Perks, who was returning to his jewellery shop in Birmingham, defeated and deflated. A local journalist also turned up, demanding to know why he'd failed. It was too much for Perks, who admired Gade's fortitude but despised the fickle British press. "All the time I was in the water," he snarled, "I never heard a cheer of encouragement."

A small crowd had gathered, not for Perks, for Gade, and

someone gave her a bouquet of flowers. Gade handed it to Perks and asked him to give the flowers to his wife. She urged him to come back next year and try again. Perks promised to think about it, but it depended less on his state of mind and more on the state of his finances. This summer had cost him a small fortune, and he didn't know if he would be able to afford another expedition in 1927. Gade sympathised with him, as she did with Mercedes Gleitze, whom she was going to see in Folkestone later in the day after her second attempt to swim the Channel had failed a few days earlier. Why, she had asked reporters during Sunday's press conference in Granville Gardens, "does not England finance an English girl so that she can have a fair chance? I feel almost sorry that I have swum the Channel. I feel it ought to have been an English girl this time." Reporters looked down at their feet or gave a nervous cough. No one knew what to say.

On Monday evening Gade gave a live radio address at the Granville Gardens that was broadcast throughout Britain by the BBC in conjunction with a programme of music from the band, drums and fifes of the First Battalion, the Lancashire Fusiliers. Three or four thousand people had crowded in and around the gardens when she and her husband arrived. She was wearing, said the *Dover Express*, "a charming green frock". The announcer was equally smitten with the swimmer and alluded in his introduction to Gade's "wonderful golden hair". For several minutes Gade described every detail of her swim, and the emotions she felt on landing, as all over Britain families sat round their wireless sets. "My success is, I believe, largely due to a sustained effort of will. I am a great believer in the supremacy of mind over matter."

She concluded by thanking the people of Dover for their hospitality over the past two months, and she singled out Harry Pearson and Billy Kellingley for praise, pointing out that without the help of these two fine Englishmen she would not have triumphed. The Corsons waved farewell to Dover on the morning of Tuesday, August 31, and took the train to London, where Gade had been booked to appear on stage at Piccadilly's London Pavilion in "Cochran's Revue". They arrived at Charing Cross unheralded by either press or public, except for a solitary correspondent from the International News Service. He helped them find a room in the Hotel Metropole in exchange for a scoop on when she would return to New York. Was it still her intention to depart at the end of September? "I've received so many fine financial offers that I'm planning to sail on the *Aquitania* on Saturday [September 4]," she told the reporter. "I want to get back to America to take advantage of these offers . . . because now my children will be able to have a good education."

That evening at the London Pavilion Theatre, Gade was brought up on stage by the American humorist Will Rogers, in the second year of a world tour. Two days earlier Rogers had sent a cable from London to the *New York Times*, which the paper printed on the same page where it reported Gade's triumph.

ANOTHER AMERICAN WOMAN JUST NOW SWAM IN FROM FRANCE. HER HUSBAND WAS CARRIED FROM THE BOAT SUFFERING FROM COLD AND EXPOSURE. SHE HAS TWO SMALL CHILDREN, THE SMALLEST A GIRL, WHO IS SWIMMING OVER TOMORROW. YOURS FOR A REVISED EDITION OF THE DICTIONARY EXPLAINING WHICH IS THE WEAKER SEX. WILL ROGERS.

Rogers introduced Gade to the audience before incorporating her into his routine.

"You tried to swim the Channel before, didn't you?"

Gade gave a nervous nod. "In 1923."

"How far did you get?"

"To within a mile and a half of England."

"You had only one child then, and now you've got two?"

Gade nodded with a smile.

"That's what did it!" Rogers yippeed. "Now, there's a boost for motherhood!"

Chapter Thirty-one

Gertrude Ederle didn't return to Amsterdam Avenue until the early hours of Saturday, August 28. After the dinner at the Roosevelt Hotel, she had been whisked off by Mayor Walker, Grover Whalen and Dudley Field Malone to the Globe Theatre for a performance of Ziegfeld's Revue; they arrived just as Charles King was starting his act, but all eyes turned to the teenager making her way to her seat, and the spotlight picked her out as the audience rose and the orchestra struck up "The Star-Spangled Banner". They left the show and encountered a crowd estimated to be fifty thousand. The police made four calls for reinforcements, and in the end it was only an impassioned plea from Mayor Walker that made the crowd give way. "Trudy is tired," he told them. "She wants to go home and so do I." If Ederle was tired, it didn't matter, for once she had been shoe-horned through the mass and into the car, she was taken to the Club Lido, to dance with the mayor as the band played "Yes, Sir, She's My Baby". There was still a gathering of two hundred people outside her front door when she was finally deposited home at 1:30 a.m., but the police guard managed to escort her inside without too much violence.

Seven hours later on Saturday morning, Ederle was peering out of the window at a street already crawling with her fans. A ring of thirty-eight policemen guarded the entrance to 108

311

Amsterdam Avenue, and an officer with a bullhorn ordered people to "keep moving, keep moving" as fruit and vegetable carts on the pavement were overturned in the scrum. Unable to get anywhere close to number 108, people did the next best thing and went into Pop's meat shop at number 110 so they could tell their friends they'd eaten some Ederle sausages.

Pop himself was flitting between the two buildings, not quite as cheerful as he had been the day before. Early in the morning a reporter from the *New York Sun* had asked him if he'd heard the latest reports of Mille Gade's swim – she was getting mighty close to Dover. Pop ignored the first couple of taunts, then snapped back, "If she's swimming, let her swim."

A reporter from the *Daily News*, Imogene Stanley, arrived to spend the day with the Ederles as part of the ongoing contract, and she found Gertrude having coffee and playing with the family's two dogs, Zip and Tiger. Two of her sisters, Margaret and Helen, were taking turns to answer a phone that never stopped ringing. Ederle asked Stanley about her red roadster: "Where is it? I've barely seen it. And I'm crazy about it." She learned that it had been smashed by the mob during yesterday's uproar and was being fitted with a new windscreen and undergoing a complete respray. "I'm almost sorry it's red," said Ederle with a sigh. "Perhaps I'd better have it painted black."

Dudley Malone bounded into the room not long after Stanley's arrival to discuss the offers he had received, which, as he had repeated parrotlike the previous day, now totalled $900,000. In a city where the average annual wage in 1926 was $1,313, Ederle's imagination couldn't grasp the enormousness of such a sum. It was beyond comprehension.

Just as they started to sift through the contracts waiting to be signed, a police sergeant knocked at the door. He was sorry to disturb them, but the reporters below insisted that he deliver a message: Mrs. Mille Gade Corson had swum the Channel in a time of fifteen hours and twenty-nine minutes. According to

Stanley, Ederle was "incredulous" at the news. "I can hardly believe it," she stammered. Days earlier swimming "experts" and well-paid columnists were confidently asserting that no woman would ever get close to her time – possibly not even a man – but here was a mother of two who not only had swum the Channel but had done so in a time that was only fifty minutes slower than her own. Instead of pursuing the offers on the table, Malone and the Ederles spent the next hour planning a defensive strategy to counter the furore that now awaited them. Ederle was no longer the one and only, but she was still the first and she was still the fastest woman to swim the Channel. It was important to appear gracious, said Malone, as he began to compose a statement for Gertrude to give to the press. And it would be wise to fire off a sporting telegram as soon as possible.

When they left the house a short while later, the reporters pounced, but years of dealing with divorce disputes had given Malone a rare talent in conciliatory noises. They were thrilled, he said, that another American woman had swum the Channel, and in fact Gertrude had just cabled her rival. Ederle told the pressmen, "I have sent my heartiest congratulations to Mrs. Corson. I am, however, very proud to have been the first woman to cross and hold the record made." Margaret was asked what she thought of Gade's effort. "Isn't it lovely?" she replied ambiguously.

From Amsterdam Avenue, Malone took Ederle and her parents to the steamship pier, where she collected her baggage that had been left on the *Berengaria*. It had been another source of upset for Ederle the previous day that she had been unable to hand out the presents she had bought for her family in Paris. During the three-hour business lunch at Malone's Mayfair apartment on Park Avenue, a band of reporters waited impatiently outside, and "occasionally one would go to a telephone and ask for Mr. Malone's apartment. A secretary would answer and say 'Mr. Malone is in conference just now.' " Ederle was driven back to Amsterdam Avenue in the late afternoon with the police again forcibly clearing a path through the hundreds of people outside her front door.

Malone finally took his leave in the evening, having persuaded Gertrude to spend the next day, Sunday, the twenty-ninth, at the home of Otto Kahn, a millionaire who was eager to inspect the first woman to swim the English Channel. Malone told Ederle that he would send his car at 10:00 a.m. Then he was gone, careering down the stairs and out of the front door past the policemen still standing guard. His place in the Ederle home was soon filled by some representatives of the "Amsterdam Avenue Arrangements Committee", a group of neighbours who had decided to throw a block party in Gertrude's honour on Monday night. They bubbled with excitement as they told her they were building a throne on which she could sit as they crowned her "Queen of the Waves".

It was late on Saturday evening when Ederle collapsed. The signs had been there throughout the day: the colour draining steadily from her cheeks, the hands that shook with every contract discussed. Unable to take any more, she curled up into a ball moaning softly. The family physician, Dr. Robert Bickley, rushed over and was shocked by what he found. He told Mrs. Ederle that her daughter was physically and mentally exhausted. He strongly advised that she should rest for at least twenty-four hours and under no circumstances should she leave the house.

When Malone's car arrived the next morning, the chauffeur was informed of Ederle's condition. In between the car departing and returning with an alarmed Malone, Imogene Stanley and Julia Harpman arrived, having been alerted to her collapse. Mrs. Ederle allowed them in to see her daughter. Harpman was horrifed to see a "semi-hysterical, nervously twitching child . . . in place of the strong, boisterous, nerveless companion of the cheerless days at Gris-Nez".

Gertrude complained about the crowd still camped outside

her front door. "They think I'm a machine," she cried, her eyes bruised with tears. "Unless I can get a little rest I'll have a real nervous breakdown, and then I won't be able to carry out any of my plans." Stanley and Harpman didn't have long with Gertrude before Malone charged in full of loud concern. "After patting her hand and urging her to take care of herself," said Stanley, "Malone was driven off to fill his weekend social engagements." As he tucked into a sumptuous spread at Otto Kahn's millionaire residence, Malone reassured disappointed reporters that Ederle would soon "be herself again", adding: "Every great athlete has a highly nervous system, and Gertrude has been on edge and in training for two years, with a constant ambition to accomplish her purpose. All she needs is a day of complete rest."

Not long after Malone had skedaddled from Amsterdam Avenue, Dr. Bickley called again and hearing how she had "rolled and tossed, then sobbed and screamed for two hours", he administered a hypodermic.

It was a much more sedate Ederle who welcomed Westbrook Pegler a few hours later. Prompted by his wife's account of her distressing encounter, he came by and found her slumped life-lessly in the front room. She was pleased to see "Peg", a man she liked for his straight-talking shrewdness. Why are they all saying these nasty things about me? she wanted to know. She had expected contrasts to be made between her swim and Gade's, but the focus she thought would have been on their ages, not on their support vessels. The *World* that morning had carried several derogatory comments from the crew of the USS *Illinois*. "I'll give credit to Miss Ederle for what she did," said one, "but I don't think she would have made it without the tugs." Another pointed out that not only had the tugs protected Ederle from the waves, they'd also kept her in the shade and prevented her from being "sunburned".

Pegler had read the same comments and sympathised with Ederle when she "wondered if she had done something criminal in swimming the English Channel first and fastest". Pegler told her to ignore people like Clem Corson and his shipmates, and think of the two million people who had turned out to welcome her on Friday. They all knew the true "Queen of the Waves".

He gave Ederle a farewell peck on her cheek and returned home to write his copy for Monday's *Chicago Tribune*. "Trudy sat in the front room of the flat this afternoon nervously fidgeting with her big, thick hands, a brave young athlete when in the water, but utterly licked in the masculine sport of slinging mud . . . the sweet flavour of victory is turning bitter in the kid's mouth. It looks like a famous naval victory."

Malone was back at 108 Amsterdam Avenue first thing Monday morning to see how the patient was. He brought with him news of another high-profile invitation, to a dinner at the Commodore Club on Wednesday night hosted by Joseph Day, who was something big in property. Malone then disappeared to discuss more deals, telling Gertrude before he left to rest for a couple of hours as she had a big day in front of her.

First was a luncheon tendered by Rodman Wanamaker at his eponymous restaurant on Ninth Street and Broadway, during which Gertrude and her parents were presented with diamond brooches. Then in the evening it was the block party. Malone arrived at around 8:00 p.m., dressed in his best finery, to escort her, along with Grover Whalen, still twirling his "topper". State Senator Abraham Kaplan, Assemblyman John J. Buckley and James J. Hagen, assistant commissioner, trotted behind as fifteen thousand people, from Broadway to Amsterdam Avenue on West Sixty-sixth Street, all searched for a sight of "their" girl. Some had a genuine wish to honour Ederle, but others had been drawn by a morbid desire to see if what the newspapers were saying was true: Was she on the brink of a nervous breakdown?

As the *Daily News* had asked in its early editions: "Is Trudy's illness a temporary inconvenience or will it prove serious? And what effect will it have on her activities for the next few weeks? Today should tell. Read the answer in tomorrow's Pink and other editions of the *DAILY NEWS*." But thousands of New Yorkers couldn't wait until tomorrow; they wanted the answer this evening.

As women tried to touch her and men shouted proposals of marriage, Ederle was pushed through a police cordon toward a platform on which stood her throne. Around her the police formed up like a New York Giants' defensive line waiting for someone to make an offensive run, and when it happened – at the moment Ederle mounted her throne – they were waiting. Women and children screamed in terror as the crowd was driven back with police batons. One of the dignitaries gave the order for the band to strike up "The Star-Spangled Banner", to drown out the yelps and curses, as the "boom-boom-boom" of camera flashbulbs provided the background beat.

Ederle sat on her throne amid the bedlam as first a diamond-studded gold badge of a special deputy sheriff was pinned on her dress by Sheriff Culkin. Putting his mouth to her ear, he shouted that she was the first woman to receive such an accolade. Then, as the police fell back under a counter-attack by the crowd, Assistant Commissioner Hagen placed upon Ederle's head a crown of tinsel. Next came John Buckley with a silver loving cup, a gift from the neighbourhood, and the platform began to wobble as the battle raged around it. Ederle was smiling and waving in the same curiously artificial way she had when she arrived home three days earlier. Suddenly, said the *World*, "she slumped in her chair and collapsed. The tinsel crown toppled from her head and rolled onto the platform". People rushed forward to offer assistance, and within a couple of minutes she was being led away by a rescue party of policemen. A smiling Malone tried to speak above the deafening chant of "Trudy!

Trudy!" The crowd quietened down for a moment, just long enough for him to say that Miss Ederle, his protégée, would be leaving New York Thursday afternoon to begin a week of exhibition swimming at Philadelphia's Sesqui-Centennial International Exposition.

⚐

When Malone woke on Tuesday, August 31, he was in need of some good news. Since he had arrived from France nearly three weeks earlier, cock-a-hoop at hearing the news midway across the Atlantic that his "protégée" had swum the Channel, little had gone according to plan. Malone had stepped ashore in New York and "waved aloft fifteen telegrams offering her jobs which ranged all the way from Chautauqua trips to the most coveted places in the stage and movie worlds".

By the time he welcomed Ederle at the Battery, the offers awaiting her signature totalled $900,000, including one of $100,000 from Marcus Loew, the owner of Metro-Goldwyn-Mayer, for a twenty-week run of exhibition swims. Malone was also being pestered daily at his office by the vaudeville impresario Edward Albee, who was offering $3,000 a week net for twenty weeks to secure Ederle's services. Not nearly enough, Malone had told him, and suggested he outbid Loew's offer if he wanted to be taken seriously. In the meantime, Loew, annoyed that Ederle was arriving back in New York without his having signed her to his stable, sent his theatre manager, Ed Schiller, to deliver a message in person to Malone early on the Friday morning before he left for the pier: unless an immediate acceptance was given to his offer, Loew must be allowed to withdraw at any time. Malone readily agreed, confident that Albee would come back with an even bigger offer.

As he waited for Albee's call, Malone spent Friday bragging to reporters about how much she was going to earn. Headlines

318

like GIRL HAS MILLIONS WITHIN HER GRASP SAYS MALONE, which appeared in Saturday's *Baltimore Post*, were exactly what he wanted to see.

But before Albee came back with a fresh offer, the news came over the wires that Gade had swum the Channel. Malone didn't have long to wait before he got a call from Loew, informing him that his contract was no longer on the table because Ederle was no longer unique, and then Albee phoned in his revised offer: $2,500 a week instead of $3,000.

Suddenly the newspaper headlines had a different hue. In his column in the *Daily News* on Tuesday, August 21, Paul Gallico wrote: "To date, I cannot see that Mr. Malone has been a conspicuous success in his handling of Trudy. There may be some juicy shekels headed for the Ederle coffers, but the girl is in a fair way to become a nervous wreck."

The headline in the *Boston Post* above Bill Cunningham's sports column was TRUDY LOSES A GOLDEN FORTUNE. Cunningham then colourfully shredded the reputations of Malone and Pop Ederle, describing them as "rank amateurs at the art of cashing in". He sympathised with them, of course, because they had "thought themselves as safe as four aces with two spares up a loose sleeve. They didn't see any need to hurry. They didn't figure any other woman living could tame those turbid tides". But one had, and now Cunningham estimated that the "thunderstruck Ederle family" could expect to write off about half of those $900,000 offers. "Trudy is still the FIRST girl to cross," wrote Cunningham, "but she's no longer the ONLY one. Trudy still holds the world's record for the event, but that unfortunate and probably unfounded contention about the tug boats still sticks to her effort, while Mrs. Corson, only 56 [*sic*] minutes slower, gets a clean bill of health in the matter of help." Still, concluded Cunningham, Malone and Pop should look on the bright side; at least "it's nice that Trudy got her big welcome home before the news came across to spoil it".

Unfortunately for Malone, he hadn't yet signed terms with Albee when he sat down to read Tuesday's newspapers. Most of them carried the same remarkable news on the front page, as the *World* did with its headline GERMAN LOWERS EDERLE TIME FOR SWIM OF CHANNEL, followed by a brief report – only cabled from England late the previous evening – about Ernst Vierkoetter's swim from France to England in twelve hours and forty-eight minutes. Albee was soon on the line to Malone withdrawing his offer of $2,500 a week.

Chapter Thirty-two

G ADE'S APPEARANCE ON A London stage had been arranged by her new manager, Arch Selwyn, whose telegram had been one of the first to reach her in Dover. She had immediately accepted his offer, cabling in reply that she stood ready to fulfil any swimming engagement that he might make. They also discussed her return date, with Selwyn advising her to hurry home as soon as possible. Gade was open to advice, but she refused to cancel the visit to see her mother in Denmark. OK, said Selwyn, leave it to me. Within a short space of time he had booked Gade and her husband on a return flight from London to Copenhagen so they would be back in England in time to sail from Southampton on Saturday, September 4.

By Monday, August 30, Selwyn had offers of $200,000 for Gade to sign, a sum that didn't diminish with the news of Ernst Vierkoetter's new record. Gade had never been the record holder in the first place; her value was as a mother. Later on Monday Selwyn issued a challenge to Ederle to race Gade around Manhattan Island at the end of September. The winner would receive $25,000, a purse offered by Walter Lissberger, Gade's backer, who could afford to be generous after placing $5,000 on her to triumph at odds of 20-1. "I believe the American people are greatly interested equally in the marvellous feat just accomplished by Miss Ederle and Mrs. Corson," Selwyn wrote in the challenge that was delivered to Malone's office. "For the reasons that Miss Ederle represents the youth, while Mrs. Corson represents the motherhood of this country." The figures being bandied around stunned Gade when told them by the reporter who met her as she got off the train in London. "It looks as though I will have more money than I have ever had before," she said, laughing, "but I am not going to be extravagant, for I am going to keep saving the nickels."

Barrett sailed from England on Tuesday, August 31, the same day that Gade had arrived in London from Dover. Having deposited their baggage in their third-class cabin, Barrett and Grace Leister set off to explore the seventy-five thousand tons of the *Leviathan*, at least those sections that weren't out of bounds to the hoi-polloi. The first-class passengers, meanwhile, reclined in the luxurious splendour of their lounge, waiting for the ship's bugler to call them to dinner. General John Pershing, returning from France, where he had been selecting sites for battlefield monuments, exchanged pleasantries with Senator Pat Harrison of Mississippi, and Supreme Court Justice Isidor Wasservogel and the French opera singer Marcel Journée mingled with rich American businessmen and minor European aristocrats.

It took a couple of days for the word to rise from the depths of third class to the great and the good of first class that Clarabelle Barrett was on board, "the girl who swam forty miles in the English Channel". The captain of the Leviathan was Herbert Hartley, an American who had been at sea since 1893, and just as Captain Rostron of the *Berengaria* had been able to relate to Gertrude Ederle through a shared experience, so Captain Hartley knew what it was to strive and to fail. Three times he had run his ships aground, including the *Leviathan*, off the French coast in 1923, and his reputation was most diplomatically described as "unlucky". But he was also a kind soul, and the moment he heard Barrett was on board, he fished her out of third class and escorted her up to the first-class deck and "proceeded to introduce her to everyone, including numerous celebrities of international repute".

On the night of Saturday, September 4, Captain Hartley invited Barrett and Leister to dine with him in the first-class lounge, and General Pershing offered to make a short speech in the swimmer's honour. After a sumptuous meal – and before the ship's orchestra began to play – Pershing rose to his feet and applauded Barrett's feat. "It was a marvellous thing," he said. "I don't know of any man that could have endured what she went through." In sum, he concluded, Barrett possessed all the characteristics of the typical American girl. Then the general smiled and produced a piece of paper from his pocket, telling Barrett that he had a little surprise for her. It was a radiogram that Will Rogers had sent Captain Hartley from London. Perhaps Rogers had been told of Barrett's courage by Gade, or perhaps he was an avid reader of the newspapers; either way, he subscribed five hundred dollars toward her expenses and asked the first-class passengers to "treat her right and see that she does not return home 'broke' and in debt . . . [as] the will to do a thing should be equally rewarded with the conquest". General Pershing proposed a toast to Barrett and then invited everyone in the first-class dining room to add something of their own on top of Rogers's pledge. By the end of the evening, the pledges totalled two thousand dollars.

The *Leviathan* arrived in New York on Monday, September 6, Labour Day, to be greeted by a crowd of several hundred people. There was a small delegation from New Rochelle to greet Barrett, as well as a few of her pupils from James Monroe High School, but the rest were there to welcome home the ship's other 2,565 passengers. The biggest cheer of the day, according to the *World's* correspondent, one of a handful of reporters on the quayside, was when General Pershing was spotted coming down the gangplank. Barrett came ashore a short while later, along with the other third-class passengers, tripping as she walked down the gangway and giving a flash of her toothy grin. Mrs. Barrett and her son embraced Clarabelle and told her that her grandmother was so sorry she wasn't there, but at ninety-four, she didn't think she could have coped with the excitement. Dr. Henry Hein, the principal of James Monroe High School, proffered his hand and said how proud the school was, and T. Harold Forbes expressed similar sentiments on behalf of the New Rochelle *Standard-Star*, of which he was editor. He then told Barrett they had a little procession planned, with a few surprises thrown in. "But I don't deserve it," said a laughing Barrett. "Oh yes, you do," replied Forbes.

For the next few minutes Barrett took questions from the reporters present, including one from the *New York Times* correspondent, who found Barrett's dress sense not quite as strong as her swimming. "She wore a brown tailored sports suit," he wrote, "obviously neither new nor expensive, a khaki-coloured blouse, a tan and brown felt hat and a pair of broad tan oxfords. Over her arm she carried a dark brown velour coat."

She didn't have "any excuses" to make for her failure, Barrett said with a smile. She simply noted that the Channel "beat" her. The reporter from *The Times* inquired whether it was true that she attempted the swim in the hope of earning the money to sing professionally. Barrett nodded. "In life we have only one or two chances to do something big, and I was willing to put my nose to the grindstone for the rest of my life for this one chance." As for her future plans, Barrett wasn't sure, especially as her employer was standing a few feet away. "I'm not going to give up my job," she declared. "Jobs are not easy to find and I guess I can find a way to take up singing . . . I want to sing and I shall, sooner or later." Then the reporters asked her about Gertrude Ederle. First, Barrett wanted to make one thing clear: In her view "a tug would not have been of any assistance in her making the swim". She was full of admiration for Ederle, and, yes, while on board the *Leviathan* she had heard of the proposed race around Manhattan, but she didn't think there was much point in her entering. Her forte was endurance swimming, not speed swimming, and she wouldn't stand a chance in that sort of race against someone of Ederle's calibre. Barrett finished the press conference by saying of course she was disappointed that she had just missed out on becoming the first woman to swim the Channel but she felt she was a success despite her failure.

The procession organised for Barrett consisted of eight brightly coloured cars drawn up on Twelfth Avenue. The *World* correspondent noted that one vehicle had a welcome-home message, but the rest were draped in unmissable banners advertising a Famous Players' production of *Beau Geste* at the Criterion Theatre. Standing to attention in front of the cars were a dozen French legionnaires, who broke into song as Barrett approached and then gave her a guard of honour. Martin Stern from the Players introduced himself to Barrett as the organiser of the procession and invited her and her family to attend an afternoon matinee of *Beau Geste*. Turning to the journalists, Stern issued a similar invitation, along with a suggestion that they might mention his play in their copy.

Before the theatre, however, there was a lunch in Barrett's honor at the modest Forty-fourth Street Hotel. A few curious bystanders gawked at the large lady in the car with the banners advertising *Beau Geste* as it drove down Broadway to the hotel. Once lunch was finished, Dr. Hein rose and made a short speech. "She symbolised the dauntless courage of the human heart," he told the small audience. "Whether the Channel is conquered or not does not matter much, but whether we have courage or nor matters very much."

The Barretts stayed the night in Manhattan and returned to New Rochelle on Tuesday once Clarabelle had signed a contract with a small group of individual theatre houses to do a four-week tour. The money wasn't bad, one thousand dollars a week, not enough to quit her job, but good enough to pay for operatic singing lessons for a year. Principal Hein had authorised a leave of absence, and best of all, at each performance she would be allowed to end with a song after she had discussed her swim. Barrett's first appearance was at the Capital Theatre in Port Chester, New York, followed by a run at Proctor's Theatre in Mount Vernon. *Variety* magazine sent one of its reviewers to a performance, and he found that her talk was "quite interestingly and modestly delivered" and she spoke in complimentary terms of Ederle and Gade. The reviewer admitted his bemusement when at the end Barrett suddenly started singing "Mighty Lak' a Rose". He imagined that it was "probably to evidence that she can do something else publicly besides swimming – for that purpose it serves".

New Rochelle extended its official welcome to Barrett on September 15 at an extravagant dinner at the Wykagyl Country Club. Mayor Badeau presented her with a sterling silver cup, and the town's prominent residents queued up to toast her health. When Barrett was called upon to make a speech, she showed that despite the attention she had received in the last few weeks, she had lost none of her humility or honesty. Without the support of Grace Leister, Barrett told the audience, she would never have got as far as she did, and the same for Walter Brickett, who gave his services for nothing, and as for dear old Captain Learmont, his "loyalty would go down in the history of Channel swimming". She added that she had been greatly moved by the generosity of New Rochelle in the last few weeks, particularly as it had allowed her to have a second attempt. It was only a pity, she said, scanning the well-fed faces around the tables, "that you have to show the world what you can do before it has faith in you".

On Monday, September 13, the *Baltimore Post* carried a brief paragraph at the bottom of page two, under a story twice the size about schoolchildren learning to typewrite. The paragraph ran: "Miss Lillian Cannon, who made two unsuccessful attempts to swim the English Channel this summer, has returned to her mother's home in the 1400 block Hollins-St. She arrived from Europe Saturday on the steamship *Caronia*, accompanied by her husband, Edwin Day."

There had been no one from the *Post* in New York to meet them at the ship because the Scripps-Howard newspaper syndicate no longer took an interest in Lillian Cannon. It had even stopped running photos of her in her bathing suit. Nor had she received any offers from theatrical agents or vaudeville impresarios. The only person to greet the couple was a friend of Lillian's husband, who had agreed to give them a lift to Grand Central Station. A reporter from the Associated Press, waiting at the quayside for the arrival of another Atlantic liner, recognised Cannon's pretty blond features and came over to say hello. She told the reporter that the fates had conspired against her and that swimming the Channel "is purely a matter of luck". She added that she had heard about the possible swimming race around Manhattan Island, and it interested her very much. Then she climbed into her friend's car and rode to Grand Central Station to catch a train back to Baltimore.

Chapter Thirty-three

As LILLIAN CANNON DROVE north up Broadway toward Grand Central Station, she might have noticed the street cleaners still clearing away the debris from the day before when thousands of people had turned out to hail Mille Gade's return. Her reception hadn't quite been on a scale to match Ederle's, but the New York newspaper reports that Cannon read as her train took her to Baltimore all spoke of a "snowstorm" of confetti as Gade paraded along Broadway.

The whole procession had borne a striking resemblance to Ederle's: the greeting by Grover Whalen on the *Macom*, an on-board press conference, a cavalcade along Broadway and an official welcome at City Hall by Mayor Walker. But Gade was more fortunate in two respects: she didn't have Dudley Field Malone breathing down her neck, nor did she have a frenzied mob launching themselves at her. After their chastening experience at Ederle's reception, the New York Police Department had taken no chances this time around. Two unbroken lines of mounted policemen had flanked Gade's car as she left the pier, and at City Hall barricades had been erected long in advance to keep the hordes at bay. Just to make sure, however, the NYPD had also recruited five hundred members of the naval reserves for the day, many of whom had been taught to swim by Gade, and as the *New York Times* wryly noted, "Their long lines of

328

rifles must have helped to stiffen the police control."

Arch Selwyn hadn't bothered to turn up to welcome Gade home; he just sent one of his associates, Cal Harris, to tell her that the offers now totaled $250,000 and that she was appearing Monday at Loew's State Theatre. Selwyn could have told her much more, but he was too busy finalising some of the two thousand deals he had received in the seven days since he had become Gade's manager. As well as the theatre bookings, he had accepted a cheque for $2,500 for the use of her name on a bathing suit, and he'd signed a contract with the United Press for a series of twenty stories carrying Gade's signature that ensured her a minimum of $7,500. Selwyn had also been busy using his thick book of press contracts to place articles in America's newspapers, portraying Gade in such a way that would only increase her commercial appeal. One such syndicated story appeared a couple of days before Gade reached New York. It ended by describing how "the Corsons have never been well off in a material way – Mrs. Corson has been very honest about swimming because she wanted the money for her children, but they have been rich in the happiness which comes from love and congeniality".

Selwyn needn't have worried, either, about Grover Whalen doing to Gade what he had done to Gertrude Ederle and separating her from her family. For a start, Clem Corson wasn't the sort of man to be pushed around by anyone, least of all a carnation-wearing dandy with an immaculately turned-out moustache and a penchant for top hats. But Whalen was wise to the fact that what had brought tens of thousands of people out onto the streets again was the wish to see America's most famous mother reunited with her two children.

They were waiting with relatives on the pier, Sonny dressed in a white sailor outfit and his sister wearing a new pink dress, as the *Macom* transported Gade and her husband from the *Aquitania* to the Battery. Inside the mayoral cutter, Gade had one eye on the Battery, searching for her children, and one eye on the throng of reporters and photographers gathered for the official press conference. One reporter commented that the swimmer "was attractively dressed in a tweed suit, light stockings, light felt hat and a brown sweater coat, and she blushed constantly as reporters plied her with questions". Gade revealed that she had reneged on her vow made in Dover never again to challenge the Channel; she would be returning to Europe in 1927 to try and become the first woman to swim the Channel the hard way, from England to France, and she confirmed that she intended to compete in the Catalina Island swim for the prize of $25,000 offered by William Wrigley Jr. She had mixed feelings, Gade told reporters, about Dudley Field Malone's decision to decline Arch Selwyn's challenge for a race around Manhattan Island; it would have been good to go head-to-head against Ederle, but she was glad she wouldn't have to swim in the Hudson's filthy water.

The *New York Times* then asked the inevitable question concerning her rival, but Gade "refused to be drawn into a discussion of the use of tugs", instead preferring to heap praise on Ederle. "It was marvellous that a girl of only 20 years [*sic*] should be able to do a thing like this," she said. "I did not believe that she could do it, but she did. There are two important phases in a woman's life. One when she is a young girl and the other when she is a mother. Gertrude swam the Channel as a young girl and I swam it as the mother of two children." The man from the Associated Press wanted to know if she had ever considered that she was too old to succeed. Gade's first response was to laugh, then she replied, "I trusted to my mind rather than my body . . . I swam with my will."

Gade closed the press conference as the *Macom* reached the Battery so she and her husband could look out of the window for Sonny and Marjorie. They spotted them waving from the top of their relatives' shoulders. At that moment, said the *New York Times*, "a mother's emotions overcame her [and] a deep flush overspread her face. Her lips trembled, her eyes filled with tears and she buried her face in the bouquet of American Beauty roses sent by Mayor Walker". As the *Macom* docked, a naval officer from the *Illinois* passed Marjorie and then Sonny through the cabin window and into the arms of their mother.

The rest of the day was enjoyable but irrelevant for Gade, now that she had her children at her side. Her two brothers and sister greeted her when she stepped down onto the pier, and an hour later she was in City Hall, receiving a gold medal and a scroll of honour from Mayor Walker, along with a fulsome tribute in which he applauded her for having bought "the only additional wreath that could be placed upon the head of American motherhood". From City Hall, the Corsons returned to the pier and boarded Eagle Boat 51, which conveyed them to the *Illinois* and a party thrown by the ship's company, to which civilians weren't invited.

The next day, Saturday, September 11, Gade spent with her children in the new apartment that had been presented to her the previous evening by the company of the *Illinois*. The three thousand dollars' worth of furniture inside the apartment, including a children's nursery, had been provided by a Third Avenue furniture company, a gesture that had Arch Selwyn's fingerprints all over it.

Two days later Gade began a week's run at Loew's State Theatre in Times Square. It was, said the *Variety* reviewer, "a hurriedly whipped-together act which does not include swimming in the routine". Gade began by reading a prepared speech and then introduced some motion pictures of her swim and her arrival in New York. The performance finished with the swimmer taking questions from the audience. Despite the spontaneity of the act, *Variety* found it entertaining. Gade showed "a quick wit and mind in her fast retorts". The audience warmed to her as well, said the reviewer, although he thought it questionable whether she should be allowed to do so much talking, "for despite her natural unaffectedness she has a slight lisp that makes certain words almost indistinct".

Gertrude Ederle was mentioned only once in the performance at which *Variety* was present, and that was when Gade said her own time across the Channel was fifty minutes slower. If the reviewer had been disappointed by the absence of jealous rivalry in the show, he didn't let on. Rather, he heartily endorsed the show and predicted she would be a draw "anywhere in the country, and those who see her will receive more in the way of entertainment than is the usual run with athletic celebrities".

Gade's five nights at the State grossed $29, 917.65, of which she earned $3,000. It was a small cut, but Arch Selwyn had said from the start that if she wanted the very best manager she would have to pay the very best prices, which in his case was a fifty-fifty split. Within hours of the curtain coming down on Gade's fifth performance, Selwyn had signed a ten-week deal with the Keith-Albee circuit that guaranteed Gade $2,500 a week, with the only stipulation being that she didn't bob her hair. When the deal was made public, *Variety* rated it "the most exceptional ever given out by the Keith office". On top of a weekly income that was almost twice the average annual wage for a New Yorker, Gade's entire expenses would be paid, "including transportation for herself and her two children, a maid for the latter, hotel bills, two advance agents, photographs and a motor car in each stand".

At the end of October, Gade's tour took her back to Bridgeport, the Connecticut town where she had stayed with her sister when she first arrived in America. The venue was a place Gade remembered well: the theatre where seven years earlier she had been laughed out of the door when she'd applied for the "yusher's" job.

Chapter Thirty-four

B Y THE END OF OCTOBER Gertrude Ederle was struggling to remember in which town she was performing. She had been granted a ten-day vacation in mid-September to recover her poise after her brief collapse earlier in the month, but since then Ederle had been touring continuously. Starting in New York, she had moved north to Boston, then west into Ohio. Soon she would be heading into Milwaukee, on to Minneapolis, Idaho, Oregon and finally to California at the end of the year. The company was good – supporting her in the act were her two friends Aileen Riggin and Helen Wainwright – but the money was poor.*

After his botched dealings with the Albee and Loew agencies, Malone had agreed to and signed a contract with the William Morris Agency for a ten-week tour across America, although this was a fraction of what the agency had originally offered. Morris, like Loew, had put $100,000 net on the table in the days after Ederle's swim, but Malone had tried to play this offer off against

---

* In an interview in 1994 Aileen Riggin recalled that she'd enjoyed the tour because as the most extrovert of the three she loved the attention. Ederle, however, said Riggin "didn't go out and greet people. She was a very reticent, retiring person . . . there was an interesting contrast between her build and personality. She was built very powerfully, but she was very quiet."

the others, only to see it withdrawn.

The second Morris deal was for $6,000 gross a week. Unlike the contract that Arch Selwyn had negotiated for Mille Gade, Ederle had to meet all expenses from her own pocket. The agency deducted its 10 per cent share, then Malone and her father both took $1,000, and once Ederle had paid her co-stars and covered travelling and living costs, she was left with about $2,200, $300 less than Gade's weekly wage.

In the meantime Malone had managed to finalise a deal with a manufacturer of bathing suits, which brought in an additional $1,000, but he'd rejected Selwyn's challenge for Ederle to race Gade around Manhattan Island for a purse of $25,000, telling him that "as soon as any woman equals or breaks Miss Ederle's record it will then be time enough to discuss a match". Malone was talking big – telling the papers that his client would be "a swimming champion, not a talking champion" – but in reality he was running scared. Selwyn admitted to *Variety* that he was puzzled by Malone's attitude; not only had he rejected the race, but he'd also turned down Selwyn's suggestion of teaming the two swimmers together on stage, not as rivals but as two disparate but outstanding examples of American womanhood.

What undoubtedly amazed Selwyn the most, however, must have been the missed opportunity to sign a contract with Carl Laemmle, founder of the Universal Pictures Company. Laemmle, one of the most powerful men in Hollywood, had been in his native Germany recovering from an appendicitis operation, when Ederle arrived to see her grandmother. Within hours he had dispatched his assistant with a contract, a blank chequebook and orders to sign Ederle at all costs because he was "personally interested" in turning her into a star. But Gertrude and her father had declined, explaining they couldn't sign anything without first conferring with Malone. As a film man himself – Selwyn was one of the three founders of the Goldwyn Pictures Corporation – he knew the sort of money Laemmle would have been willing to pay, and it staggered him to think of the opportunity Ederle had blown.

Instead of spending the autumn being feted in Hollywood, Ederle and her two companions were being shunted from one town to the next, performing on a drab stage in a glass tank that was fifteen feet long, ten feet wide and seven feet deep. (Ederle had to buy the tank out of her wages for six thousand dollars.) None of the three women swimmers enjoyed the experience, particularly Riggin and Wainwright who had to do a series of dives as a curtain-raiser to Ederle demonstrating her famous crawl stroke. Riggin said it felt like being in a "fish bowl". On a couple of occasions the organisers hadn't been able to heat the water properly, so the girls held their breath and jumped into a tank that felt colder than the English Channel. Westbrook Pegler had seen the show and walked away dismayed at Ederle's humiliation in having to perform "in a one-stroke tub [that] suggests a whale doing a marathon in an eye-cup."

A writer from the *Christian Science Monitor* joined Ederle for a few days in late October and was stupefied, not just with the act, but with the way the conqueror of the Channel was being treated. "It is possible to wonder at her continued and immense good nature in the face of what may appropriately be called a condition of servitude," she wrote. None of them were allowed any time to enjoy the places they were visiting; instead they were held to a schedule of photography and superficial interviewing, and deprived of their friends and family.

At least Gertude had her sister Helen for support, but the latter was finding the tour as arduous as the swimmers. "We hardly know from one week to another where we'll be," Helen told the reporter. "They want us to go to California but we don't want to. We like it at home." The greatest shame, in the opinion of the *Christian Science Monitor*, was that Gertrude was too polite to disobey "the desires of a host of people to whom her phenomenal achievement was but the beginning of things".

But slowly Ederle's sunny disposition began to darken. At the end of October she filed a suit against Sheriff W. E. Robb, the proprietor of Avon Lake in Iowa, accusing him of having paid her only $36 of the agreed fee of $750. A couple of weeks later, the tour train stopped at Milwaukee, and her compartment was invaded by hollering photographers and reporters. Ederle refused to cooperate and, turning to one of her friends, said: "Being posed for pictures and interviews has been the bane of my life. I think newspaper people are damned nuts." Perhaps she had wanted the journalists to hear, or perhaps with her poor hearing she had just blurted it out in that voice that Westbrook Pegler had once likened to the famous bodyguard Wild Will Lyons.

Either way, Ederle's comments weren't well received, and in December *Variety* ran a story titled "Trudy Getting It Wrong With Dailies", which described how her recent faux pas hadn't gone down well with the newspapers.

She was still a draw as the year came to a close, but the numbers coming to see the show were dwindling. More than anything, people wanted to see her swim, not in a tank but in the ocean. The obvious answer was for Ederle to compete in William Wrigley Jr.'s Ocean Marathon Swim, the inaugural twenty-two-mile race from Avalon on Catalina Island to Point Vicente on the Californian coast, which had been inspired by the race to cross the English Channel. When Ederle arrived in California in December, everyone was desperate to know if she would be one of the hundred swimmers competing for the $25,000 purse on January 15. Clarabelle Barrett and Mille Gade had both entered their names, so what better way to settle the argument as to who was the world's greatest female swimmer?* But Ederle declined the invitation. Of course, she would love to put her rivals in their place, she told the *Los Angeles Times*, but she was just too busy with her theatre engagements. She was also acting under instruction from Malone, who knew that Ederle's aura was

Newspapers called the swim in Catalina, "Our Own Channel Swim".
Clarabelle Barrett is visible in the small circle inset (with hat)
on the far left side

already diminishing and that if she were to be beaten by another woman, her reputation as the world's greatest female swimmer would be irreparably shattered.

The New Year was barely a fortnight old when Ederle received further bad news: Uncle John, who four months earlier had celebrated her swim with an impromptu street party on Amsterdam Avenue, lost control of his car in Long Island and smashed into a truck. He was killed in the accident and his wife, Sophie, and another of Gertrude's uncles, William, were badly injured. Not that Ederle had much time to grieve as she was obliged to continue her slog across America, although as winter turned to spring, the bookings began to diminish and the nation's newspapers were ever more fixated on the sordid divorce battle between the fifty-one-year-old property heavyweight Edward "Daddy" Browning and his sixteen-year-old bride Frances

---

* In fact Mille Gade withdrew from the race when it was announced that female competitors would be allowed to swim naked provided they covered themselves in black axle grease. "I positively will not enter a swimming match and compete with any woman who won't wear a bathing suit," said Gade, living up to her image as the morally impeccable mother. Barrett did compete, along with eighty-seven men and fourteen other women, but only one swimmer finished the course: the seventeen-year-old Canadian George Young. Barrett was one of the last to quit after fourteen hours in the water.

"Peaches", who, among a string of eyebrow-raising revelations in court, disclosed that "Daddy" was in the habit of keeping an African goose in their bedroom.

At the start of May, Ederle's contract with Malone expired, and she didn't seek an extension. When Westbrook Pegler spoke to her in June, a year after they had left New York together bound for Cape Gris-Nez, Ederle was only too happy to chat. "Thank God that's over," she said of the end of her partnership with Malone. She told Pegler that she was "resting" for the moment, enjoying driving through New York in her red roadster without being mobbed by hordes of screaming fans. She hadn't been swimming, proper swimming as opposed to a dip in a tank, for three months. She had a small part in a film, playing a swimming instructor with Bebe Daniels as the lead, but apart from that and a couple of vaudeville engagements later in the summer, things were pretty quiet.

Pegler had been curious to know how much she had earned since swimming the Channel, so together they worked it out on a scrap of paper. The total amount was $64,000; that was the easy part. Then they deducted Malone's cut, her father's, the cost of the glass tank, and all the other expenses, until they were left with Trudy's net earnings: $19,793. "The showmen of the sport business all feel sorry for Trudy as the victim of an awful job of mismanagement," Pegler wrote a while later, anxious to tell America how their heroine had been exploited. "The girl might have had a huge fortune . . . but for the officiousness of the people she thought were her best friends, this girl has had worse luck than any other performer in the athletic department of the great American show business. She discounted about a quarter of a million dollars' worth of ballyhoo for twenty thousand dollars, and the chance will never come again."

But Pegler's noble words fell on deaf American ears. His article appeared in the same June week that Charles Lindbergh arrived back in New York, having left a month earlier in the

October 1953, Westbrook Pegler presented Gertrude Ederle with a
chart of her swim drawn by his wife and Ederle's companion,
Julia Harpman

Spirit of St. Louis on the first solo, non-stop flight across the
Atlantic. When Lindbergh stepped off the ship that brought him
back to New York, Grover Whalen was there to meet him and
escort him up Fifth Avenue for the official welcome by Mayor
Walker, as thousands of tons of ticker tape descended from the
skies he had so recently conquered. Two days later, on June 15,
tucked away on page twenty-eight of *Variety*, there was a small
story about Lindbergh's homecoming.

Hundreds of thousands of people were banked on Fifth Avenue and up and down all the cross streets anywhere near it. They still had hours to wait. Somewhere in the Forties someone scowled at a stout, husky girl, trying to squeeze through to a better place of vantage. She seemed surprisingly strong. That was what attracted those around her. Then someone who had a camera eye looked again, and closer. "Hey, Miss, aren't you . . . aren't you the girl that . . .?" "Yes," she panted. "I'm Gertrude Ederle. Please help me get through."

Epilogue

IN THE SPRING OF 1936 Westbrook Pegler went to Europe on assignment. Coming up from Paris to Boulogne to catch the Channel ferry, he decided to break his journey and spend an afternoon revisiting Cape Gris-Nez. He hired an automobile and drove along the winding, potholed lanes that hadn't seen a workman in the ten years since he'd last made the trek.

The summer season was still a few weeks off, so the Hôtel du Phare was deserted except for one or two hardy souls who had come for a weekend's hiking. Pegler found Madame Blondiau in the kitchen shaking up some omelets for a wedding party in the neighbouring village later that day. Her husband, Amédée, was out walking their dogs, but when he returned the three of them retired to the bar. Pegler gave a hoot of nostalgic joy when he saw the old artesian beer pump was still there. So was the sign propped up against the till: LET CONSCIENCE BE YOUR GUIDE. The walls were decorated with some of Art Sorenson's photographs, now yellow and faded, from that unforgettable summer a decade earlier. As Monsieur Blondiau filled three glasses with beer, he began to bemoan the fact that Channel swimmers rarely stayed at his establishment anymore. The romance was gone, and with it the hefty hotel bills that had made him one of the wealthiest men on the Cape. In the last ten years only nine people had swum the Channel, five of them women, and most had been British, so they trained in Dover and only stayed in Gris-Nez long enough to change into their bathing suit. Not even Helmy came anymore, noted Blondiau; it was three years since he'd last checked in at the Phare.

Pegler asked the Blondiaus for news of the people he remembered from 1926. Bill Burgess still came every summer, although the golf course he had talked of building at the Cape had never come to fruition, and Jabez Wolffe and Billy Kellingley were still earning a living as Channel coaches. Jack Wiedman was long dead – nine years – but Joe Costa, the tall-story-telling captain of the *Alsace*, had died only a few months earlier, and the stories in Boulogne were that he had gone to his grave without a dime to his name.

And the Americans, asked Blondiau, how are they? Pegler's wife, Julia Harpman, was fine, although she no longer worked as a journalist, preferring the role of his personal secretary. Pegler hadn't bumped into Arthur Sorenson for a while, although his photos had been frequently in the papers when Bruno Hauptmann was tried for the murder of Charles Lindbergh's baby. Pop Ederle, Pegler believed, still ran his butcher shop on Amsterdam Avenue but now lived in a bigger house. Margaret was OK, too. In fact, everyone was fine, said Pegler, except Trudy. Life hadn't been kind to her in the last ten years.

By flying across the Atlantic, Charles Lindbergh had turned Ederle into a twenty-year-old relic. Almost overnight Channel swimming lost its glamour. It was prosaic, old-fashioned, even, compared with the thrill of what mankind might achieve in tandem with a machine. "I think it inane to swim across the Channel when there are ships and aeroplanes to take you across," said Winifred Sackville Stoner, founder of the League for Fostering Genius, in October 1927. She, like an increasing number of her sex, believed women should strive for intellectual parity, not sporting equality. As interest in Ederle receded, so did the bookings, although she still traipsed around America now and again, shivering in her glass tank, and feeling more and more like a circus act.

In 1928 Ederle's hearing started to deteriorate as rapidly as her nerves, but she let herself be talked into competing in an all-female international swim in Toronto that August, her first race since the Channel triumph. Ederle came in sixth in the ten-mile swim, nearly an hour behind the winner. Not long after, she suffered a total nervous breakdown. She cancelled a tour to Europe that she was about to undertake and retreated into the bosom of her family, and her boyfriend, "a six-foot athletic type", with whom she had fallen in love. For several months, America heard nothing of Ederle.

Then a headline appeared in New York's *Daily News* on March 21, 1929: TRAFFIC WARRANT TO TEST MISS TRUDIE'S CRAWL STROKE, with an accompanying story explaining that a warrant had been issued for her arrest after her failure to appear in court to answer a charge of speeding in February. The publicity brought Ederle to court, as it did several dozen New Yorkers, all curious to see what punishment she would receive from Magistrate Abraham Rosenbluth. What ensued, said the *Daily News* reporter, would have been farcical, had it not been so pitiful. Ederle couldn't hear what Magistrate Rosenbluth was saying; it reached the point where he "shouted in her ear to make her understand that he had suspended sentence against her after she pleaded guilty". Her deafness, Ederle explained, was the reason she was speeding in the first place; she had been late for an appointment with her specialist, who had been treating her for several months. Outside the court, on a beautiful sunny March day, Ederle tried to make light of the incident. "The worse part of it," she joked to reporters, "is that I can't hear the nice things my best beau says to me — unless he shouts it, so we have absolutely no privacy."

Later in the year Ederle was joking about her deafness again, this time to her boyfriend as they discussed the possibility of marriage. "With my poor hearing it might be hard on a man," she chided him. She'd expected a reassuring hug in return, "but instead he said 'I guess you're right, it would be hard on a man' " and left.

Ederle was devastated by the abandonment and became even more withdrawn. Her misery was complete when the New York Board of Education refused to allow her to become a swimming teacher, even though she had passed the exams; it didn't think she would be able to hear if a person was in distress. She got a job earning fifty dollars a week as a hostess and instructor at Rye Playland Baths in Westchester County, the owners trading on the last vestiges of her celebrity.

Nearly four years to the day after she'd swum the Channel, Ederle was visited by a reporter from the Associated Press who wanted to write an anniversary piece. Four years of setbacks had stripped Ederle of what Julia Harpman had once called her "strong, boisterous, nerveless" character. Now she was morose and apathetic, even to the point of spiritless. The reporter found that already her voice had begun to take on the flat quality of a deaf person as she described her life. She'd earned about $150,000 from all her vaudeville and personal appearances – including the $14,000 she received for a small part in a Hollywood film in 1927, which she'd donated to the Women's Swimming Association as a thank-you for all the support it had given her. Of that amount, she told the reporter, she'd "got less than $50,000," and a fair percentage of that had gone on medical bills for her hearing. Her father still ran his butcher shop, but he had moved the family into a house in the Bronx.

Her outstanding recollection from the summer of 1926 was of everyone standing on the deck of the *Alsace* singing her favorite song, "Let Me Call You Sweetheart." On the odd occasion she went dancing with her sisters or friends, she could just about hear the tune if the band played it. The trouble was that then the happy memories would come flooding back, and she'd burst into tears on the dance floor.

The reporter asked Ederle what she wanted to do with the rest of her life; she was still only twenty-three, after all. "What I'd like would be for someone to build a pool and maybe name it after me and let me be head instructor there. But I guess it would be pretty hard to get any backing now."

But surely, the reporter persisted, it must make you proud to know you were the first woman to swim the Channel, and that your record still stands. Ederle shook her head. "I'm not sorry I did it. Only, if I'd known how it was going to be, that I'd lose my hearing, I don't think I'd have done it. It wasn't worth while."

For the next few years Ederle's humdrum life at the Rye Playlands continued. From time to time, a sportswriter dredged his memory to bring her up in some article, but for the most part the world left her alone. Then on December 12, 1933, Ederle went to visit some friends at the Justine Apartments in Hempstead, Long Island. As she was leaving, she slipped on a loose tile on the second-floor stairway and tumbled down fifteen steps. She picked herself up, dusted herself down, and walked home to her own nearby apartment. Two days later the pain in her back was so great Ederle couldn't get out of bed. She slept on the floor for a week, hoping that might fix the problem, but when it didn't she went to the doctor. He prescribed a sacro-iliac strap, but two months later the pain was as bad as ever. When she went for a second opinion, it was discovered that everything from the fifth vertebra down was pressing against the sciatic nerve. She was encased in a cast, and a dozen specialists said the chances of her ever swimming again were virtually nil.

345

It was a wretched note on which to leave Cape Gris-Nez, Pegler admitted to Monsieur and Madame Blondiau, but he had a ferry to catch. Before he left the hotel Pegler asked where they had finally erected Ederle's statue, the one that the good folk of Kingsdown and Gris-Nez had been bickering over in the days and weeks after the swim. Blondiau shook his head. There wasn't one. It had all been just talk.

A few hours later, as Pegler headed toward England, he ruminated on his return to Cape Gris-Nez. "The old Channel lay placid as a table top as the ferry started off for Folkestone in the dusk," he wrote. "Half-way to England we were still getting flashes from the old lighthouse above the beach where she walked boldly into the surf, and smacked the Channel firmly on the chin."

Four years later the German army occupied Cape Gris-Nez and commandeered the Hôtels du Phare and Sirène. The beach where Ederle had set out for England-and Lillian Cannon had played golf – was strewn with mines, and on the cliffs above, a battery of huge naval cannons was installed, ready to support the invasion of England when it came. The Germans also brought a railway gun to Cape Gris-Nez, with a seventy-foot barrel, which rained down shells on Dover in the summer of 1940. It wasn't until the end of September 1944 that the Canadian army ousted the Germans from the Cape and liberated the small village and its two hotels.

The year before, Jabez Wolffe had died in his sixty-seventh year from natural causes. The Englishwoman Sunny Lowry, who was coached by Wolffe on her three attempts to swim the Channel – the last of which, in 1933, was successful – says in all the time she knew him, Wolffe never once mentioned the incident with Gertrude Ederle in 1925. In his later years he patented a balm which was sold in pharmacies at five shillings a bottle and which was advertised in newspapers as: "Jabez Wolffe's Channel Embrocation – indispensable to all sufferers from Rheumatism, Sciatica, Lumbago, Muscular Sprains etc".

In July 1946 Clarabelle Barrett died at her home on Young Avenue, Pelham, after a short illness at the age of fifty-four. The newspapers that carried her obituary got her age right this time, perhaps because her mother was no longer around to knock off a few years here and there, but the *New York Times* and the New Rochelle *Standard-Star* misspelled her name "Clarebelle". She would have probably grinned at the mistake. Barrett left a husband, Price Shaver, a New York Central Railroad employee whom she had married a few years earlier, but there were no ambitions left unfulfilled. The operatic career to which she had aspired had not been glittering, but in June 1940 Barrett realised the dream that had kept her going for nearly twenty-two hours in the English Channel fourteen years earlier: she performed as a soloist in the Malone Monthly Musicale at the Carnegie Chamber Music Hall in New York City.

Her death was front-page news in New Rochelle's *Standard-Star*, which gave a long account of her valiant struggle in the foggy waters of the Channel twenty years earlier. What would have pleased Clarabelle even more, perhaps, was its description of her as a "possessor of a fine, deep contralto voice."

Jimmy Walker, the mayor of New York from 1926 to 1932, endured a spectacular fall from grace. He fled the United States in 1932 to escape likely criminal charges arising from corruption while in office, and the following year he married a chorus girl in Cannes, France. They returned home in 1935, with Walker ill and penniless, and for a while raised chickens in Northport. Walker divorced his chorus girl in 1941 and died in 1946.

Grover Whalen had no such misfortune and died in 1962 at the age of seventy-five. By then he was known throughout New York as "Grover the Greeter", having continued to welcome the great and the good to the city until the 1950s. In an interview in 1957, Whalen told the *New York Times*, "Over the last forty years, I can't recall anyone in sports who matched Gertrude Ederle's tremendous impact on this city."

Dudley Field Malone died in October 1950, having become for the American press a figure of fun. He had divorced and remarried in 1930 — a music student twenty-three years his junior — and gained a reputation as a bon vivant who liked to be seen in only the best places drinking only the finest liquor. But as the *Chicago Tribune* noted in its obituary, "His high spending days ended when he filed as a bankrupt in 1935, listing liabilities of $261,370 and assets of $62,500, although one of his creditors filed charges in a federal court in 1937 that Malone had 'knowingly and fraudulently concealed' assets." Malone moved to the West Coast in the late 1930s and in 1943 played the part of Winston Churchill in the film *Mission to Moscow*, a movie that President Roosevelt wanted made because it cast Stalin's Russia in a favourable light.

A number of other protagonists from that summer also died in the 1950s, among them Walter Lissberger (in 1951), the man who had financed Mille Gade's attempt, and Arch Selwyn, a man of similar business acumen to Lissberger, who helped Gade reap the reward she deserved from her swim. Selwyn died in 1959, the same year as Arthur Sorenson, who, before suffering a fatal heart attack at the age of sixty-five, had spent several years with the publicity department of the National Broadcasting Company. Their passing came four years after that of Captain Learmont, the gruff Scot who had piloted Clarabelle Barrett to within sight of the French coast, and two years after the death of Bill Burgess in 1957.

Burgess had continued to train swimmers for a few years after Ederle's triumph, and in 1928 he finally got Ishak Helmy across the Channel. He spent the last years of his life living just outside Paris and was eighty-five at the time of his death. In the 1960s

Paul Gallico, who had been a sportswriter for the *Daily News* in 1926 and a friend of the Peglers, wrote about America's sports stars of the 1920s in a book called *Golden People*. In describing Ederle's conquest of the Channel, Gallico was unable to decide if Burgess had ordered her out of the water for the sake of "sheer humanity" or "obstruction". Although it is impossible to know for sure, it seems unlikely that Burgess would have tried to sabotage Ederle's swim. Why would he? He wasn't a particularly patriotic man – he had moved to France as a young man – and it wouldn't have mattered to him if the first woman across the Channel was American, English or French.

But he did want the cachet of being the coach who guided that woman across, especially as Jack Wiedman was in charge of Lillian Cannon. And, of course, he hoped to receive a fat bonus from Ederle if she was successful. If anything, Burgess was overprotective of Ederle because he feared that if she suffered unnecessarily on her first attempt, she might not be able to have a second crack that summer – and that would mean no bonus. The fact that Ederle refused to give Burgess a bonus is a delicious irony, although perhaps Burgess had the last laugh. Ederle never got her statue, but at the entrance to the Sheffield Road swimming pool in Rotherham, in the north of England, there is a handsome bust of local lad Bill Burgess. A tradition has sprung up among visitors to the pool that if you give Burgess's nose a rub as you pass by, it will bring you a bit of luck in the water.

Burgess's nemesis, Julia Harpman, the person who never forgave him for his double-cross, quit journalism in the late 1920s and devoted herself to her husband's flourishing career. She accompanied Westbrook Pegler on his many trips around the United States and all over the world, acting as his secretary and adviser. Increasingly, however, she suffered from ill health, although she felt strong enough to travel with Pegler to Europe in the fall of 1955. It was during this trip, as they visited Rome, that she died of a heart attack at the age of sixty. Harpman's other enemy from the summer of 1926, Minott Saunders of the United Press, had died in 1947 at the age of fifty-seven.

By the time of his wife's death, Westbrook Pegler was one of America's most widely read writers, having won the Pulitzer Prize (the first columnist to do so) in 1941 for exposing racketeering in Hollywood labour unions. The older he got, the more invective and controversial Pegler became. He loathed Franklin D. Roosevelt, nicknaming him "Moosejaw" or when he was feeling particularly cantankerous, the "feeble-minded Fuehrer". The president's wife he referred to as "La Boca Grande" (the big mouth), while Roosevelt's successor, Harry Truman, was a "thin-lipped hater" and Dwight Eisenhower, "wormy".

In the 1950s he was sued for libel by his former friend and fellow writer Quentin Reynolds, after Pegler had described him in print as a coward and a war profiteer. The action cost Pegler $175, 000 and was later turned into a Broadway play called *A Case of Libel*. Just about the only person spared the Pegler vitriol was Gertrude Ederle, whom he continued to admire and respect. "She was heroic in the true sense of the word," he wrote in an article in 1949, before going on to list a raft of people in American public life who weren't. Pegler married twice more after the death of Julia, but he never had any children, and died of stomach cancer in 1969.

Mille Gade was the only one of the four American swimmers who returned to the English Channel. In 1927 she arrived in Dover with her husband and two children – having first toured Denmark to great acclaim – promising to become the first woman to swim from England to France. But despite the best efforts of Harry Pearson and Billy Kellingley, Gade quit after ten hours in the water and never again took on the Channel. The year between her success and her failure had been good to Gade – thanks to the nous of Arch Selwyn and her own smiling geniality – and even if she had become the first woman to swim the Channel in both directions, it probably wouldn't have caused much excitement in Europe or America.

The next time Gade was in the news was June 1928, when she and four other prominent American swimmers – including Ethelda Bleibtrey, the woman arrested in 1919 for rolling down her stockings on Manhattan Beach – took a midnight swim in the Central Park reservoir as part of a stunt conceived by the *Daily News*. The paper wanted the authorities to allow the reservoir to be used for public swimming, and so it paid the five a small amount of money to go for a midnight swim. When they were seen and arrested by a policeman (perhaps it was more than just a coincidence that he happened to be on the scene so quickly!), the *Daily News* gave the story extensive coverage the next day. Twenty-four hours later it launched its campaign to turn the reservoir into a public pool, enlisting the help of various swimming organisations. By the time Gade and her four accomplices appeared in court a week later, even Magistrate Louis Brodsky was on their side, passing a suspended sentence and declaring that "that part of Central Park has been neglected too long . . . the reservoir should be serving the public good".

Thereafter Gade slipped out of the public eye when she and her family moved to Suffern in rural New York. She was a judge at local swim meets and was very active in the local community as a volunteer. An article about her appeared in the *New York Times* in 1941, when she awarded medals to the underprivileged and crippled children of the city's rotary club for their efforts in the swimming classes.

Clem Corson died in 1960 and his wife in Croton-on-Hudson, New York, in 1982, at the age of eighty-five. Little Sonny inherited his mother's love of water and swam competitively in his youth. After the Second World War, he served for thirty-three years as a pilot in New York Harbour and ended his career as captain of the Sandy Hook Pilots of New York. He died in July 2005 in his eighty-third year. His little sis, Marjorie, was alive and well at the time of writing this in 2007.

She and her brother got the decent education for which their mother had striven. "I went to college and became a chemist," says Marjorie, "and even now I still work as a volunteer in museums, something I got from my mother who had a passion for volunteer work."

During the idyllic childhood in the country – "my brother and I loved it, building lean-tos and exploring all the woods" – Marjorie's mother occasionally told her children stories of her Channel swim, but she never gave the impression it was the defining act of her life. "My mother was very driven in everything she did," recalls Marjorie. "When she had an idea, then she made things happen. But she could get frustrated if things didn't go well. She liked to do well!"

Intriguingly, the story that sticks in Marjorie's mind about her mother's Channel swim was told her by her father. Clem Corson had always been very proud of the fact that his wife's swim was an "open water" swim, accomplished with a motor boat and not a tug. He emphasised the point on several occasions both in Dover and on their return to New York, sometimes with a passion that bordered on the ungracious. But there was a reason, he once told his daughter, for his fervour. Mille Gade had intended to hire a tug in England, but there were none available, nor were there any in France. Patterson's newspaper syndicate had bought up every tug for the summer in a calculated attempt to wreck Gade's (and presumably every other) attempt to swim the Channel, though it had been too late to prevent Cannon from hiring *La Morinie*.

Two of Gade's friends from that summer failed to emulate her success. Louis Timson got nowhere near swimming the Channel during his September bid and never tried again. He died in 1980 at the age of ninety. Frank Perks didn't give up on the Channel, but despite two further summers in Dover, in 1927 and 1928, his dream was never realised.

Mercedes Gleitze became the first Englishwoman to swim the Channel when she crossed from France to England in 1927 in fifteen hours and fifteen minutes. By then, however, the appeal of Channel swimming had ebbed in Britain as it had in America, and she received scant acclaim. *The Times* of London gave Gleitze half a column and noted dryly that her success had come only after seven previous failures. A feature of Gleitze's swim was that it was the first to be authenticated by the Channel Swimming Association, the body established in 1927 – in response to the criticism levelled at Ederle the previous year-to regulate all future Channel attempts.

With the Channel defeated, Gleitze sought fresh challenges, and in 1928 she became the first person to swim the Straits of Gibraltar. She retired from swimming in 1932 with many records to her name and used the money she had earned to found the Mercedes Gleitze Home for the Destitute, a block of eight apartments in central England. With the outbreak of the Second World War, many of her apartments were used to house refugees from mainland Europe. In November 1940 they were destroyed in a German air raid, and before the war had ended, news reached Gleitze that her mother had been killed by Allied bombs in Germany. Gleitze died in London in 1980 at the age of eighty, living as a recluse for the last few years and never sharing her swimming memories with her children.

Ishak Helmy finally swam the Channel in 1928, his seventh attempt, in twenty-three hours and forty minutes. Upon landing at Dover, Helmy immediately sat down on the beach and ordered a bottle of champagne so he could toast himself. Even after his success – which turned him into a national hero in Egypt – Helmy kept returning to the Channel for the next few years, a lost soul trying to recapture the carefreeness of the 1920s. His last visit was in 1975, when he attended a party at Dover Castle to mark the centenary of Captain Webb's inaugural crossing, the only representative from the swimmers of 1926.

No one heard anything of Lillian Cannon for eighteen months after her return from Europe. If she felt humiliated by her efforts, others were equally deserving of scorn. The *Baltimore Post* had turned a competent local swimmer into a potential Channel champion without ever stopping to ask if she was as good as it was making her out to be. The reality was that Cannon, as a swimmer, wasn't in the same class as Ederle, and when she found herself at Cape Gris-Nez, the focus of so much attention in America and Europe, she must have realised she was out of her depth, metaphorically and literally. But instead of letting it worry her, Cannon decided to enjoy herself – it was, after all, her first time out of America – and soak up French culture. Within a short time she had recovered from the Channel experience and returned to the more docile waters of Chesapeake Bay. In early 1928 she was appointed swimming coach of the Jewish Community Centre in Washington, and that summer she won a race across the Bay, in the process reclaiming the record for the fastest time for a woman. Cannon's husband, Eddie Day, meanwhile, had enlisted in the US Air Force, and over the next thirty years he rose through the ranks to become a brigadier general. He died in 1989 at the age of eighty-five, and Lillian died a year later in her eighty-seventh year.

The humiliation Lillian Cannon endured in 1926, when she returned a fallen idol to Baltimore, was nothing compared to that which Gertrude Ederle faced on January 28, 1937. Three years after her fall in Hempstead, Ederle arrived at a courthouse in Mineola, Long Island, to pursue a claim for negligence against the owners of the Justine Apartments. "The spotlight of forgotten fame played today on a plump, blue-eyed woman in a raccoon coat," wrote a *Washington Post* correspondent, one of a dozen reporters drawn to New York's own Greek tragedy, "as she limped to the witness stand with the aid of a heavy cane and said: 'I am Gertrude Ederle.' Necks craned in a hushed courtroom as the famous 'Queen of the Waves', who has been the unluckiest woman in the world since her historic battle across the English Channel 11 years ago, told simply why she wanted $50,000 because of a fall in an apartment house."

Ederle described to the judge how she had spent over two years as an invalid, unable even to walk without the aid of her heavy cane. The only time she left the house was to visit the hospital to have her spine drained of fluid. Justice Thomas Cuff asked Ederle to explain that procedure, but as she began to speak she broke down and wept. The judge ordered a recess so the witness could compose herself. When she returned to the witness stand, Ederle described in a meek, faltering voice how she had to lie like a baby on her side, with her knees drawn up to her chest, as the fluid was sucked from her spine with a syringe.

The case dragged on for a year until an out-of-court settlement was eventually reached. In the meantime, something had changed in Ederle's character. In the months after her fall, she had nearly lost the will to carry on; there was nothing left for which to strive. The specialists said she might walk again without the use of a cane, if she was lucky, but swimming was out of the question. Then one day Ederle woke up and decided to prove them wrong. She started to set herself goals. "It was torture to take steps, but I did it," she said. "After many months I was able to walk a block, then two, then three." The reporter who knocked on the door of Ederle's Queens apartment on August 5, 1937, wanted an interview with "poor old Trudy", but instead he found himself confronted by a steely-eyed woman who agreed to talk but warned, "I don't want any sob stories written about me." Two years later, on August 6, 1939, Gertrude Ederle swam the length of a swimming pool at the New York World's Fair. Even before she was halfway across the placid turquoise water of Billy Rose's Aquacade pool, the audience of ten thousand were on their feet, clapping and cheering. Ederle hauled herself out, and someone passed her a towel. She lifted up her goggles, the same ones she had worn thirteen years earlier, and dabbed away the tears with the towel. Later, when she had put in her hearing aid, she told reporters that learning to swim again had been "something like swimming the Channel – only harder". What impressed the reporters most was Ederle's demeanour. There was no bitterness, no cynicism, despite everything that had befallen her. If anything, she seemed a more contented person now than the one who had swum the Channel. "I'd be stupid if I hadn't realised that people can't stand for ever on street corners playing brass bands," she said, laughing, when someone asked if she missed being famous. And anyway, Ederle said, almost as an afterthought, "I wonder why Broadway doesn't bring out its band and throw tickertape on some of those real heroes who overcome great physical handicaps – paralysis and sickness and things like that."

In 2001 a journalist from the *New York Times* did what countless other reporters had done since Gertrude Ederle swam the English Channel, and went in search of the "Queen of the Waves", whose reign had lasted until 1950, when another woman finally beat her record. He found her, shrunken and shrivelled, in a New Jersey nursing home, her spindly legs wrapped under a red blanket. She happily answered the reporter's questions, smiling as she recalled how someone on the boat – her trainer, perhaps, whatever his name had been – had told her to quit because of the rough water, and she always answered, "What For?" The thing with her trainer, added Ederle, was that he, like the rest of them, didn't think a woman could swim the Channel. "I wanted

August 1951, twenty-five years later, Gertrude Ederle looks over the scrapbooks of clippings that honour her incredible achievement

to prove it could be done. It took a Yankee to show them how."

There was no one left alive now from that summer of 1926. Ederle had outlived them all. Her parents were dead by the early 1950s, and Margaret had died in 1999. "I miss her so much," whispered Ederle in her feathery voice. "I adored Meg." Ederle passed her days in the nursing home, watching television and perhaps, from time to time, reflecting on a life that had peaked three-quarters of a century earlier, at least if the yardstick by which a life is measured is the quantity of newspaper headlines generated.

In the sixty-odd years since Ederle had swum at the World's Fair in New York, her name had appeared in print usually only on August 6, and then it was a cold-hearted chronicle of her plight: a deaf spinster, living with two other old maids in a Queens apartment, whose only job was to teach deaf children to swim. What a tragic downfall, was the tone, for a girl who for a few mad weeks had been the most famous woman in the world. But in Ederle's eyes, her misfortune had been her enrichment. What she lacked in material wealth, she made up for in spiritual strength. It had taken a while for the realisation to dawn, she had said in an interview in 1960, but "slowly I came to know that the depth of our heartbreaks determines the depth of our faith. God gives us everything to conquer the big and little hurts of life".

Gertrude Ederle died on November 30, 2003, at the age of ninety-seven, and for the first time in seventy-seven years her name flashed around the world. Some newspapers, such as *The Times*, carried lengthy obituaries and printed grainy black-and-white photographs. Others mentioned her passing in a few brief lines. The *New York Daily News* ran a 350-word piece, describing her swim as a "daredevil feat" and boasting that it was the paper that had given Ederle a shiny red roadster. There was no mention of all the misery and pain she had suffered, nor of the great faith that had sustained her throughout. The article finished by recalling what Ederle had said to a reporter who came calling one warm August day in the 1950s hoping for a sob story. "I have no complaints. I am comfortable and satisfied. I am not a person who reaches for the moon as long as I have the stars."

Acknowledgements

Thanks first to my agent, Gail Fortune, who recognised instantly what a good story *The Great Swim* was, and kept faith with it even when countless publishers rejected it for being "just a book about swimming". Fortunately, Michele Lee Amundsen and George Gibson at Walker Books shared Gail's foresight, and I'm grateful for their enthusiasm and encouragement. All three then allowed me to crack on and turn the story into a book without interference. Thank you, and I also thank Liz Peters at Walker for her diligent editorial efforts.

Sandy Vercruyssen offered some pithy advice early on when I was writing the synopsis for potential publishers. It was good advice, too, as her advice usually was during six good years. Go well, sweetheart.

Doloranda Pember, the daughter of Mercedes Gleitze, provided me with many documents, notes and photos about her mother and her myriad swimming achievements, for which I am thankful. Similarly, Mille Gade's daughter and granddaughter – Marjorie and Susan Andreen, respectively – were patience personified in answering all my questions, and I hope they find this book a fitting tribute to brave and bold Mille.

Sunny Lowry fielded many questions about Jabez Wolffe, more than seventy years after he had coached her across the Channel. A remarkable memory and a remarkable lady.

In New York I would like to thank all the staff of the New York Public Library for their assistance during my research, and for showing a slow-witted Englishman how to work the microfilm copier. The day I spent at the New Rochelle Public Library was also made easier by the helpfulness of the staff.

Not for the first time in my career, I am in debt to the staff at the British Library's National Newspaper Library in London for their speed and efficiency, while Mark Frost at the Dover Museum not only unearthed many fascinating documents and photographs but was also a mine of information on all things Dover.

Thanks to Alison and Michael Reid at the Channel Swimming Association, and I tip my hat especially to Julie Bradshaw, the secretary of the association, and one of *the* great Channel swimmers, who was kind enough to share some of her experiences with me.

Peter and Ellis Lohmann in Copenhagen generously gave of their time to translate several Danish newspaper articles into English, for which I am very grateful, as did Damon Allen with the German reports.

I must say thanks to the owners of La Sirène, the seafood restaurant that now stands on the site of the old hotel at Cape Gris-Nez. They might not have been able to tell me anything about the history of the place, but the seafood was excellent and the views spectacular.

Tom and Julie Tudor gave me use of the "executive suite" during my research trips to London and fed me royally at the same time. Who needs hotels? Tom Schoff and Jenny Chammas provided me with hospitality and support while I was in New York, which made the research feel less painstaking. Here's to rainy Wednesday evenings in the Village drinking beer.

Finally, for my wee daughter, Margot. Take a sprinkling of Ederle's determination, a soupçon of Barrett's honesty, a flavouring of Gade's courage and a dash of Cannon's joie de vivre — and you'll go far in life, my girl!

Notes

PROLOGUE

9   "Five shillings' worth of nourishment gone to Neptune": *Los Angeles Times*, August 19, 1925.

10   "Too fast! Too fast! It's not a 1500-metre race!": *New York Times*, August 19, 1925.

11   "I am sorry she has not followed stricter training but her ideas have frequently been opposed to mine": *Baltimore Sun*, August 18, 1925.

12   "There's too much": ibid

12   "I just couldn't do it": ibid, August 19, 1925.

CHAPTER ONE

14   THE VILLA OF CROSS-CHANNEL SWIMMING: The sign was first mentioned in the *Iowa City Press* on December 15, 1924, in an article that described Burgess's ten-room wooden house in Cape Gris-Nez and the fact that four of the rooms had been leased for the following summer by the Anglo-Argentine swimmer Lillian Harrison and her entourage. She failed to swim the Channel in 1925 under the guidance of Burgess.

15   The improvements were all upstairs on the first floor: the descriptions of the Hôtel du Phare are taken primarily from articles by Gertrude Ederle in the *Daily News* on June 11, 1926, Julia Harpman in the *Boston Post* on July 20, 1926, and a reminiscence by Westbrook Pegler in the *Syracuse Herald* on March 25, 1936. Other details concerning the Cape were gleaned from snippets contained in newspapers of the time, or from the author's own visit to Cape Gris-Nez in July 2006. The village, one sensed, had changed little in eighty years.

CHAPTER TWO

18   "Sure, I'll make it": *Baltimore Post*, August 20, 1925. The *Post* and the *Baltimore Sun* gave extensive coverage to Cannon's swim.

20   "It's tough going": *Baltimore Sun*, August 21, 1925.

20   "At that time": New Rochelle *Standard-Star*, May 19, 1926.

21   "There is just a chance": *Standard-Star*, May 21, 1926.

22   "Shucks": Ibid., May 18, 1926.

24   "He was selected": *Baltimore Post*, May 12, 1926.

27   "Come on, Drake, come on!": *World*, May 14, 1926.

28   Over the hubbub: The *Baltimore Sun*, June 15, 1926, carried Ederle's *Chicago Tribune-Daily News* column in which she talked of the surprise sprung on board the liner.

CHAPTER THREE

31   Lack of confidence: The details on Gade's early life were found in the Danish newspaper *Berlingske Tidende* in its edition of August 29, 1926, and the website www.royalden mark.us.

31   The manager sniggered: *Sheboygan Press*, October 30, 1926.

32   "Help the lady out": *Standard-Star*, September 8, 1926.

34   "Whoever you are": *World*, August 29, 1926.

36   Lissberger identified with Gade: several newspapers mentioned Lissberger's role in sponsoring Gade, but the most extensive account was in the *Hartford Courant*, September 12, 1926.

CHAPTER FOUR

38   "because you are a mother": *World*, August 31, 1926.

38   "revive the good old-fashioned dances like the waltz": *New York Times*, September 20, 1925.

39   In Jamestown, North Dakota: *Baltimore Post*, September 7, 1925.

39   "Any girl I catch smoking": *Duke University Chronicle*, December 17, 1924.

39   "They didn't show our knees": *Baltimore Post*, May 19, 1926.

CHAPTER FIVE

50   that had inspired him during his war service: Patterson served first as a second lieutenant and then a captain, taking part in five major engagements and being gassed and slightly wounded. In London he paid a courtesy call to a family friend, Lord Northcliffe, the man who had founded Britain's first tabloid, the *Daily Mirror*, a few years earlier. Northcliffe suggested to Patterson that the time might be ripe for launch ing the first American tabloid. This information was con tained in Patterson's obituary, published in the *New York Times*, May 27, 1946.

50   Patterson knew this because he often dressed: George

Douglas, The Golden Age of the Newspaper (Westport, CT:GreenwoodPress, 1999).

53   "screaming woman running down the street": Westbrook Pegler's obituary in the *New York Times*, June 25, 1969.
"With a 'Pullman-car' name": *Los Angeles Times*, June 25, 1969.

55   He owned a butcher shopon Amsterdam Avenue: Westbrook Pegler wrote a lengthy description of Pop Ederle in the mag azine *Liberty*, which appeared on July 24, 1926. Although they did dine together on this and every night aboard the ship, I have speculated that the conversation took place in the dining room.

56   "I merely am not acquainted": Gertrude Ederle's column in the *Daily News*, June 4, 1926.

56   Pegler had scarcely had a chance: during the summer of 1926 Westbrook Pegler drew a discreet veil over Ederle's hearing problem, and it was only afterwards that he revealed, sympa thetically, the extent of her deafness.

CHAPTER SIX

63   "Come along, girl": The *Baltimore Post* pretended that Burgess was still coaching Cannon two weeks after the Ederle row and on June 23 published an article alongside an old photo of Burgess and Cannon (yes, in her bathing suit!) drinking hot chocolate.

64   "I spend hours gazing": Lillian Cannon in the *Baltimore Post*, June 15, 1926.

65   "not quite kissing friends": Westbrook Pegler in the *Atlanta Constitution*, July 5, 1926.

65   She dangled a stained napkin: Julia Harpman in the *Boston Post*, July 20, 1926.

65   "brilliant crawl stroke": *Baltimore Post*, June 30, 1926.

66   Ederle solved the dilemma: the *Standard-Star* published the photograph on June 23 with the caption "Two Channel Swimmers and Their Trainer".

68   Cannon was forced to flee: Neither Cannon nor Ederle revealed whether Cannon checked out of the Hôtel du Phare of her own accord, or whether pressure was exerted by the Ederle camp.

68   With the connivance: Gertrude Ederle in her *Daily News* column, July 3, 1926.

69 Her coach and one or two concerned members: Louis de Breda Handley tells this story in the essay he wrote on swimming in the 1920s for the book *Sports Golden Age*, edited by Allison Danzig and Peter Brandwein (New York: Harper and Bros., 1948).

69 There they loaded up the car: Gertrude Ederle's column written on June 17 and published in the *Daily News*, June 18, 1926.

CHAPTER SEVEN

70 "Unquestionably Miss Ederle": *New York Times*, June 7, 1926.

72 With the war over, Barrett trained: Nathan Barrett's obituary which appeared in New Rochelle's *Evening Standard* on October 17, 1919.

73 One of Nathan senior's few remaining pleasures: Clarabelle Barrett described her father's unusual instruction methods in an interview with the *Dover Standard* on August 5, 1926.

74 Galligan, like Barrett, was a member: Louis de Breda Handley gives a good account of the formation of the WSA in *Sports Golden Age*, edited by Danzig and Brandwein.

75 "What is the best way to acquire": The question-and-answer session was in the February 1923 edition of the Women's Swimming Association News.

76 In the report of Barrett's funeral: New Rochelle's *Standard-Star*, October 21, 1919.

76 In need of money: The *World*, August 3, 1926, and the *New York Telegram*, August 2, 1926, both described Barrett's reasons for becoming a teacher.

77 "Miss Barrett is of superb physique": *Standard-Star*, May 28, 1926.

78 Twenty of Barrett's friends: *Atlanta Constitution*, September 7, 1926.

CHAPTER EIGHT

81 From Bournemouth: in her *Baltimore Post* column of June 29, Cannon said the dogs had now been returned to America and also gave details of the contents of some of the letters she had received from British dog lovers.

81 "had spread over several": *Baltimore Post*, June 19, 1926.

82 Cannon joined in the insolent fun: *Standard-Star*, June 23, 1926.

82 "He said the [American] flag": *Baltimore Sun*, June 15, 1926.

82   It had been an embarrassing disclosure: *Baltimore Post*, June 16, 1926.

84   He was too old now: *Syracuse Herald*, August 31, 1919.

86   "thus displaying her amazing": *World*, June 16, 1925.

86   Training went well at first: *New York Times*, August 2, 1925.

87   "[Wolffe] contends that Miss Ederle": *Syracuse Herald*, August 13, 1925.

88   "Her remarkable speed": *Baltimore Post*, August 18, 1925.

89   "It was funny the way I sank": ibid., August 19, 1925.

89   "You guys are crazy": *Dallas Morning News*, August 20, 1925.

89   The United News correspondent: Ibid.

90   "I was swimming with": *World*, September 19, 1925.

90   "Just imagine his coming": ibid.

90   "I absolutely refuse": Ibid.

91   "I'm all right, Elsie": *New York Times*, September 21, 1925.

91   She had "many suspicions": Ibid., September 24, 1925.

91   "It seemed to me that Wolffe": *World*, September 24, 1925.

92   "Come ,Trudie, let bygones be bygones": *New Smyrna Daily News*, August 9, 1926.

92   Wolffe reacted churlishly: *Oklahoman*, July 8, 1926.

93   A few days later Ederle described: *Daily News*, July 18, 1926.

CHAPTER NINE

94   She would be reunited: *New York Herald Tribune*, August 29, 1926.

95   "You bet I will swim": (London) *Star*, August 8, 1926.

96   Gade's boarding house: *Sunday Times*, August 29, 1926.

97   For most of the year: *Dover Express*, August 20, 1926.

98   The week after Gade arrived: *Dover Express* and *East Kent News*, July 2, 1926.

98   His first sally across the Channel: Ibid.

CHAPTER TEN

101   Gleitze had been born in Brighton: interview with Doloranda Pember, Gleitze's daughter, June 27, 2006.

102   "My plan was to walk": Gleitze family private papers.

102   "How can one suddenly still a drive": Ibid.

106   On July 11 she embarked: *Daily Chronicle*, July 12, 1926.

109   "I do get fed up on the Channel-swim talk": Gertrude Ederle's *Chicago Tribune-Daily News* column, July 12, 1926.

110   "I can forget all about the croakers when I sit down to read": Ibid.

110   In her darker moments: Julia Harpman first revealed some of the darker goings-on at the Cape in her exclusive report for the *Daily News* on August 28, 1926, when they arrived back in New York.

110   He was one of the twenty-one children: Gertrude Ederle in the *Daily News*, June 23, 1926.

111   Nor was Pop immune: Gertrude Ederle in the *Sunday News*, June 27, 1926.

112   "I shall be glad to welcome her": *Standard-Star*, July 7, 1926.

112   "Madame Sion and Perrault": Ibid., July 30, 1926.

113   Her sister disappeared to Paris: *Daily News*, June 25, 1926.

114   "I suppose you are all as disgusted": *Chicago Tribune*, June 30, 1926.

114   It was costing Patterson: in an article in the *New York Times* on August 9, 1926, Alec Rutherford mentioned that Cannon had a second option on the *Alsace*. Westbrook Pegler's recollections of Costa were described in his syndicated column which appeared in the *Syracuse Herald* on March 25, 1936.

115   Creeping down to the beach: *Daily News*, July 2, 1926.

116   SEA MONSTERS CAPTURED: Ibid., July 9, 1926, and a similar article appeared in the *Boston Post*, July 20.

117   When she had sailed from New York: ibid., June 3, 1926.

118   "I don't want anyone to suggest": *Boston Post*, July 19, 1926.

120   In the second half of July: the Gloria Swanson–like photo appeared in the *Baltimore Post* on July 19, although the most gratuitous bathing shot photo was undoubtedly the one looking up at Cannon halfway up a ladder, which the *Post* published on July 21 with the caption: "Lillian Cannon, for diversion, climbing ladder to Cape Gris Nez."

120   One male correspondent from Pittsburgh: *Baltimore Post*, July 19, 1926.

121   "Swim'er? 'Tis a hard job": ibid., June 17, 1926.

121   Meanwhile John Hayward: ibid., July 24, 1926.

121   "It has reached a stage now": ibod, August 1, 1926.

CHAPTER TWELVE

122   "walk up and down": *Boston Sunday Post*, July 18, 1926.

122   he was "beginning to believe": *Standard-Star*, July 29, 1926.

126   The previous year Learmont had accused the mayor: *Dover Express*, July 25, 1925.

126   Within a short space of time: *New York Times*, July 31, 1926.

126   "I cannot leave such a splendid woman": ibid.

127   Ideally, Barrett would have swum: one of the most concise contemporary reports of the Channel tides was written by Louis de Breda Handley in the *New York Times*, August 23, 1925. I also gleaned much information from Julie Bradshaw, the secretary of the Channel Swimming Association who swam the Channel in 1979, age 15, in a time of ten hours and nine minutes.

127   If Barrett had a magpie memory: *New York Times*, August 23, 1925.

129   The air temperature: *Daily Chronicle*, July 27, 1926.

CHAPTER THIRTEEN

132   The *Dover Standard* grumbled: *Dover Standard*, July 16, 1926.

132   The London *Star* blushed in reporting: Star, July 14, 1926.

132   One American innovation: *Baltimore Post*, June 25, 1926.

133   Many took with them: *Herald Tribune*, August 22, 1926.

135   "Miss Gleitze found herself among the steamers": *Folkestone Herald*, July 17, 1926.

135   She was pulled on board: ibid.

137   The British newspapers dubbed it "Channelitis": (London) *Daily Mirror*, August 2, 1926.

137   "It's becoming a joke": (London) *Daily Express*, August 2, 1926.

137   "I would like to swim": (London) *Daily Mirror*, August 2, 1926.

138   He had many exceptional feats: *Dover Chronicle*, August 7, 1926.

CHAPTER FOURTEEN

139   The incident was widely reported: *Philadelphia Inquirer*, August 31, 1926.

140   Grace Leister, wearing a navy-blue dress: Although all three Dover newspapers devoted much coverage to Barrett's swim,

the *Dover Standard*'s edition of August 5 was the most detailed. I also obtained information from watching the British Pathe newsreel film of Barrett's departure from Dover.

141 "I know I have a hard job ahead": *Dover Standard*, August 5, 1926.

142 The *Dover Express* reckoned: *Dover Express*, August 6, 1926, and *Dover Chronicle*, August 7, 1926.

143 As Learmont steered: *Dover Standard*, August 5, 1926.

143 She even had a speech prepared: Ibid.

143 The reporter from the *Dover Standard*: Ibid.

144 A few hours later the final editions: *New York Telegram*, August 2, 1926.

145 She provided the *Sun*: *New York Sun*, August 2, 1926.

145 But Brewster and his pilot: Dover Chronicle, August 7, 1926.

146 "Miss Barrett is the giantess of Channel swimmers": *New York Times*, August 4, 1926.

147 Dense shoals of the creatures: *Dover Standard*, August 5, 1926.

148 "I didn't think much": ibid.

148 Brickett leaped to his feet: ibid.

149 Learmont noticed that every steamer's fog horn: ibid.

149 She enjoyed the sensation: ibid.

151 "Tell me the truth": ibid.

151 "I am sorry I've failed": ibid.

151 "I shall never come back again": ibid.

152 "It was the fog entirely": ibid.

CHAPTER FIFTEEN

156 In July Ty Cobb: *Boston Post*, July 24, 1926.

157 Two days later a pitched battle: ibid., July 27, 1926.

157 The dispute had reached an impasse: *World*, July 24, 1926.

157 The *Boston Post* lamented: *Boston Post*, August 4, 1926.

158 So America turned its gaze: *New York Sun*, August 4, 1926.

158 "I have made up my mind": *Herald Tribune*, August 7, 1926.

159 On the morning when she'd heard: Washington *Evening Star*, August 4, 1926.

160 "Another celebrity is just routine work": *Standard-Star*, July 27, 1926.

160 "There is the keenest rivalry": *Washington Post*, August 6, 1926.

161   "This is where I will have to call on her": although this quote
      was reported by Westbrook Pegler in *Liberty* on July 24, there
      is no doubt that Burgess would have repeated the strategy to
      other journalists on the eve of the swim. The *Boston Post* of
      August 6, 1926, carried a description of her intended route,
      provided by "Burgess, her grizzled trainer".

161   Tomorrow morning, replied Burgess: *Boston Post*, August 6,
      1926.

162   At the beginning of July: *Daily News*, July 2, 1926.

163   "Don't let anybody": *Oklahoman*, August 5, 2001.

163   " 'England or drown' is my motto": *Boston Post*, August 6,
      1926.

163   "If she can last 14 hours": ibid.

CHAPTER SIXTEEN

164   By the time they had negotiated the lane: naturally, the most
      detailed accounts of Ederle's swim came from the *Chicago
      Tribune-Daily News* syndicate in the form of Ederle's own
      columns or Harpman's dispatches.

165   Her sister was still asleep: *Daily News*, August 7, 1926.

167   When Julia Harpman appeared: I have speculated that the
      confrontation occurred on the beach; it might have occurred
      in the hotel shortly before they departed for the beach, but
      what is without doubt is that Harpman waited until the
      morning of the swim before revealing her intentions. There
      is nothing to suggest in the other reporters' behaviour – drink
      ing beer with Burgess in the Hôtel du Phare on Thursday
      evening and drinking coffee with the Ederle camp on Friday
      morning – that they had any foreknowledge of the trick, and
      that is why *La Morinie* was late in joining the swim.

168   "I feel just like a grease ball!": *Herald Tribune*, August 7, 1926.

168   "For heaven's sake": *World*, August 7, 1926.

168   Like any man with a psychological hold: *Philadelphia Inquirer*,
      August 7, 1926.

170   "This is now or never": *Daily Sketch*, August 7, 1926.

171   "Entering the water": *Daily News*, August 6, 1926.

171   "Please God, help me": Gertrude Ederle interview in the *New
      York Times*, August 6, 1961.

171   "I invented the two-piece": *New York Times*, August 15, 1975.

171   "Take your time, Miss Ederle": *World*, August 7, 1926.

174   "Nothing comes easy in this life": Gertrude Ederle interview

in the *Dallas Morning News*, March 18, 1960.

CHAPTER SEVENTEEN

175   "Come on, Pop": *Daily News*, August 7, 1926.

178   "Tell me when it's noon": Ibid. 178 "The water is wonderful": ibid.

178   Arthur Sorenson took off his shoes: *Daily News,* August 28, 1926.

180   In fact, Burgess told Harpman: ibid., August 7, 1926.

180   Rutherford wrote that at 1:30: *New York Times,* August 7, 1926.

180   Only Minott Saunders of the United Press: *New York Sun*, August 6, 1926.

181   The jellyfish, which waltzed: *Daily News,* August 7, 1926.

181   Ederle was having a drink of hot chocolate: ibid.

182   *La Morinie* was now fifteen yards away: ibid.

183   "You damned loafers": *Chicago Tribune*, August 30, 1926.

183   if he had a gun, he would shoot everyone: John Hayward in the *Daily Sketch*, August 17, 1926.

183   "Have I got to take you into training, too?": *Boston Post*, August 7, 1926.

185   "It must have seemed": *Chicago Tribune*, August 9, 1926.

185   "After that I felt I had": *Herald Tribune*, August 8, 1926.

186   He confronted Gertrude's father: *Washington Post*, August 7, 1926.

186   Ederle "pointed out that Gertrude"· *Reader's Digest*, September 1958.

186   Harpman said later: *Washington Post*, August 7, 1926.

CHAPTER EIGHTEEN

187   "I never dreamed": New York *Sunday News*, August 8, 1926.

187   "What For?!": *Daily News*, August 7, 1926.

187   "I am going right through with it this time": John Hayward in the *Daily Sketch*, August 7, 1926.

187   Eventually when Burgess realised: ibid.

188   Rutherford had seen Burgess: *New York Times*, August 7, 1926.

189   Ederle had already experienced: *Sunday News*, August 8, 1926.

189   "God Almighty": *Daily News*, August 7, 1926.

190   "the worst luck possible": *Daily News*, August 7, 1926.

190   "It was very difficult": *Herald Tribune*, August 8, 1926.

191   "No man or woman": *Daily News*, August 7, 1926.

192   She had read of Freyberg's heartbreaking collapse: *Boston Sunday Post*, August 8, 1926.

192   "Assured": *Daily News*, August 7, 1926.

192   "You are sure to make it": ibid.

192   "Won't mamma be glad?": ibid.

194   "with the tide in her favour": (London) *Daily Mail*, August 8, 1926.

194   "Everything seemed to depend": *Westminster Gazette*, August 8, 1926.

CHAPTER NINETEEN

196   "She gave all she had": *Washington Post*, August 7, 1926.

197   Margaret screamed: ibid.

197   On board *La Morinie*: *Atlanta Constitution*, August 7, 1926.

198   Ederle was disorientated and bewildered: *Daily News*, August 7, 1926.

198   "I'm all right": ibid.

198   She understood the excitement: *Sunday News*, August 8, 1926.

199   "I just knew if it could be done": *New York Times*, August 7, 1926.

200   "Gee, have I got to get up just for that?": *New York Telegram*, August 7, 1926.

200   as if they were criminals: *Boston Sunday Post*, August 8, 1926.

CHAPTER TWENTY

201   It was a breathless, rambling dispatch: Washington *Evening Star*, August 6, 1926.

202   Other dignitaries leaped on board the bandwagon: *New York Times*, August 7, 1926.

203   "Bully! That's great": *Herald Tribune*, August 7, 1926.

203   Another reporter telephoned: ibid.

204   "it just goes to show": ibid.

204   At the Ederle meat shop: *New York Times*, August 7, 1926.

205   She answered all their questions: most newspapers carried quotes from Mrs. Ederle, although it was the *World* on August 8 that specified how Ederle was pronounced.

205   "It was Ed-er-ly": *World*, August 8, 1926.

206   He showed the reporter a facsimile: *Boston Post*, Aug 7,1926.

206   In fact the reason it was harder to swim: from an interview with Julie Bradshaw, secretary of the Channel Swimming Association on July 1, 2007.

207   "It's marvellous": *New York Times*, August 7, 1926.

CHAPTER TWENTY-ONE

209   "fair women are usually more frivolous": *Boston Post*, August 7, 1926.

211   Once Ederle had finished her bath: probably the best account of the "morning after" appeared in the *Chicago Tribune* on August 8, 1926.

211   "I'm not a bit lame and none the worse": ibid.

211   "Well now, a wire": *Sunday Times*, August 8, 1926.

211   "I was determined for Burgess's sake": *Chicago Tribune*, August 8, 1926.

212   "It's a lot easier to swim": ibid.

213   The first one was predictably banal: Nearly every British and American newspaper carried accounts of the press conference on August 8 and 9, although some conveyed the impressions to their readers that it was an exclusive. However, the exact same quotes from Ederle appeared in several other newspapers. What I have done here is to round up the quotes to form the probable pattern the conference followed.

215   "You certainly did a fine swim": *Sunday Times*, August 8, 1926.

215   "She has shown splendid courage": *Herald Tribune*, August 8, 1926.

216   "If I live a thousand years": *Washington Post*, August 8, 1926.

217   "she felt like running away": *Chicago Tribune*, August 8, 1926.

217   "Gee, it's hot": ibid.

218   Cape Gris-Nez had never witnessed a party: *Daily News*, August 9, 1926.

218   "I lost $5000 on last year's swim": *New York Sun*, August 7, 1926.

218   "He made $25,000": *Mansfield News Journal*, Nov 18, 1958.

CHAPTER TWENTY-TWO

219   Cannon had returned to Boulogne: *New York Times*, August 8, 1926.

219   "splendid sport": *Boston Sunday Post*, August 8, 1926.

219   "Gertrude was absolutely wonderful": (London) *Star*,

August 7, 1926.

220 "She declared today": *Atlanta Constitution*, August 9, 1926.

220 "definitely decided not to abandon her attempt": *New York Times*, August 9, 1926.

220 "frail in comparison": ibid., August 8, 1926.

221 The previous day Burgess had rhapsodised: *Chicago Tribune*, August 9, 1926.

221 Harpman later told a colleague: Bill Cunningham's column in the *Boston Post*, August 26, 1926.

222 "I congratulate you with all my heart": *Atlanta Constitution*, August 9, 1926.

223 "If she tries this again": *Standard-Star*, August 11, 1926.

CHAPTER TWENTY-THREE

225 "I am not afraid": *New York Times*, August 11, 1926.

225 "I will never again try to swim": *Baltimore Post*, August 11, 1926.

225 Dr. Hugh Cumming: *New York Sun*, August 7, 1926.

226 "epoch-making things": *World*, August 12, 1926.

227 "In a men's washroom": *Chicago Tribune*, July 18, 1926.

227 "needn't accept without question:" *Oakland Tribune*, August 9, 1926.

227 ON YOUR TOES, MEN: *Daily News*, August 19, 1926.

228 An editorial in the *Morning Post*: *Herald Tribune*, August 9, 1926.

228 The French authorities: Washington *Evening Star*, August 12, 1926.

229 William Randolph Hearst's New York *Daily Mirror*: *Daily Mirror*, August 9, 1926.

230 "Trudie was indignant": *Sunday News*, August 8, 1926.

231 The *Daily News* ran a series: the articles began on August 9, 1926, and continued for most of the week with Ederle giving her views on "petting" in the edition of August 10.

231 "now that I'll have more time to fall in love": the unnamed British newspaper was quoted in the August 9 edition of the *Herald Tribune*.

231 "Who says woman is the weaker sex?": ibid.

232 WE DID IT, MOTHER!: the *Daily News* printed a facsimile of the cable in its edition of August 25, 1926.

234 "Mademoiselle, permit me": *Dover Express*, August 20, 1926.

234 "the glasses of champagne": ibid.

264   "I am not going home": *New York Times*, August 21, 1926.

266   "I am sure I can make it this time": *Standard-Star*, August 23, 1926.

267   She covered three miles in the first hour: the account of Barrett's brief and unsuccessful attempt was carried by the *Dover Standard* on August 26, 1926.

269   "I give her [Ederle] credit for swimming across": ibid.

269   "the sight of Mrs. Corson's boat": *New York Times*, August 24, 1926.

270   "a cheery party romping on the sands": ibid.

270   "I cannot help feeling": ibid.

271   "The game is up for this year": *Baltimore Post*, August 24, 1926.

CHAPTER TWENTY-SEVEN

272   "gave the impression that she knew": *Herald Tribune*, August 21, 1926.

272   "Papa told Gertrude not to talk to reporters": Ibid.

272   "The *Chicago Tribune* acquired all the rights": *Le Grand Echo du Nord de la France*, August 24, 1926.

274   "I didn't know how much": *Boston Post*, August 23, 1926.

274   "I am going to train": *Herald Tribune*, August 23, 1926.

275   "I am so afraid. I'll think I'll jump": Ibid.

275   "What am I living for now?": *Daily News*, August 28, 1926.

277   "Overwhelming applause greeted": *Boston Post*, August 26, 1926.

279   "he jumped a little too far forward": *New York Times*, April 28, 1957.

279   the mayor preferred to spend his mornings in bed: on August 22, 1976, the *New York Times* published an article by Warren Moscow, who in 1926 had been an eighteen-year-old reporter covering mayoral business. Like most New Yorkers, Moscow had a certain amount of affection for the affable Walker, but nonetheless called him "perhaps the city's most amoral mayor with regard to sex". While Walker's wife was secreted at the family home in St. Luke's Place, he "lived, loved and slept in a succession of posh uptown-hotel suites".

CHAPTER TWENTY-EIGHT

280   "Hello, pal!" she cried: Paul Gallico in his column in the *Daily News*, August 30, 1926.

280 "It is a matter of particular pride": *World*, August 28, 1926.

281 "What more is there?": ibid.

281 "Men's hands caught the edge": *Herald Tribune*, August 28, 1926.

282 Amid the sea of straw hats: ibid.

283 As ambulances were summoned: most New York newspapers described the bedlam, but the *Herald Tribune* and the *World*, both August 28, 1926, were particularly thorough.

284 "When history records the great crossings": *Herald Tribune*, August 28, 1926.

286 "curiously artificial": *World*, August 28, 1926.

286 "I'm tired," Ederle pleaded: *Herald Tribune*, August 28, 1926.

287 "You just lie down and get rested": *World*, August 28, 1926.

290 "There is never a duel": original trial transcripts reproduced on the Internet by various legal websites.

290 TO GERTRUDE EDERLE, "MY INFANT": *Herald Tribune*, August 28, 1926.

290 "declaring to the host of reporters": *Daily News*, August 12, 1926.

291 "When Trudy opened a New York newspaper": *Chicago Tribune*, August 28, 1926.

292 "You can't get a good manager for 12 1/2 per cent.": ibid., August 25, 1926.

CHAPTER TWENTY-NINE

294 When she woke there were tears: *Dover Express*, September 3, 1926.

294 "I'm very hopeful of success": *Daily News*, August 31, 1926.

295 "Watch out for the dogfish": *World*, August 30, 1926.

295 "12.32am: two miles northwest": ibid., August 29, 1926.

296 "Get the life belt ready": *Dover Standard*, September 2, 1926.

297 "Make the pain go away, please": *World*, August 30, 1926.

297 "There's old England": *Dover Chronicle*, September 4, 1926.

297 "I've written a song for you": *Dover Standard*, September 2, 1926.

298 "Another mile for Sonny": ibid.

299 "You are doing a marvellous swim": *New York Times*, August 29, 1926.

CHAPTER THIRTY

301   "Large crowds were seen gathered": *World*, August 29, 1926.

302   "You must do it": *Dover Standard*, September 2, 1926.

302   "Whoever you are": *World*, August 29, 1926.

303   "Staggering about from side to side": ibid.

303   Over a couple of flickering candles: ibid.

305   "whenever I got downhearted": *Dover Express*, September 3, 1926.

305   "it would have broken my heart": *Dover Standard*, September 2, 1926.

305   "I would not do it again for a million pounds": *Dover Chronicle*, September 4, 1926.

305   "Mrs. Corson holds the record for an open sea swim": *World*, August 30, 1926.

305   "We trained hard for it": *Daily Sketch*, August 30, 1926.

306   "I didn't swim for America": *World*, August 30, 1926.

306   "shook hands with anyone and everyone": *Daily Mirror*, August 30, 1926.

307   "All the time I was in the water": *Daily Express*, August 30, 1926.

308   Why . . . "does not England finance": *Daily Sketch*, August 30, 1926.

308   "a charming green frock": *Dover Express*, September 3, 1926.

309   "I've received so many fine financial offers": *Standard-Star*, August 31, 1926.

309   "You tried to swim the Channel before": *Dover Express*, September 3, 1926.

CHAPTER THIRTY-ONE

311   "Trudy is tired": *Oakland Tribune*, August 28, 1926.

312   "If she's swimming, let her swim": *New York Sun*, August 28, 1926.

312   "Where is it? I've barely seen it": *Sunday News*, August 29, 1926.

312   "I'm almost sorry it's red": *Daily News*, August 30, 1926.

313   "I can hardly believe it": *Sunday News*, August 29, 1926.

313   "I have sent my heartiest congratulations to Mrs. Corson": *Chicago Tribune*, August 29, 1926.

313   "occasionally one would go": *World*, August 29, 1926.

314   "a semi-hysterical, nervously twitching child": Paul Gallico reporting the comments of Julia Harpman in his column in

the *Daily News,* August 31, 1926.

315   "They think I'm a machine": ibid., August 30, 1926.

315   "After patting her hand": ibid.

315   "Every great athlete has a highly nervous system": *Hartford Courant,* August 30, 1926.

315   "rolled and tossed": *Baltimore Post,* August 30, 1926.

315   "I'll give credit to Miss Ederle": *World,* August 29, 1926.

316   "Trudy sat in the front room": *Chicago Tribune,* August 30, 1926.

317   "Is Trudy's illness a temporary inconvenience": *Daily News,* August 30, 1926.

317   Ederle sat on her throne: most American papers drew a discreet veil over Ederle's collapse on the platform; only the *World* on August 31 reported the incident in full.

318   "waved aloft fifteen telegrams": *Daily News,* August 12, 1926.

319   TRUDY LOSES A GOLDEN FORTUNE: *Boston Post,* August 30, 1926.

CHAPTER THIRTY-TWO

321   "I believe the American people": *Herald Tribune,* August 31, 1926.

322   "It looks as though I will have more money": *Standard-Star,* August 31, 1926.

323   "It was a marvellous thing": *New York Times,* September 7, 1926.

323   "treat her right": *World,* September 7, 1926.

324   She didn't have "any excuses": ibid.

324   "In life we have only one or two chances": *Atlanta Constitution,* September 7, 1926.

324   "I'm not going to give up my job": *New York Times,* September 7, 1926.

324   "A tug would not have": *Hartford Courant,* September 7, 1926.

325   "She symbolised the dauntless courage": ibid.

326   "quite interestingly and modestly delivered": *Variety,* September 28, 1926.

326   "that you have to show the world": *Standard-Star,* September 16, 1926.

327   "is purely a matter of luck": *Hartford Courant,* September 12, 1926.

CHAPTER THIRTY-THREE

328   "Their long lines of rifles must have helped": *New York Times*, September 11, 1926.

329   "the Corsons have never been well off ": *Standard-Star*, September 8, 1926.

330   "was attractively dressed in a tweed suit": ibid., September 10, 1926.

330   "It was marvellous that a girl": *Atlanta Constitution*, September 11, 1926.

330   "I trusted to my mind": ibid.

331   "the only additional wreath": *New York Times*, September 11, 1926.

331   "a hurriedly whipped-together act": *Variety*, September 15, 1926.

332   "the most exceptional ever given out": ibid.

CHAPTER THIRTY-FOUR

333   In an interview in 1994 Aileen: interview with Dr. Margaret Costa, Amateur Athletic Foundation of Los Angeles, in November 1994.

334   "a swimming champion": *Herald Tribune*, August 31, 1926.

334   Selwyn admitted to *Variety*: *Variety*, September 15, 1926.

334   What undoubtedly amazed Selwyn: Julia Harpman first mentioned the Laemmle offer in her report for the *Daily News* on August 19. "Ederle was offered a movie contract by a personal representative of Carl Laemmle ... Miss Ederle is considering this offer, but will make no decision until she reaches New York and confers with her attorney, Dudley FieldMalone."

335   "It is possible to wonder": *Christian Science Monitor*, October 18, 1926.

336   "Being posed for pictures and interviews": *Variety*, November 10, 1926.

336   "Trudy Getting It Wrong With Dailies": ibid., December 1, 1926.

336   But Ederle declined the invitation: *Los Angeles Times*, December 10, 1926.

337   "I positively will not": *New York Times*, December 6, 1926.

338   "Thank God that's over": *Chicago Tribune*, June 19, 1927.

338   Pegler had been curious to know: in fact, Pegler wrote an article on April 12, 1927, which was widely publicised, in

which he and Ederle had worked out her earnings, and presumably kept in touch with her during the following weeks before the piece appeared in the *Chicago Tribune* on June 19

338   "The showmen of the sport business": ibid.

340   "Hundreds of thousands of people were banked": *Variety*, June 15, 1927.

EPILOGUE

341   In the spring of 1936 Westbrook Pegler: *Syracuse Herald*, March 25, 1936.

342   "I think it inane to swim across the Channel": *Atlanta Constitution*, October 15, 1927.

343   "a six-foot athletic type": an interview in the *New York Times* on August 6, 1958.

343   "The worse part of it": *Daily News*, March 23, 1929.

344   "With my poor hearing it might be hard": *New York Times*, August 6, 1958.

344   Four years of setbacks had stripped Ederle: *Los Angeles Times*, July 29, 1930.

345   "I'm not sorry I did it": ibid.

346   "The old Channel lay placid": *Syracuse Herald*, March 25, 1936.

347   but the *New York Times* and the New Rochelle *Standard-Star* misspelled her name: *New York Times*, July 18, 1946, and *Standard-Star*, July 17, 1946.

347   "possessor of a fine, deep contralto voice": *Standard-Star*, July 17, 1946.

348   "His high spending days ended": *Chicago Tribune*, October 6, 1950.

351   When they were seen and arrested: the story first appeared in the *Daily News* on June 12, 1928, under the giant headline NAB STARS IN PARK SWIM, and the paper followed it through to the court appearance on June 19.

352   "I went to college and became a chemist": interview with Marjorie Andreen (née Corson), January 24, 2007.

352   Intriguingly, the story that sticks: Ibid.

353   *The Times* of London gave Gleitze half a column: Unfortunately for Mercedes, a few days after her authenticated swim another Englishwoman, Dr. Dorothy Logan, claimed to have swum the Channel in thirteen hours and ten minutes. Suspicions were aroused, however, when the doctor

couldn't produce any witnesses, and, under pressure from the newspapers, she confessed it was all a hoax. Mercedes' swim also came under the spotlight, even though she provided doubters with a boatload of witnesses. Angered by the scepticism, Gleitze set out to repeat the feat on October 21 wearing a Rolex "Oyster" wristwatch, said by the manufacturers to be the first waterproof watch in the world. Though the watch stood up to the buffeting, Gleitze succumbed to the coldness of the water, and there was more bad news when she returned to her London flat: she had been burgled, and among the items stolen were several swimming medals and the logbooks of all her swims. Happily, the Channel Swimming Association validated her initial swim, and thus she was officially the first non-American woman to swim the Channel.

355   "It was torture to take steps": *Chicago Daily Tribune*, August 7, 1939.

355   "I don't want any sob stories written": this syndicated story appeared in many newspapers, including the *Fitchburg Sentinel* on August 6, 1937.

356   "something like swimming the Channel": *Oklahoman*, August 7, 1939.

356   "I'd be stupid if I hadn't realised": ibid.

356   "I wanted to prove it could be done": *New York Times*, April 30, 2001.

358   "slowly I came to know": *Dallas Morning News*, March 18, 1960.

358   "I have no complaints": *Daily News*, December 1, 2003.

Selected Bibliography

Danzig, Allison, and Peter Brandwein, eds. *Sport's Golden Age*. New York: Harper and Bros., 1948.

Douglas, George. *The Golden Age of the Newspaper*. Westport, CT: Greenwood Press, 1999.

Fass, Paula. *The Damned and the Beautiful: American Youth in the 1920s*. New York: Oxford University Press, 1977.

Gallico, Paul. *Golden People*. New York: Doubleday, 1965.

Holyoake, Gregory. Bygone Kent, June 1981.

Leinwald, Gerald. *1927: High Tide of the 1920s*. New York: Four Walls, Eight Windows, 2001.

Smith, Lissa, ed. *Nike Is a Goddess: The History of Women in Sports*. New York: Atlantic Monthly Press, 1998.

Watson, Kathy. *The Crossing: The Glorious Tragedy of the First Man to Swim the English Channel*. London: Penguin Putnam, 2000.

Williamson, J. A. *The English Channel: A History*. London: William Collins Sons & Co., 1959.

Wolffe, Jabez. *Swimming Short and Long Distance*. Harrow, England: Foulsham, 1937.